THE
MAGNIFICENT
MIND

OTHER BOOKS BY GARY R. COLLINS

Beyond Easy Believism
Christian Counseling: A Comprehensive Guide
The 60-Second Christian

GARY R. COLLINS

THE
MAGNIFICENT
MIND

WORD BOOKS
PUBLISHER
WACO, TEXAS
A DIVISION OF
WORD, INCORPORATED

THE MAGNIFICENT MIND
Copyright © 1985 by Word, Incorporated

Printed in the United States of America

Unless otherwise indicated, scripture quotations in this book are from the New International Version of the Bible (NIV), copyright © 1978 by the New York Bible Society. Used by permission.

Those marked KJV are from the King James Version of the Bible. Those marked NASB are from *The New American Standard Bible*, copyright 1960, 1962, 1963, 1968, 1971, 1972, 1975 by the Lockman Foundation. Those marked TLB are from *The Living Bible, Paraphrased*, copyright © 1971 by Tyndale House Publishers, Wheaton, Illinois. Those marked RSV are from the Revised Standard Version of the Bible, copyright © 1946, 1952, © 1971 and 1973 by the Division of Christian Education of the National Council of Churches of Christ in the U.S.A.

Library of Congress Cataloging in Publication Data

Collins, Gary R.
  The magnificent mind.

  1. Christian life—1960–   . 2. Intellect.
3. Christianity—Psychology. I. Title.
BV4501.2.C6434   1985   233'.5   84-21598
ISBN 0-8499-0385-8

In Memory of

DR. JAMES D. LINDEN
1929–1983

CONTENTS

INTRODUCTION

Every summer, usually in early June, a tall gray heron arrives at the edge of the pond near our house and spends a few days fishing. The bird is slender, stately, and inclined to wade knee-deep into the water and stand motionless while he watches the fish swim by. When he judges that the time is right, his (or is it her?) long neck darts into the water, spears a fish, and deposits the wiggling catch on the cool grass.

I have always been intrigued by this little drama, and more than once have been distracted from my work so I could watch. I have wondered why the bird studies the scene so carefully before moving to make the catch, why some fish are selected and others get away, why some are small enough to be swallowed in one gulp but others are bigger and probably harder to digest.

One day it occurred to me that I have had to face similar questions while working on this book. A few years ago, the mind was not a popular topic in psychology and almost nobody was writing about it. Then things began to change. Suddenly the mind returned to favor and an avalanche of articles and research papers began to appear, describing its characteristics and capabilities. After reading many of these reports and presenting my ideas to college, church, and lay audiences, I began to feel like that heron—standing before a whole lake of tasty morsels but not knowing what to select, realizing that some good things might get away but uncertain about how to separate the easily digested ideas from those that are larger and harder to grasp.

In the following pages, I have tried to include a lot of information about the mind, but I have had to be selective and in some cases brief in my presentations. Almost every chapter could be expanded into one or more books—but that would involve the production of an entire library that nobody would have the time or inclination to read. Like the heron on the pond, therefore, I have had to make choices and have been forced to let some ideas get away.

I have tried, however, to make my choices interesting, accurate in terms of psychology and theology, carefully documented for those who want to read further, practical, challenging at times, informative, encouraging, entertaining, and fun to read. Many years ago I learned that the best authors don't try to pad their works by adding irrelevant information; instead, they write from an abundance of background research and work to pare down their research findings to make their writing both concise and interesting. I hope that my paring down has resulted in a fascinating, accurate, and useful book.

To help me with this, several people have read the entire manuscript and offered valuable suggestions for improvement. I am grateful to David McKay, C. S. Burdan, and my wife Julie Collins, for their encouragement and long hours of work in reviewing this project. In addition, Brian Boone, Daniel Lerom, and Laura Myer read sections of the book and gave helpful recommendations.

My friends at Word, especially Al Bryant and Ernie Owen, showed their usual support and encouragement as this book took shape. I continue to be grateful for their editorial expertise, and for the competent team of people in Waco, Texas, who work so efficiently to get a project like this into print and into the hands of readers.

Once again, I deeply appreciate my family. They have watched me write a lot of books and they still stand solidly behind me when I face deadlines. They do a magnificent job of encouraging me—and screening out the phone calls. I especially appreciate their prayer support, as well as the prayers of so many others who prayed for me and for this book as it was being written.

Shortly after beginning the manuscript, I learned that my friend, Dr. James D. Linden, had died of cancer. Jim was a professor of psychology at Purdue University. He accepted me as his first doctoral student, guided me through my study at graduate school, supervised my dissertation, and remained a colleague and an encourager long after I had departed with my diploma. Jim Linden respected my desire to integrate psychology with my Christian faith and he was consistently supportive of my work—especially my writing. This book is dedicated to his memory. I am sorry that I was not able to dedicate a book to him before his untimely death.

GARY R. COLLINS

1
THE
REMARKABLE
MIND

Nobody could have predicted that Phineas Gage would end up in a circus.

He was described at the time—over a century ago—as a healthy, strong, active, trustworthy, and religious young man who was popular with his friends and admired by his employer. His home was in rural Vermont where he worked as foreman of a railroad gang. Their job was to blast rock and lay tracks for the new Rutland and Burlington Line.

One fall morning, in September of 1848, Phineas Gage was peering into a blasting hole when the dynamite charge exploded prematurely. With missilelike force, a thirteen-pound, three-and-a-half-foot-long pointed "tamping rod" tore through the air, pierced the cheek of the hapless foreman, passed through his brain, and emerged from his skull to continue its flight through the air.

Bleeding profusely, Phineas Gage was carried to a nearby oxcart, but he sat up during the three-quarter-mile ride to his hotel and asked about the whereabouts of his rod. He got out of the cart by himself, walked up a long flight of stairs, pointed to the hole in his cheek, and calmly informed the doctor that an iron bar had "passed through my head."

The local physician, Dr. John Harlow, could hardly believe what he saw. Even though he was able to insert his fingers into the poor man's skull, the patient and doctor carried on a conversation as the wound was treated. For a few days Phineas Gage was seriously ill because of infected wounds and blood loss, but soon he began to show signs of recovery. The local cabinet-maker, who had done the work of producing a coffin, discovered that it wasn't needed. Within three months, the patient was free of headaches, his physical health was good, and he was ready to go back to work.

But something was different. His employers, who once regarded Mr. Gage as their most efficient and capable foreman, now "considered the change in his mind so marked that they could not give him his place again." No longer self-controlled and sensitive to others, he was described in the doctor's colorful words as "fitful, irreverent, indulging at times in the grossest profanity (which was not previously his custom), manifesting but little deference for his fellows, impatient of restraint or advice when it conflicts with his desires, at times . . . obstinate, yet . . . vascillating, devising many plans of future operations, which are no sooner arranged than they are abandoned in turn for others. . . . His mind is radically changed, so decidedly that his friends and acquaintances said that he was 'no longer Gage.'"[1]

Unable to find a niche in the world, Phineas Gage earned a living in the only way possible. He jointed the P. T. Barnum circus and exhibited himself as a medical curiosity. When he died, his skull and the famous tamping rod both went to the Harvard Medical School museum where they remain on display to this day.[2]

THE MYSTERIOUS MIND

The complexities of the human mind have fascinated people for centuries. The Bible is filled with references to the mind; ancient and more modern philosophers have pondered its power and existence; psychoanalysts from the time of Freud have attempted to uncover its mysteries; neurophysiologists have explored its relationship to the brain; and a new generation of computer specialists has been studying its similarity to "high-tech" data-processing systems.

According to the dictionary, *psyche* is the Greek word for mind, and *psyche*ology is a field of science devoted to the study of the mind. When I enrolled in my first psychology course, however, the professor apparently hadn't read that dictionary definition. Swept along by the philosophy of behaviorism, my instructor—like most others in his profession—focused our attention on behavior and even joined those who denied that the mind existed.

But all of this is changing. In what has been called "a silent revolution,"[3] many psychologists are forsaking traditional behaviorism and joining psycholinguists, neurophysiologists, computer scientists, and others in an attempt to study the mind. They call their new interest "cognitive science," and are fond of saying that the brain and the mind are the last of this world's unexplored frontiers. As we will see, this exploration is fascinating. But it also poses some problems.

Consider, for example, the fact that no one knows what the mind is. It has tremendous power, but it cannot be seen, felt, weighed, or surgically dissected. It is affected by the kind of brain damage that Phineas Gage experienced; it somehow is related to intelligence and personality; according to the Bible it can be Christlike[4] or evil;[5] it is able to be molded and manipulated[6] and it can give rise to the genius of an Einstein, the creativity of a Beethoven, or the barbaric brutality of a Hitler.

The mind influences how each of us lives and thinks. There is clear evidence the mind can be controlled—by others or by ourselves—twisted by distorted thinking, and molded by God.

In the pages that follow we will take a tour of the magnificent mind, looking at its marvelous capabilities and mysterious workings, but pausing periodically to consider how all of this applies in practical ways to our own lives.

THE MEANING OF "THE MIND"

Have you ever thought about how we use the word "mind" in everyday conversation? The word is used in so many different ways that it is almost meaningless:

"I can't bring the details to *mind*," he stated apologetically, "but she acted like she was out of her *mind*.

"It was *mind*-boggling. *Mind* you, at first I had a *mind* to give her a piece of my *mind*. I didn't think she would *mind* my saying what was on my *mind*. But it soon became clear that her *mind* was made up, and even though it may be true that great *minds* think alike, she and I were not of the same *mind*. I knew she would never *mind* me, however hard I might try to change her *mind*.

"But never *mind*," he concluded. "I will just try to *mind* my own business and let someone else try to change her *mind*."

In these few sentences, the word *mind* takes on a variety of different meanings. And the problem is made even more confusing by our habit of using adjectives to describe the mind. We talk, for example, of brilliant minds, troubled minds, mature minds, aggressive minds, academic minds, creative minds, or even "the American mind." In addition, we talk at times about things and people that are mind-less, mind-ful, or mind-expanding.

So what do we mean by the word *mind*? Since the term has so many diverse meanings, it is unlikely that any one definition can satisfy everyone. In this book, however, let us assume that *"mind" refers to the total of all our mental activities—including thinking, learning, problem-solving, willing, perceiving, concentrating, remembering, attending, and experiencing thoughts and emotions*. The mind does not exist in a tangible form. Instead, *mind* is a word that we use to refer to human thinking, knowing, and feeling. Like "electricity," or "gravity," it is something none of us can see with our eyes, few of us understand, but all of us know about and use. And when the mind is abused, understimulated, deeply troubled, or damaged, we can become like Phineas Gage—unable to think clearly or live fulfilled and productive lives.

THE WORKING OF THE MIND

When I was very young, I was told that warts come from handling frogs, and that the way to get rid of warts is to rub them with a penny. It was a beautiful theory, except for one problem.

It was wrong.

Some people get warts even though they have never seen a frog (it is probable that warts come from viruses), and there is no evidence that a penny provides effective treatment.

But it is possible to "buy" a wart from a child. To do this, offer to pay a quarter for the wart (in these inflationary times you can't buy anything with a penny), hand over the coin and announce that the wart is now yours. "But how will you get it?" the amused or bewildered child may ask. Simply reply nonchalantly that within a few days the wart will come off all by itself. And it often will.[7]

There is no scientific reason to explain why such a "treatment" should work.[8] Physicians are able to remove warts by burning them off or by other medical treatment, but for centuries warts have also yielded to the power of suggestion, the influence of superstition, and the belief in magical cures. In some unconscious way, it appears that the mind is able to influence a part of the body and bring changes, like the removal of a wart—sometimes in exchange for a quarter.

How does the mind do this? At present no one knows for sure, but a small army of cognitive scientists is working daily to understand how the mind works. And some things are already clear.

The mind can receive sensations. Psychological studies of sensation and perception show that the sense organs are constantly bombarded by stimulations that come both from the world around us and from inside the body. My eyes and ears let me know what is happening in the room; internal sensations tell me when I have a stomachache or a gnawing worry about some persisting problem.

If we paid conscious attention to all of the stimulations that we encounter, there would be mental confusion and an inability to concentrate. To prevent this, a part of the brain "weeds out" most of the stimulations, so they aren't even noticed. Others are handled automatically—like the eye that closes a little when light gets brighter, the hand that pulls back when it gets too near the stove, or the heart that beats a little faster when we are in danger or in love. These reflex actions occur instinctively, "before we know it," and often without our ever being aware of what the nervous system is doing. The ancient psalmist was right: We are fearfully and wonderfully made.[9]

The mind interprets. It thinks. As we get older, more experienced, and wiser, we learn how to interpret events in the environment. We are able to make sense of other people's actions, and we know what can be done about awkward social situations, danger, stomach upsets, or headaches. Long before we reach adulthood, we form ways of looking at events or issues and reach conclusions about what is significant, dangerous, good, threatening, or unimportant. We learn that people may be friendly, aggressive, stupid, brilliant, perceptive, or insensitive. When we experience pain, we reach conclusions about its meaning and possible influence on our lives. We form opinions about ourselves and conclude, for example, that we are capable, incompetent, intelligent, ugly, or attractive to the opposite sex.

It probably is true that we talk to ourselves all of the time, and often tell ourselves things that may or may not be based on facts. Think, for example, of what life is like for people (perhaps you or me) who keep telling themselves:

- I'm no good.
- I'll never be successful.

- Nobody likes me.
- God doesn't care about me.
- I must get a lot of money in this life.
- I'm too old and stupid to learn anything new.
- Life is meaningless if you are single.
- I'm the best (or worst) Christian in the church.
- I'm a failure.
- I'm irresistible to the opposite sex.

Frequently such conclusions are based on little or no accurate evidence, but sometimes they are held firmly. Often they are made unconsciously and in response to the opinion of someone else. For example, if a mother repeatedly tells her son that he never will be a success in life, he eventually may believe what he hears. He begins to notice things that support this conclusion, and because he expects to fail, he may never try anything that would lead to success. Sometimes, it seems, he even acts in ways that are almost certain to bring the failure that his mother predicted.

This shows another activity of the mind.

The mind makes decisions. After we form opinions in our minds and make interpretations about the world, we almost always decide (sometimes unconsciously) to act in accordance with these interpretations.

The person who thinks, "I'm too stupid to do this job," often gives up trying, and this brings on failure. The individual who concludes, "Nobody likes me," frequently acts in accordance with this belief, is unpleasant to other people, and ends up without friends. The perfectionist often sets such high standards that he never is satisfied with his work, and this leads to frustration and feelings of failure.

Psychologists sometimes call these "self-fulfilling prophecies." They often begin when we are very young. An adult or another child, for example, may say repeatedly that you are stupid, ugly, or incompetent. Maybe there are also some experiences that make you feel inadequate, and because the brain is not well developed, you can't evaluate these experiences or criticisms. Before long, therefore, you start looking for evidence to see if the beliefs about yourself really are true. You find evidence to confirm the beliefs and soon you start acting like everybody expects you to act. This, in turn, brings about the result that others had predicted and that you had learned to expect.[10]

We don't have to be left in a state of hopelessness or futility, however, because there is another important activity of the mind.

The mind can control its own thinking and this, in turn, can influence behavior. This conclusion is at the core of Norman Vincent Peale's popular philosophy of "positive thinking."[11] It is the basis of Robert Schuller's theology of "possibility thinking."[12] It is central to the "positive mental attitude" approaches to success.[13] And it is the foundation assumption in a host of recent stress-management books and seminars. It is even the major idea in a popular approach to counseling.

In the early 1950s, a clinical psychologist named Albert Ellis had become discouraged because his clients weren't getting better. In accordance with his psychoanalytic training, Dr. Ellis had tried helping people understand the significance of their early childhood experiences, and sometimes they were able to get good insights into the causes of their problem behavior.

Why, then, were they not improving? The answer, Ellis concluded, was that the people continued to hold irrational, self-defeating ideas about themselves. To change people, the new theory stated, it is necessary to change thinking.

Ellis concluded that we human beings are verbal creatures who silently talk to ourselves all the time. Often, we tell ourselves things that are self-defeating, unrealistic, stupid, and wrong. To change ourselves, or to change a counselee, this self-defeatist thinking must be challenged. "Who says you are incompetent?" Ellis might ask a client. "Where is the evidence that you can't learn, will never be successful, or are unable to get along with people?"

Rational-emotive therapy (sometimes called RET) was the new approach to counseling that Ellis proposed. It still is a controversial kind of treatment, not only because it deemphasizes many emotional and unconscious influences on our lives, but also because Dr. Ellis is so bombastic, anti-religious, prone to use profanity, and seemingly insensitive. He is not hesitant to argue with a client, attack ideas, or "vigorously pound away" at any self-talk that he considers to be harmful.[14] Nevertheless, many people respond positively to this "no-nonsense" approach, and even those who prefer a more gentle therapy have concluded that some of the core ideas in RET are valid.

We *do* talk to ourselves and this affects how we act.

We *do* reach many conclusions that are harmful, self-defeating, and inaccurate.

We *can* change our thinking, and this in turn can lead to changes in behavior.

We human beings *can* change our minds.

THE INFLUENCE OF THE MIND

When I was growing up, my parents took me to Sunday school every week, and it was there that I started to learn Bible verses. I'm sure Isaiah 26:3, 4 didn't mean much to me at the time—especially since we used the King James Version of the Bible—but the message has stuck throughout the years. God keeps people in "perfect peace" when their minds trust in him.

A few days before his crucifixion, Jesus gave the same message to the disciples. He announced that he would be leaving, but he promised that the Holy Spirit would come to bring comfort and teaching.[15] Then he told them that he would be giving his followers a remarkable gift: peace of mind. This "peace of mind . . . isn't fragile like the peace the world gives," Jesus promised. "So don't be troubled or afraid."[16]

The world is filled with people whose minds are not at peace. Even within the churches there are people who have anxious minds, confused minds, envious minds, or minds that are controlled by anger, discouragement, pressure, lust, or cynicism. When we have no peace of mind, our lives are tense, our days are unfulfilling, and our contacts with others tend to be strained. Surely it is true that many of our problems begin with the mind, and it is there that the problems must be tackled.

Violence and decisions to break the law first arise in the mind, and they do not completely disappear until thinking and emotions are changed.

The lust and sexual temptations with which so many people struggle, begin and must be controlled in the mind.

Psychological problems, poor self-concepts, bad attitudes, distorted thinking, bitterness—each of these can arise in the mind, and the mind is where each must be attacked.

Before turning to a more detailed discussion of issues such as these, however, it can be helpful to consider an intriguing question that has concerned philosophers for centuries. It is a question that interests modern cognitive scientists, and it has fascinated generations of neurophysiologists. It is the question of the mind's location.

Is the mind somehow lodged in the tissues of the brain?

Is "peace of mind" nothing more than stability of the chemical activity within the human skull?

Is the mind something bigger than the brain?

When Phineas Gage lost part of his brain, did he also lose his mind?

To answer questions like these, we must consider the captivating issue of the human brain and how it works. To this subject we turn in the next chapter.

2
THE
PHYSICAL
MIND

It has happened for over half a century. Every year in late December, the editors of *Time* magazine announce their choice for "Man of the Year."

The title usually goes to some political or military figure who has made a significant contribution during the previous twelve months. At times, a woman has been selected, sometimes the honor has gone to an entertainer, and on occasion, the editors have selected a group of people, such as the Hungarian Patriots (in 1956) or the Young (in 1966).[1] E. T., the popular little movie creature from "extraterrestrial" space, almost made it one year but he (or was it she?) didn't get enough votes.

Instead, the editors surprised everyone by naming the computer as "Machine of the Year." The cover story summarized what many people were seeing in their own lives: There continues to be a phenomenal growth in the number and capabilities of computers.

Described by some as the most significant invention since the printing press, the computer "predicts the weather, processes checks, scrutinizes tax returns, guides intercontinental missiles and performs innumerable operations for governments and corporations." The *Time* article noted that computers have "beeped and blipped their way" into homes, schools, and offices, bringing with them the world-wide "information revolution" that futurists have long been predicting. Largely because of the computer, we have shifted from an industrial to an "information-processing society."[2] Our lifestyles have been influenced by computers, and so have our standards of living and our ways of thinking. Because of computers, predict the *Time* editors, our "entire world will never be the same."[3]

This enthusiasm about computers has not been without critics. In his book *The Third Wave*, Alvin Toffler wondered if computers would transform our minds or perhaps even cause them to waste away.[4] He wrote that computers are not superhuman. They break down and make errors. Yet with all their qualifications, writes Toffler, they are "amazing and unsettling . . . for *they enhance our mind-power. . . .*"[5]

But in spite of its complexity and wonderful capabilities, the computer is not nearly as complicated as the human brain. With its millions of neurons, "its largely unknown symphony of biochemical and biophysical interactions," and its ability to handle massive quantities of information, the human brain is far more complex than any computer.[6] It has been called "the most mysterious, intriguing area of our universe"[7]—a mystery that lies not in the farthest reaches of outer space, but within the inner space of the human skull.

THE INCREDIBLE BRAIN

Tucked beneath the skull in each of our heads is a three-pound, jellylike mound that looks like crinkled putty, but is actually a collection of between 10 billion and 100 billion neurons. Each neuron is as complex as an entire small computer,[8] and consists of a central nerve-cell core attached to a long tail and several thousand wispy "dendrites." These dendrites reach out to make contact with other dendrites, and if we could count the number of contact points (scientists call the connecting points "synapses"), it is estimated that there may be as many as 1 quadrillion in every human brain.[9]

In itself, each of these synapses is a marvel of complexity. The dendrites do not actually touch, but they are able efficiently and rapidly to pass messages to each other. Information comes down the dendrite in the form of an electrical impulse. This impulse triggers the discharge of a chemical secretion. The chemical floats across the tiny space between synapses, bumps into the neighboring dendrite, and starts another electrical charge that sends the message on its way. This whole process takes less than one-thousandth of a second.

All of this is so complex that the brain cannot even begin to comprehend its own complexity. According to one writer, the number of connections within one human brain rivals the number of stars and galaxies in the universe, while the number of neurons is several times greater than the population of earth.[10] In the course of one day, it is estimated that adults lose about 100,000 brain cells due to aging,[11] but so many cells are left that we are fully capable of normal thinking well into old age. Phineas Gage could still function mentally even after that rod went through his head and destroyed perhaps millions of brain cells.[12]

If we could cut away the skull and look directly at the brain, we would see something like the drawing that is labeled Figure 2-1. Cut the head right down the middle, and you would see some-

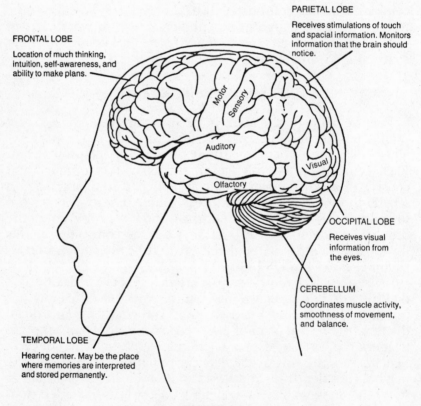

FRONTAL LOBE

Location of much thinking, intuition, self-awareness, and ability to make plans.

PARIETAL LOBE

Receives stimulations of touch and spacial information. Monitors information that the brain should notice.

Motor
Sensory
Auditory
Visual
Olfactory

OCCIPITAL LOBE

Receives visual information from the eyes.

CEREBELLUM

Coordinates muscle activity, smoothness of movement, and balance.

TEMPORAL LOBE

Hearing center. May be the place where memories are interpreted and stored permanently.

FIGURE 2-1
An external view of the human brain.

thing like Figure 2-2.[13] It isn't surprising that attempts to un-ravel the complexity of the brain present scientists with one of their greatest challenges.

THE LOBOTOMIZED BRAIN

In 1935, at a conference of neurologists in London, two speak-ers described how they had calmed the temper tantrums and experimental neuroses of chimpanzees by surgically removing a part of their frontal lobes. At the end of the talk, a Portuguese neurologist named Antonio Egas Moniz rose to his feet and asked if a similar operation could work to remove anxiety in humans. Nobody could respond to the question, but Dr. Moniz

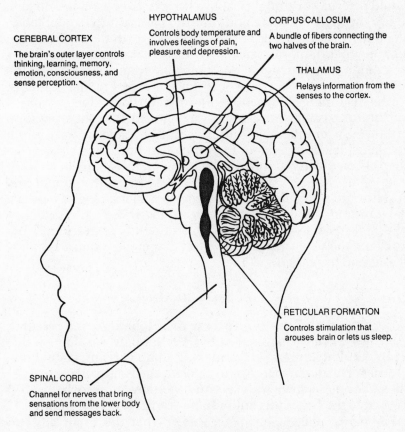

HYPOTHALAMUS
Controls body temperature and involves feelings of pain, pleasure and depression.

CEREBRAL CORTEX
The brain's outer layer controls thinking, learning, memory, emotion, consciousness, and sense perception.

CORPUS CALLOSUM
A bundle of fibers connecting the two halves of the brain.

THALAMUS
Relays information from the senses to the cortex.

RETICULAR FORMATION
Controls stimulation that arouses brain or lets us sleep.

SPINAL CORD
Channel for nerves that bring sensations from the lower body and send messages back.

FIGURE 2-2
An inside view of the human brain.

was determined to find his answer. Back in Portugal, he did brain operations on anxious patients and reported enthusiastically that almost all were less agitated and easier to handle.

Suddenly this surgical technique, known as the lobotomy, became tremendously popular. In the twenty years between 1935 and 1955, approximately 70,000 lobotomies were performed in the United States and Britain alone.[14] Over 3,500 of these were done by an American named Walter Freeman who once remarked that an enterprising neurologist could do 10 to 15 lobotomies in a single morning. And in the midst of all this activity, Dr. Moniz got the Nobel prize for the discovery.

After a while, the procedure became so routine that it could be done in the doctor's office without assistance, and with electroconvulsive shock used instead of anesthesia.[15] The physician would insert a surgical pick above the eye, and use a little mallet to tap through the bone and into the base of the frontal lobes. Then the pick would be swung back and forth to cut the fibers, and the operation was over.[16] Since there were no tranquilizers or antidepressant drugs at that time, lobotomies were one of the few ways to treat violent or severely disturbed mental patients. At the beginning, few people questioned their value.

As time passed, however, it was noticed that the operation produced a number of side effects. The patients were often apathetic, less affectionate than they had been, and more irritable. Often there was impaired judgment, less ability to concentrate or to think clearly, reduced creativity, and a loss of any belief in life's meaning. It was suggested that a new psychiatric classification should be used to describe these patients. They became known as people having "frontal lobe syndrome." Before long the surgical procedure was dropped—almost as quickly as it had appeared.

THE SPLIT BRAIN

In the midst of the controversy over lobotomies, a research team at the California Institute of Technology was doing a different kind of surgery—and making some very interesting discoveries. Headed by Dr. Roger Sperry, the California researchers had done surgery with cats and monkeys to see what would happen if the brain was cut in half—right down the middle.

For many years it has been known that the brain has two parts—a left and right "cerebral hemisphere"—that are joined together by a bundle of fibers known as the corpus callosum. If you could look at the brain from the top, you wouldn't see the corpus callosum (it is inside the brain), but you would see something that looks like Figure 2-3.

Sperry and his associates found that if you cut the corpus callosum in animals, and thus divided the brain in half, intellectual functioning was not impaired. Would the same be true for humans?

Of course such questions could not be answered by experimental surgery on humans, but the California researchers reasoned that people with severe epilepsy might have a reduction in seizures if their brains were split. So the surgery was done and the results were as expected. At first, the patients had mental fatigue and a short-term memory loss, but all showed a substantial reduction in epileptic attacks, and there were few side effects.[17]

Once split brain surgery had been done with both animals and humans, scientists were able to investigate something that had

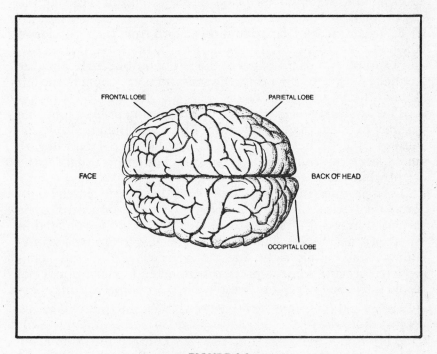

FIGURE 2-3
Top view of the human brain.
The Corpus Callosum is buried beneath the
line that divides the two hemispheres.

been suspected for decades: that at least for most right-handed people the two halves of the brain are not duplicates of each other as had once been assumed.[18] Usually the two brain halves work together, but when the corpus callosum bridge was cut surgically, it became possible to study undamaged halves of the brain to see if each side has a specialty.

In hundreds of clinical cases, it had been found that injury to the left side of the brain produced symptoms that were different from those that appeared when the right side was damaged. With the split brain people it was possible to see that there really are differences between the two brain sides. The results of these studies have been reported widely in popular magazine articles.

The left brain. The research has shown that the left side of the brain tends to handle logical thought, language, abstract thinking, analysis of details, and one's ability to do mathematics. The left hemisphere controls the ability to speak and write—so much so that people with left brain damage often are unable to use language. More recent research has suggested that the left side is associated with happiness, positive feelings,[19] and even the ability to spell.

Perhaps you are aware that information from the right side of the body goes to the left hemisphere of the brain. Your right ear, for example, sends messages to the left hemisphere. If you gaze to the right side of the room, the sensations are going to the left side of the brain.

This knowledge lets you do a little experiment. Ask someone to spell Mississippi or to divide 144 by 6 and then multiply the answer by 7.[20] There is a good chance that the person will gaze into space while thinking of a response. The gaze is usually to the right while the left brain does its work.

The right brain. In contrast to the left side of the brain, the right brain deals with the ability to appreciate and produce art, to be oriented in terms of space, to be creative, to be coordinated in sports or mechanical abilities, and to be able to appreciate anything visual.[21] The right side has been called the "sad hemisphere" because some depressed people tend to have abnormal brain waves on the right side and when people are deep in reflection or unhappiness they tend to gaze left (as the right side of the brain is stimulated).[22]

Is it possible that the right hemisphere is also the side of the brain that is most aware of the complexities of morality and evil? Some evidence suggests that this might be so.[23]

Armed with this knowledge, a novelist once wrote a murder

mystery, based on his interpretation of the split brain experiments. The main character in the novel tried to deny his involvement in the crime when he spoke (using his left brain), but he felt a lot of guilt on the right side. According to the novelist, the poor man had disagreements within his own head.[24]

Perhaps that novel is a good example of the extremes to which some people have taken the right brain-left brain differences. They seem to have assumed that the brain is a battlefield of warring factions, with two opposite and antagonistic brain halves working against each other.

But the human brain is an integrated unit, even though it tends to specialize in terms of its functioning. The left side usually deals with language and the right side with spatial awareness, but not always. We do know, however, that in normal human beings the two sides usually work together in harmony. It is only then that we are able to "appreciate the moral of a story, the meaning of a metaphor, words describing emotion, and the punch lines of jokes."[25]

The harmony between hemispheres is especially apparent when an attempt is made to understand musical abilities. Appreciation for pitch and timbre appear to be right side features. Sensitivity to rhythm is housed in both hemispheres. Ability to read notes or compose a score may be left brain capabilities. Clearly music cannot be localized in one part of the brain.

THE MIND AND THE BRAIN

But what about the mind? Can it be found in the right or left hemisphere? Is the mind included in the brain at all?

Philosophers have debated these questions for decades. Augustine was interested in "the mind-brain" problem, and so were Descartes, Leibnitz, and an American named William James who called this "the ultimate of ultimate problems."[26] If we could understand how the mind relates to the brain, James suggested, this would be "the scientific achievement before which all past achievements would pale."

The work of Wilder Penfield. Some of the most interesting ideas on the mind-brain problem have come not from philosophers but from the writings of a Canadian neurosurgeon named Wilder Penfield.

Dr. Penfield had studied under the finest neurologists in the world, and during the course of a distinguished career he did hundreds of brain operations. In such surgery, it sometimes is essential to have the patients awake so they can communicate with the doctor and guide as he or she tries to locate a part of the brain that may trigger epileptic seizures or bring other physical problems. Since the brain feels no pain, such surgery can often be done under local anesthesia.

During one of these operations, Penfield "stumbled upon the fact"[27] that when certain parts of the brain were stimulated (by very mild electric currents), the patients had "flashbacks" to vivid memories from the past. One lady, for example, described a scene from her childhood in detail, just as if she were back in the past. A young man remembered sitting at a baseball game watching a little boy crawl under the fence to join the crowd. A woman reported that she was hearing a symphony in a concert hall. Penfield stimulated the same spot about thirty times and each time the woman saw the scene, heard the music, and was able to hum along with the melody.

Before long, Penfield was keeping a record of his findings— mapping out what happened when different parts of the human brain were stimulated. At the close of his career as an operating neurosurgeon, the doctor discovered that, using local anesthesia, he had explored the brains of 1,132 patients who had had operations to treat their epilepsy.

Throughout his career, Penfield had "struggled to prove that the brain accounts for the mind,"[28] but in reviewing his life work, he began to have second thoughts. "It seems to me certain that it will always be quite impossible to explain the mind on the basis of neuronal action within the brain," he wrote. "The mind seems to act independently of the brain in the same way that a programmer acts independently of his computer."[29] Penfield concluded that when brains and bodies are growing older and wearing out, minds are often reaching their fullest potential.[30] He even wondered if minds might survive after death, and concluded that "there is no good evidence, in spite of new methods, such as the employment of stimulating electrodes . . . that the brain alone can carry out the work that the mind does."[31]

The conclusions of Howard Gardner. Penfield had an unusual way of seeing how the brain works, but it also is possible to study the human brain without ever making a surgical incision or probing with electrodes. Like Phineas Gage's doctor, who had dramatic opportunity to see how one man was influenced by brain injury, innumerable researchers have investigated the thinking of people who have been victims of brain disease, accidents, or strokes.

Howard Gardner, for example, is a Harvard University psychologist whose book, *The Shattered Mind,* is a moving account of his contacts with brain-injured people.[32] Because of the brain damage, many couldn't talk or walk, but they clearly were alert, aware of themselves or others, and often able to think clearly.

According to Dr. Gardner, when you or I talk about "my mind," we seem to be thinking of something inside our heads—a unique set of feelings, ideas, plans, beliefs, and thoughts that are personal. To most of us, the words "myself," "I," and "my mind" tend to mean pretty much the same thing.[33] Is it possible, Gardner wonders, that the mind is a slow accumulation of ideas about ourselves and about our experiences? Each of these ideas comes originally into the brain, but as we acquire more information, as we build on past experiences, and as mental ideas interact with each other, we build an awareness of "who I am." This awareness of self, which might also be called the mind, has a chemical basis in the brain, but appears to have an independent existence.

Every part of the brain contributes to this awareness of the mind and self, but the frontal lobes are perhaps of greatest importance. This was the area that Penfield investigated most thoroughly, and it is the part of the brain that, when damaged, brought the most dramatic changes in the patients whom Gardner studied. They were the people whose "minds" tended to be most disrupted.

THE MIND AND COMPUTERS

Can we conclude, then, that the mind is something based in the brain but able to rise beyond the chemical and anatomical structure of the nervous system? Is it valid to conclude, as one writer has, that the mind is to the brain as digestion is to the stomach—the brain (like the stomach) is what exists, but the mind (like digestion) is what the brain *does*?[34]

Think of the page that you are now reading. These sentences are, in one sense, only dots of ink on a paper. In another sense, however, they convey ideas that mean something more than ink dots. The dots are like the brain; the ideas are like the mind—larger than the ink dots, but dependent on them. If all of this seems complicated, then join the crowd of people who for centuries have been trying to unravel the mind-brain relationship. There still are many questions, and the debate continues.[35]

Recently there has come a new, potentially exciting, entry to the debate: computers. Some scientists believe that the computer may provide a key to unlocking the brain's secrets and solving the mind-brain problem. Other scholars aren't so sure. In some ways the brain is like an unusually sophisticated computer, but does it follow that the mind is then the computer programmer and operator?[36] If so, the human skull houses the most remarkable computer of all—a computer that completely programs itself.

Maybe the editors of *Time* made a mistake when they named the computer "Machine of the Year." Perhaps they should have honored the human mind instead!

It is amazing that consciousness, creativity, understanding, the appreciation of art or music, the capability of planning for the future, the ability to analyze the past—these and a host of other marvelous human capabilities—are all housed in a mass of cells that decay and sometimes get damaged. Nobody knows why this is. But as Wilder Penfield concluded near the end of his life, many questions about the mind are beyond the ability of science to answer.[37]

Before going any farther, therefore, perhaps there could be value in taking at least a brief look beyond science. What have ancient writers, especially the biblical writers, said about the human mind? That is the theme of the next chapter.

3
THE
BIBLICAL
MIND

I suppose it shouldn't surprise me anymore. Colorful advertising has been landing in my mailbox for years. But I am constantly amazed when I read the kinds of things that people are trying to sell.

"YOU CAN DISCOVER THE BEAUTY OF YOUR MIND'S LIMITLESS POTENTIAL," a letter addressed to me recently proclaimed. In exchange for $275.00, I could receive all that was needed to expand my memory, spiral my creativity, and experience joyful learning. Another brochure advertised "love tapes." The manufacturer promised that these would help me to use both halves of the brain and would stimulate "effective mind development." If I listened carefully, the tapes would bring more happiness, health, success, loving relationships, and peace of mind.

A magazine advertisement tells me that I am not alone in the universe. "Somewhere out there are other minds," the Rosicrucians proclaim. And, I am told, in this world, each of us has the power to experience "profound" peace of mind.

One fascinating catalog recently offered a variety of cassettes that would help me to speak "Spanish, French, German, Italian, or Hebrew in exactly twenty-four hours," lose weight through subliminal subconscious mind control, dramatically improve my vision so I could throw away my glasses, become a professional hypnotist, "win big money in casinos . . . time after time," learn karate, become twice as smart as I am now, conquer fears, control phobias, eliminate all sex problems, learn about "universal mind power," and release my "creative mind potential." All of this was as near as my phone and could be charged on my MasterCard.

I confess that much of this colorful advertising makes me skeptical. Do I really use only 5 percent of my brain capacity, as the brochures proclaim? Is it really possible that "there is a hidden Einstein, Rembrandt, and Hemingway in everyone," ready to be pulled out through new techniques of mind development? Do the advertisements promise something that is really possible, or are the cassette sellers overly impressed with the potential of making a fast buck from gullible MasterCard holders?

It is undoubtedly true that our minds can be more productive and efficient. Surely there can be great value in looking at modern methods of learning, intellectual stimulation, creativity building, and mind development. (One purpose for this book is to describe some of these modern developments.) But there can also be value in pondering the wisdom that has persisted through the ages. There is truth in the old idea that an awareness of the past can help us plan for the future and avoid errors in the present.

But in turning to the past, where do we look to find useful information? There would be value in studying the ancient philosophers and historians, but there is no literature more widely read, respected, debated, and analyzed than the pages of the Bible. It should come as no surprise to discover that this ancient Book is filled with insightful statements about the mind.

THE BIBLE AND THE MIND

Several years ago I was invited to give a series of talks at a local church. "Choose any topic you want," the caller suggested, "but a few of our people have been wondering if you could include something about the mind."

I hung up the phone, reached nonchalantly for a Bible index, and turned to the "M's." To my amazement I discovered that there are roughly two hundred biblical references to the word "mind."

If we could understand the original Hebrew and Greek languages in which the Bible was written, we would discover that no one word in either language is equivalent to the English term "mind." In the King James Version of the Bible, for example, six different Hebrew words are translated "mind"—and sometimes these same ancient words become "soul," "heart," and "attitude" when they are translated into English.[1]

Perhaps this helps to explain why "mind" has different connotations when used in the biblical writings. Sometimes the word refers to *determination*. (In Nehemiah 4:6, for example, we read that the people "had a mind to work."[2]) In parts of the Old Testament the word "mind" is used to mean *memory*. (Isaiah 46:8, 9 tells readers to "remember" the past and "fix it in mind." Lamentations 3:21–23 reminds readers of God's love, compassion, and faithfulness. "I call this to mind," the writer states, "and therefore I have hope.")

In the New Testament there are several references to the mind as something related to *emotional stability*. According to Mark 5:15 and Luke 8:35, when Jesus healed a demon-possessed man, the people were amazed and afraid when they saw him "in his right mind." Later, the brother of Jesus wrote about the man who is "double-minded" and thus "unstable in all he does."[3]

Elsewhere in the Bible, "mind" refers to *thinking* (as when Mary "cast about in her mind" to discover the meaning of the angel's message),[4] to *intellectual alertness* (as seen by the people in Berea who were open-minded),[5] and to *commitment* (as shown by the person who loves God "with all your heart and with all your soul and with all your mind").[6]

Reading further, we see that the biblical writers often used an adjective to describe the mind. They wrote, for example, about the evil mind, blinded mind, corrupted mind, wicked mind, hardened mind, doubtful mind, reprobate mind, vain mind, and fleshly mind.[7] Sometimes the adjectives were more positive. The New Testament writers referred to the willing mind, the lowly mind, the humble mind, the sound mind, the pure mind, and the mind that is renewed.[8]

The Bible also gives instructions for mind development and makes promises to people whose minds are focused on spiritual issues. You will experience "perfect peace," the book of Isaiah states, if you put your trust in God and let your mind think about him.[9] In terms of our beliefs and lifestyles, it is best if we can each be "fully convinced" in our own minds of what we think.[10] In several places we are told that there can be benefits to individuals who are able to work together united "with one mind."[11] And the Christian is given the remarkable statement that "strange as it seems, we Christians actually do have within us a portion of the very thoughts and mind of Christ."[12]

Each of these Bible references would be consistent with the definition of mind that we gave in chapter one; each refers to our thinking, inner attitudes, and mental abilities. But the biblical writers were not trained in psychology, and their ideas about the mind almost always suggested action rather than only a passive reflection and contemplation.[13] We learn, for example, that anxious minds lead to anxious behavior;[14] that people with foolish minds say stupid things, spread error, and are involved in evil actions;[15] that the sinful mind leads to acts that are hostile to God;[16] that people with corrupt minds love conflict;[17] that we can make up our minds not to worry;[18] and that our minds can be controlled and readied for activity.[19]

Are all of these ways of saying that our minds control behavior and mold our personalities? Wise King Solomon once wrote that our thinking influences our actions and determines what we are like.[20] The mind is not something that can be discussed in a book and then ignored in everyday life.

William James once concluded that the greatest discovery of his generation was the fact that "human beings can alter their lives by altering the attitudes of the mind." The quality of our lives is closely related to the quality of our thinking. In large measure, how we think with our minds determines how we live, view the world, see ourselves, and get along with others. And with our minds we decide what to do with God and whether or not we will think now about life after death.

HUMAN NATURE AND THE MIND

In his famous theory of psychoanalysis, Sigmund Freud divided the human personality into three parts: the id, the ego, and the super-ego. More recently, the popular transactional analysis approach to therapy has made a similar proposal. Within each of us, this view maintains, there are three conflicting forces: the "child," the "adult," and the "parent." Does the Bible make a similar division?

According to some people the answer is yes. Human beings are assumed to be "tripartite," composed of three parts. There is the *body*, the *spirit* (the supernatural part of our natures), and the *soul* which is assumed to include the emotions, the will, and the mind.[21]

Such a viewpoint is based not on the Bible but on Greek philosophy.[22] It assumes—incorrectly I believe—that the Bible attempts to give a scientific view of human nature.[23] It fails to realize that biblical writers apparently used different words (including the words that are translated "mind," "heart," "soul," and—in the Old Testament—sometimes even "bowels" and "liver") to mean the same thing: "the inner self, or the mind that controls the self."[24]

It is accurate, writes Professor G. C. Berkouwer of the Free University of Amsterdam, to conclude that the Bible sees human beings as holistic individuals who are described in different ways and with different, sometimes overlapping words. (Such as "heart," "soul," "flesh," "spirit," "conscience," and "mind.") He also writes that "the Biblical view of man shows him to us in an impressive diversity, but . . . it never loses sight of the unity of the whole man." Instead, it brings out and accentuates this unity. No part of the person is emphasized as being independent of other parts.[25]

But even though the Bible has a holistic view of human beings, it seems to portray a struggle between our mental inclinations and our actions. Saint Paul confessed to his own conflict between what his mind wanted and what he did in practice,[26] and Jesus taught that outward behavior begins with one's private thinking.[27] Once again we see the influence of the mind on our lives and daily ways of living.

What are some of the ways in which behavior is controlled by thinking? In the remainder of this chapter, we will consider just two of the mindsets or ways of thinking that are described in the Bible. Each of these can have practical relevance for life today.

THE PREPARED-ACTIVE MIND

When I was a student living in London, I made my way one Sunday evening to Regent Street and an Anglican church known as All Soul's Langham Place. To my surprise, the place was packed, and I soon discovered why. The preacher was a man named John R. W. Stott. At that time he wasn't as well known as he is today. Instead, he was serving as a parish rector whose in-depth preaching captivated his congregations week after week.

In a book titled *Your Mind Matters*, Dr. Stott tells the story of a man who once described his feelings whenever he went to church. "I feel like unscrewing my head and placing it under the seat, because in a religious meeting I never have any use for anything above my collar."[28]

Such mindless religion never existed in Stott's church and neither is it endorsed in the Bible. Dorothy Sayers, a member of a writers' group that included C. S. Lewis and J. R. R. Tolkien, once listed what she considered the most conspicuous "virtues" of ordinary church members. These included mental timidity, childishness, dullness, sentimentality, fault-finding, depression, and a need to be considered respectable.[29] These qualities are in sharp contrast to those implicit in the advice of the apostle Peter. "Prepare your minds for action," he wrote. "Be self-controlled; set your hope on the grace to be given you when Jesus Christ is revealed."[30] At least three very practical ideas can be found in his words.

First, we should be mentally alert. The *King James Bible* uses the words "gird up the loins of your mind." This is a quaint expression but it conveys a vivid picture.

In the ancient Middle East, as in some countries today, men wore long flowing robes that hindered fast progress and could get in the way whenever strenuous activity was necessary. But around the waist, the men wore a broad belt into which the robes could be tucked if there was a need for freer movement.

Thus, the Bible is telling us to "gird up" our minds and get ready for action. The instructions were written to people who already were followers of Christ,[31] and the message was clear: Their minds should be alert and sharp. They were not expected to unscrew their heads when they went to church.

William Barclay, the noted Bible scholar from Glasgow University, once described what may have been in Peter's mind as he wrote.

> Peter is telling his people that they must be ready for the most strenuous mental endeavour. They must never be content with a flabby and unexamined faith; they must . . . think things out and think them through. They must never be content with an easy and superficial acceptance of faith. They must think things out. It may be that they will have to discard some things. It may be that they will make mistakes. But that with which they are left will be theirs in such a way that nothing and nobody can ever take it away from them.[32]

Second, we should be mentally self-controlled. The Bible writer apparently was concerned about people who were morally and intellectually inclined to be intoxicated with the latest fad or newest craze. There is nothing wrong with being aware of the intellectual trends around us, but the careful thinker does not let his or her mind get carried away by some person's new theory or cassette program. Careful investigation is the mark of an alert mind.

Third, we should be mentally hopeful. Hope seems to be in short supply in modern times. There is much around us to cause mental despair and hopelessness.

Some people, I suspect, might criticize believers for putting their hopes in God and in the expectation that Christ will someday return. But whether or not one accepts this theology—as I do—it is hard to dispute the fact that a mind filled with hope is a mind that avoids futility and despair. The mind that "hopes fully" in Christ has some purpose for living in the present and for looking forward to the future.

At the end of his life, Charles Darwin lamented the fact that he had become so intent on proving his theory of evolution, that he had lost the ability to appreciate poetry, music, and art. "My mind seems to have become a kind of machine for grinding general laws out of large collections of facts," he wrote. As a result of his overemphasis on work, Darwin sensed an increased sadness, a loss of intellectual alertness, and a decline in his emotional sensitivity.[33] Any of us could fall into the same trap of narrow, constricted thinking.

Far better, and richer, is the prepared-active mind—especially the mind that has hope because it has something, and someone, in which to believe.

THE RENEWED MIND

The Book of Romans is a biblical statement of theology with a powerful, practical postscript at the end. The first two verses of chapter twelve begin the practical section by stating that it is possible to be "transformed by the renewing of your mind." Then the writer, Paul, gives some instructions about how mind renewal can take place. The instructions focus on the physical, social, and spiritual issues in our lives.

First, mind renewal is linked to how we care for our bodies. The Bible's words at first sound somewhat mystical: "I urge you . . . to offer your bodies as living sacrifices, holy and pleasing to God."[34]

In the ancient Jewish religion from which Christianity arose, the worshipers presented sacrificial animals at the temple. These were not to be crippled animals or rejects from the herd. Instead, God was to be given the best animals the people could find.

When Jesus came to earth, he claimed to be God's Son. He offered to give his own life in death on the cross, and in this way—because he was a perfect sacrifice—he paid for the sins of all future generations of believers.[35] Animal sacrifices would no longer be necessary to pay for human sins.

In writing his epistle, therefore, Paul reminds the readers of "God's mercy." Because God is so good to us, Paul writes, believers should worship God by keeping their own bodies holy, pleasing to their Maker, and offered to him as an ongoing, living sacrifice.

Obviously this is written to people who were followers of Christ. But is it possible for anyone to have a clear mind if the body is steeped in pollutants and enslaved by what the Bible and some modern psychiatrists call "sin"?[36]

Second, mind renewal is linked to how we relate to other people. Once again the Bible gives a challenging directive: "Do not conform any longer to the pattern of this world, but be transformed by the renewing of your mind."

It takes no effort or force of character to go with the crowd. Anybody can float along with the opinions, values, fads, and customs of the masses. But the "patterns of this world" may not always be good or healthy. Sometimes we need to stand out from the crowd, instead of letting others squeeze us into their mold.[37]

We can only resist the squeeze when our minds are "renewed." In another part of the New Testament,[38] Paul reminds his readers that they once were corrupted by their selfish desires, but now they have a new "attitude of mind" that brings about a change in behavior. As a result of this change, people are different—much more inclined to be characterized by goodness and right living.

It is possible, no doubt, to bring about some of these changes through a willful determination to alter our ways of thinking. But the Bible is clear in stating that mental willpower, by itself, has limited effectiveness. When we really want to change our attitudes, and then our ways of living, we need to ask God for help.[39] Soon people are likely to notice that their thinking and behavior are being "transformed"—for the better.

The remainder of Romans 12 gives us a useful guide to the kinds of thinking and behavior changes seen in people whose minds are transformed. They have a more realistic self-image, an awareness of their strong points, a sensitivity to the needs of others, a new zest for living, a natural willingness to be helpful, and a better ability to get along with people. The list, and its promises, are impressive.[40]

Third, mind renewal is linked to how we get along with God. According to the Bible, God has a "good, pleasing, and perfect will" for people. We are able to live in accordance with this will, when we keep our minds open and are willing to have them renewed by God.

To the person steeped in religion, all of this may make perfect sense. To the reader who has not studied the Bible in detail, this will sound strange and new.

But these biblical ideas are also thought-provoking and practical, as are the Bible's teachings on the pure mind, the heavenly mind, the Christian mind, the envious mind, and even the troubled mind.

In the chapters that follow, we will return again to these ancient themes and contrast them, at times, with modern psychological, physiological, educational, and religious perspectives on the mind. We might even discover that some of those mind-improvement products and cassette tapes we read about in our mail are not as unrealistic or as idealistic as they seem at first.

4
THE
POSITIVE
MIND

Everybody in Garden Grove, California, knows about the Crystal Cathedral. Only a few miles from Disneyland, and clearly visible from the busy Orange County freeways, the imposing, sixteen-million-dollar all-glass structure dominates the landscape of its southern California community.

Every Sunday the Reverend Robert H. Schuller, resplendent in flowing blue robes, mounts the flower-decked platform to deliver his sermon. Only a third of the church's 10,000 members are able to be seated in the massive auditorium, under its 10,660 panes of glass. There are other worshipers who sit in their cars, listen on the radio, and view the preacher through an opening in the building created by two ninety-foot glass doors that swing silently aside at the start of each service. Millions more, throughout North America and overseas, watch on television. They are part of what has been called the largest congregation in the world. The "Hour of Power" morning service is the most watched of all televised church services.

It wasn't like this when the present pastor started preaching at a nearby drive-in theater only a few years ago. The first congregations were very small, and for a while the preacher struggled with self-doubt and fear of failure. But within his mind there was a dream—a determination to create something big and beautiful.

THE POWER OF POSITIVE THINKING

The magnificent Crystal Cathedral was built, debt-free, as a "service center for God," but today it also stands as a monument to the power of a positive mind. Dr. Schuller talks frequently about "possibility thinking," but he would be among the first to acknowledge that the notion of a positive mindset did not originate with him.

It could be argued that possibility thinkers have existed since the dawn of history, but the idea was catapulted to popular attention by another clergyman—Norman Vincent Peale.

Born in a small Ohio town at the turn of the century, Peale was a "preacher's kid" who struggled for a while with self-doubt and feelings of inadequacy.[1] But he overcame this, chose to enter the ministry and quickly established himself as an outstanding preacher. In the late 1930s he published two slender little volumes that met with only moderate success, but a 1948 book went through twenty-five printings and Peale's delighted publishers urged him to try again.

When *The Power of Positive Thinking* appeared in October of 1952, the reviews were friendly but not enthusiastic. Who could have predicted what would happen next? The book jumped to the top of *The New York Times* best seller list and stayed there long enough to break the all-time record. Sales moved into the millions and the book was translated into more than thirty languages. Through his writings, newspaper columns, radio talks, public lectures, and sermons, Dr. Peale became known as the "minister to millions." He appeared on the covers of *Newsweek* and *Look* magazines, was showered with acclaim and honorary degrees, was inundated with mail, and found himself swamped with invitations to speak.

The publisher had pushed the book enthusiastically, and the author had a captivating writing style—with short sentences, frequent anecdotes, enthusiastic phrases, unpretentious simplicity, and great clarity. But the book's real popularity came because of its message.

"Altogether too many people are defeated by the everyday problems of life," Peale's introduction stated. "They go struggling, perhaps even whining, through their days with a sense of dull resentment at what they consider the 'bad breaks' life has given them. In a sense there may be such a thing as 'the breaks' in this life, but there is also a spirit and method by which we can control and even determine those breaks."[2] That "spirit and method" could be summed up in two words: *positive thinking.*

The first few words in the book showed the optimism and hope that permeated the following chapters. "BELIEVE IN YOURSELF!" the author began. "Have faith in your abilities!" With "sound self-confidence you can succeed."[3] The book offered "simple procedures" that promised to bring readers peace of mind, improved health, a never-ceasing flow of energy, and a life filled with joy and satisfaction.[4] The chapters dealt with ways to "create your own happiness," stop fretting, break the worry habit, learn to relax, get people to like you, have constant energy, solve personal problems, and get the power that comes from "a peaceful mind." As a clergyman, the writer did not hesitate to make references to "prayer power," the help of God, and the importance of drawing upon "that Higher Power;" but his emphasis was on how to change mental attitudes, develop optimism, and, of course, learn to think positively. In the years to follow there would be an avalanche of self-help books. However, *The Power of Positive Thinking* not only was one of the first, it was the most influential.

It is difficult to encounter the ideas of Norman Vincent Peale—or Robert Schuller—and not feel buoyed with confidence and hope. The possibility thinkers are motivators who know how to communicate and who believe, without hesitation, in their message.[5] They use phrases that spur people on to action:

- "Develop the happiness habit. . . . Out of the happiness habit comes a happy life."
- "Do not fume. Do not fret. Practice being peaceful."
- "Take a positive, optimistic attitude toward every problem."
- "God is actually with you and helping you. . . . RECEIVE power from Him."[6]
- "Remember, always remember: You can if you think you can."
- "When you have a problem . . . never quit."
- "Keep on believing in yourself."
- "Never think of failing. You don't need to!"
- "You have what it takes to meet obstacles."[7]

Moving beyond Peale's practical writings, Schuller wrote a "theology of self-esteem," and proposed that there should be a "theology of possibility thinking." He boldly proclaimed that his work could usher in a "new Reformation," and hinted that this would be as significant as the Protestant Reformation of Luther and Calvin.[8]

For the doubters, both Peale and Schuller can point to their own considerable achievements through positive thinking. And each has a host of anecdotes and case histories to show that possibility thinking works.[9]

POSITIVE MENTAL ATTITUDE AND THE PROMISE OF SUCCESS

It would be wrong if we got the impression that positive thinkers are all connected with the church. Educators, athletes, entertainers, political leaders, and a host of others have seen and proclaimed the value of developing a positive mind. But nowhere has this been more apparent than in the world of business.

W. Clement Stone, for example, is a fabulously wealthy Chicago businessman who started with $100.00 and built a multimillion-dollar corporation. At the age of sixteen he sold his first insurance policy. By the time he was twenty, he had established an insurance agency, and a short time later he created his own national sales organization. And to what does Stone attribute his success? He believes in having a positive mental attitude—something which is abbreviated PMA.

W. Clement Stone has written several books, and it probably will come as no surprise for you to learn that these are best sellers. They all have variations of the same message: It is possible for anyone to have success through a positive mental attitude.[10] Like his friends Norman Vincent Peale and Robert Schuller, Stone punctuates his books with practical suggestions, stories of success, and slogans that motivate. He writes about preparing salesmen to become outstanding successes by "motivating them to become self-builders."[11] He suggests that anyone, even a child, can be taught to develop a positive mental attitude by filling the "subconscious mind with self-suggestion." To do this, we need to repeat positive phrases such as this:

Day by day, in every way, through the grace of God I am getting better and better.

Stone freely admits that this idea originated with the autosuggestion theory of Emile Coué.[12] He does not claim that PMA is his idea. It is an approach to life that is seen in the experiences of "the most successful persons our nation has known." It is a mental attitude that does not arise naturally. It comes easiest to people who have a belief in God, and it must be practiced by those who have learned a basic principle of PMA: Success is achieved and maintained by those who keep trying.[13]

A more recent addition to the PMA speakers' roster is a man named Zig Ziglar. He is a dynamic, enthusiastic, entertaining speaker who radiates charisma and reportedly travels 350,000 miles every year preaching the message of success through a "right mental attitude."[14] The cognitive scientists that we mentioned in chapter one rarely pay much attention to the motivators like Zig Ziglar. But could it be that this man, and the other apostles of PMA religion, are the most influential shapers of thought in America today?

SOME PERSPECTIVES ON THE POSITIVE MIND

Shortly after Robert Schuller published his theology of possibility thinking,[15] an influential preacher, also from Southern California, published a powerful attack on the book.[16] The critic pointed out, correctly many would agree, that Schuller's enthusiasm for possibility thinking had led him to redefine the basics of Christian theology. Original sin, his book stated, has nothing to do with wickedness but really is the same as a negative self-image. To be born again is to change from inferiority to self-esteem and to move from a negative to a positive self-image. A person in hell is one who has lost self-esteem, and salvation means "to be permanently lifted from sin (psychological self-abuse with all of its consequences . . .)" and moved to a state of self-esteem.[17] Surely there was merit in the criticism that Schuller was attempting to fit God into a man-made philosophy. And could it be true that the world's greatest preacher of possibility thinking had really invented a new gospel that is "quasi-Christian, proud humanism without transactional redemption"?[18]

Similar questions had been raised earlier, long before Schuller's book appeared. Dr. John Stott, in his Presidential Address to the Inter-Varsity Fellowship Annual Conference, argued that the positive thinkers had replaced a faith in God with a faith both in ourselves and in the ability of human beings to change their own thinking. Stott questioned Peale's "worry breaking formula" which proposed that the first thing we should do every morning is jump out of bed and say out loud, "I believe, I believe, I believe." But what do we believe in? Who do we believe in? The answer, presumably, was to believe in our own capabilities.[19]

Psychologist Paul Vitz would agree with this criticism. He maintains that the possibility thinkers emphasize faith in self and reduce God to "a useful servant" who is helpful in letting us reach our personal goals.[20]

Several years ago I attended a two-day PMA workshop. The seminar leader was humorous, enthusiastic, and absolutely convinced of the value and all-encompassing power of a positive mind. Although some of us who attended the meeting were less convinced (and probably less positive in our attitudes) than our leader, we still came away realizing that positive thinking can have tremendous practical implications for day-to-day living.

SO WHAT CAN WE SAY ABOUT PMA?

As we will see, there can be problems with the positive-thinking approach, but let's not begin with the negative. Instead, can we see what is positive about the positive mind?

The positive mind produces hope. I have a friend whose life has not been easy. Family problems, financial burdens, career disappointments, and health failures have all combined to make things difficult. It isn't easy for my friend to maintain a bright and cheerful perspective on life. Sometimes it seems that he goes about his days waiting in tension for the next disaster to strike.

Is it possible, however, that my friend contributes to his own hopelessness? He expects the worst and acts on the assumption that his circumstances will never be better. So he has given up trying to change and he wallows in misery—without hope.

When I was a young college teacher, I asked my students to read Viktor Frankl's account of his three grim years in a Nazi prison camp.[21] Frankl was a Jewish psychiatrist who lived each day with the realization that he might be among those who would march next to the human incinerators. Such knowledge drove some prisoners mad, while others gave up hope and died.

But not Viktor Frankl!

Sometimes he would peer through the broken slats in the wall of his cold hut and take pleasure in the beauty of a sunset. He worked to develop a sense of humor so he could laugh—even in his misery. He thought about life after the war and concluded that "the prisoner who had lost faith in the future—his future—was doomed."[22] He tried to find meaning in his suffering, and he looked for opportunities to help others.

After his release, Frankl developed the famous theory of logotherapy. It rests on the assumption that each of us needs to have meaning in life, even when circumstances are bad. Frankl never used the term "positive thinking," but that certainly described his mindset during the years in prison. Positive thinking kept him alive because it gave him hope.

The positive mind reduces pessimism and helps us cope with the pressures of life.[23] Do you remember the story of Pollyanna? In a tremendously popular book that first appeared in 1912, Eleanor Porter told the adventures of a little girl who saw the bright side of everything—even when she was mistreated by a stern aunt and seriously injured in a car accident.

Today, such thinking tends to be laughed at. Everybody knows that Pollyanna was simplistic and naive, so we look with mild disdain on people who are "Pollyanna-ish" in their thinking. But that fictional little girl was buoyed by her bright perspective and she lifted the spirits of everyone she met. Maybe Pollyanna's positive attitude is something that many of us lack—and feel we need. Perhaps this need is what attracts millions to the PMA seminars and books.

One of the most powerful sentences in the Bible was written by Paul when he, like Frankl, was confined to a prison. "Whatever is true, whatever is noble, whatever is right, whatever is pure, whatever is lovely, whatever is admirable—if anything is excellent or praiseworthy—think about such things."[24] This is not a Pollyanna-like suggestion. It is, instead, a command from a man who knew how to cope with pressure. For those of us who believe that the Bible is the Word of God, this statement is a divine indication that there is value in training our minds to dwell not on the negative but on thoughts that are good, right, and positive. Such thinking can help us cope with life's stresses.

The positive mind can stir us to action. Everybody knows that young children like to hear stories—and most parents, I suspect, aren't opposed to reading to their offspring at bedtime each evening.

But parents like variety; their kids often do not. Little people tend to ask for the same story over and over again (or they play the same record repeatedly), until their thoroughly bored parents are ready to scream.

One of the favorites in our house was the story of a little train engine who wasn't sure if he had the energy to get over a hill. Drawing on all of his strength and almost bursting with effort, he puffed, pushed himself, and kept repeating, "I think I can, I think I can, I think I can . . ." (if you read the words fast, they're supposed to sound like a train) until at last he reached the top.

The writer of that children's story was teaching a basic PMA principle: We can win by determination. Dr. Peale expressed the same idea in the title of one of his books: *You Can If You Think You Can.*[25] Motivated by this belief, thousands of people have overcome their lethargy, have refused to quit or talk about defeat, and have gone on to accomplish great and significant things. The history books are filled with stories of people who persisted in spite of failure, obstacles, and temptations to quit. Such persistence is a distinguishing mark of successful people. Their positive mental attitude motivates them to keep going.

The Negative Side of the Positive Mind

The admirable enthusiasm that radiates from possibility thinkers often hides the fact that there can be another side to the PMA picture.

The positive mind can lead us to ignore problems and to deny reality. By looking at things optimistically, it is possible to overlook real danger and miss seeing severe problems. This happened repeatedly in the Old Testament. The preachers and prophets would call rebellious people to repentance, but they would prefer to see things positively and to ignore the evidence showing political corruption and moral decline in their society.

Many people make a similar mistake today. Positive about their work and inclined to overlook family problems, too many men fail to see that their marriages are falling apart, until it is too late. Convinced that things will get better, business people ignore problems and go further into debt, until they are faced with bankruptcy. Enthusiastic about their church programs, many believers do not see the spiritual and personal needs of the hurting people who smile across the aisle on Sunday mornings.

Sometimes even without our conscious awareness, positive thinking becomes a smoke screen that hides reality, enables us to deny our weaknesses, and provides an excuse to do nothing about problems that may, in time, be destructive.

There can be no doubt that the advocates of a positive mental attitude have done much that is of value. They have encouraged a lot of people, motivated others to action, and challenged the poor-little-me-I-can't-do-anything mentality that plagues too many of us. But there has also been a tendency, at times, for the positive thinkers to ignore dangers and to overlook the fact that in spite of their PMA, some people simply do not have the abilities, training, or opportunities to attain their unrealistic dreams or to reach their lofty goals. Like all enthusiasts, the possibility thinkers emphasize success stories, but fail to tell us about people who had a positive mindset—and failed.

The positive mind can undermine basic Christianity. The same possibility thinking that can reduce pessimism, help us cope with pressure, and stimulate action, can also ignore and even undermine some basic Christian teachings.

The Bible teaches that God loves us, values us, cares for us, and gives us hope. The God who created the world and us is still in control, holding all things together by his power.[26] Because they believe this, Christians have every reason to shun pessimism and to think positively—about themselves, about the world in which we live, and about the future.

It doesn't take long for the reader to discover, however, that the Bible is very realistic. It warns of life's dangers, freely deals with unpopular topics like sin, and alerts us to the end results of immorality. It calls readers to repentance and commitment, shows that people in themselves are powerless apart from God,[27] and realistically points out that believers may be persecuted—even though some well-meaning Christian leaders may claim otherwise. The Bible demonstrates that some of history's greatest saints—like John the Baptist, Paul, and Jesus—did not "make it to the top" in terms of the values of their society, even though they served God diligently and had a positive mindset.

The advocates of PMA overlook some of this realism. They say little about obedience, discipleship, or the cost of commitment. And they rarely mention the will of God for individual lives.

The Bible never implies that God wants us to have a positive mental attitude that ignores him and sends us off on our own self-centered schemes to get pleasure and success. God wants obedience, sensitivity to his leading, and a recognition of the sin and realities of life. Christ himself taught that the way to be great is to be a servant,[28] even though this may not lead to a life of ease, acclaim, and positive thinking. With him, all things are possible—even things that are impossible for humans to do on their own.[29] The Christian's responsibility is to yield to God's control and direction, knowing that he will give a realistic-optimistic perspective on life.

SOME CONCLUSIONS ABOUT THE POSITIVE MIND

It would be foolish to ignore the benefits and power of the positive mind. It would be equally foolish to ignore the realities of life and to assume that we can do all things through PMA and possibility thinking.

What we need, instead, is a balanced perspective. This is the recognition that most of us need to think more positively, without losing sight of realism and the will of God in human affairs.

Nowhere is this balance more needed than in our thinking about sickness. Can a positive mental attitude heal? Does the positive mind sometimes keep us from facing the realities of sickness? These questions lead us to the fascinating issue of the mind's influence on illness and healing. That is the topic of chapter five.

5
THE
HEALING
MIND

David Oligani is a short, pleasant, soft-spoken, middle-aged man with olive complexion and jet black hair. His home is not far from Baguio, the mountain resort center north of Manila, where wealthy Filipinos and thousands of American military personnel vacation every year.

Few of the vacationers have heard about David Oligani, but to his own people, he is well known. Deeply religious and heavily involved in the Espiritista Church, David is a psychic surgeon who claims to operate on people using his bare hands. There are no anesthetics, but the surgery is painless. Immediately following each operation, the incision appears to have healed, the patient steps down from the table, and the next person comes in for treatment. On a normal day David does seventeen or eighteen operations, but on Sunday, the number more than triples. He admits, without hesitation, that his powers come from God.

Several years ago, the psychic surgeons attracted great interest in Australia, Japan, Europe, and North America. Service clubs and church groups watched films of the healers at work, and literally thousands of people—some of whom were very sick— flew on charter flights to the Philippines in search of instant healing.

One of the travelers was a Minneapolis surgeon with impeccable medical credentials. Dr. William Nolen, a man who had performed several thousand operations in the United States, wanted to investigate the psychic healers for himself. The films of psychic surgery had been impressive, and many people were praising the healers' incredible powers and abilities. Nolen knew, however, that those of us who are not medically trained could easily be fooled, so the American decided to watch the operations with the eyes of an experienced surgeon.[1] The investigation took him on an eight-thousand-mile journey that eventually brought him to the home of David Oligani.

According to Dr. Nolen, David's operations, and those of the other psychic surgeons, were all pretty much the same. The patient would enter the house, or come forward after a church service, and describe the symptoms. Usually, the person would then be instructed to lie down and his clothes would be pulled back just enough to expose the abdomen or other part of the body being prepared for surgery.

David would bow in prayer, then swab the skin with alcohol. While one of his hands remained on the patient's flesh, the other would make a slashing gesture in the air, apparently to make the incision. Soon a dark red liquid would begin to ooze from the healer's fingers. For a few minutes there would be kneading of the skin, "just as one might knead dough," then something would be pulled from under the surgeon's fingers and identified as a blood clot, an appendix, a tumor, or some other kind of "bad tissue." The "tissue" would be removed by an assistant, David would use a little cotton to mop up the red liquid, and the operation would be over. There would be no cut, no stitches, no scar, no pain.

And the patient immediately felt better.

As you might have guessed, Dr. Nolen was skeptical, and so were members of the medical community in the Philippines. A television documentary, filmed by a British crew from the BBC and shown widely in the United States and Canada, raised questions about the healers' abilities.[2] Many of those who thought they had been healed discovered later that they still had their original medical problems. Before long the charter flights stopped, and the overseas popularity of psychic surgery faded.

But the surgeons still work in the villages of the Philippines, Mexico, and Brazil. Even today, as you read, hundreds of people will be visiting psychic surgeons, quack healers, and primitive medicine men around the world—and many of these sick people will get better. The improvements will not be a result of scientific medicine. The pain relief, sometimes accompanied by actual recovery, comes because the mind is able to influence the body.

THE MIND AS A CAUSE OF DISEASE

Before we consider how the mind can bring healing, it may be helpful to ponder some of the ways by which the mind creates sickness.

Almost everybody has heard about voodoo deaths and the curses that bring sickness and death in some primitive societies. When a tribe decides to punish one of its members, for example, the witch doctor may be called to recite some incantations and point a "magic bone" at the hapless victim who is then assumed to be under the spell of death.

"The man who discovers that he has been 'boned' is a pitiable sight," one explorer wrote. "He sways backwards and falls to the ground . . . he writhes as if in mortal agony and, covering his face with his hands, begins to moan." Later, he regains his composure, crawls to his hut, sickens, frets, and dies a short time later.[3]

Dr. Walter Cannon, a Harvard physiologist, has suggested that voodoo victims get sick and die because of the body's reaction to fear and the loss of support from the tribe. The heart beats faster and the capillaries eventually are damaged. Blood pressure drops and the vital functions cease. Having been left alone to die, the victim has no emotional support or physical help. Death is the only alternative.[4]

In 1884 an eminent London physician compiled a scholarly book titled *Illustrations of the Influence of the Mind upon the Body*. The author summarized what was then scientifically known about the mind's power over the body.[5] But it isn't necessary to read outdated medical books or to visit remote primitive tribes to see how the mind can bring sickness. The existence of psychosomatic illness is well recognized in our society, and there are hundreds of research studies to show how the stresses of life affect us physically.

It is now widely accepted, for example, that worry, fear, insecurity, anxiety, uncertainty, excitement, and a host of other emotions can influence the body in a variety of ways. Heart attacks, migraine headaches, hypertension, ulcers, colitis, constipation, diarrhea, diabetes, allergies, cancer, backaches, arthritis, and perhaps even accident proneness may all have known physical causes, but each of these is more likely to appear in people whose minds are under emotional stress.[6] There is overwhelming evidence that although the mind heals, it can also attack us physically.[7]

Consider, for example, the problem of headaches. These come at times because of clear physical influences such as fatigue, hormone imbalances, unhealthy diets, or changes in the menstrual cycle. More often, however, headaches result from emotional tension. According to one report, 90 percent of all headaches, including migraine headaches, come when we feel anxious, tense, angry, frustrated, threatened, or unable to control our circumstances.[8] At such times, and for reasons still being studied, muscles tighten in the head, normal blood flow through the arteries is hindered, and nearby nerve endings are stimulated to create pain.[9] Clearly, one's state of mind can create headaches, and the mind can reduce them as well.[10]

The findings of psychoneuroimmunology. Within recent years a relatively new field of science—with a long name—has arisen. Psychoneuroimmunology studies how the mind and body work together, often to immunize us against disease.

It used to be assumed that the "immune system" of the body worked on its own to fight disease, destroy bacteria or viruses, and keep the body healthy. Now it appears that the immune system works in conjunction with the central nervous system. Someplace within the brain, most likely in the hypothalamus, the two systems get together (along with the endocrine system) and influence each other.[11]

Whenever we encounter stressful situations, the central nervous system sends a message to the hypothalamus and this, in turn, sends out small chemical messages that alert the brain to the problem. Some of these chemicals help the body rise to defend itself against further disease and damage, but other chemicals affect the immune system and reduce its ability to fight disease. This helps to explain why people (and laboratory animals) are more likely to get sick when they are under stress.

Cancer patients are an example of this. The possibility of a connection between cancer and the mind has been the most intensively studied issue in psychoneuroimmunology. Some of these research investigations have supported the conclusion that mental stress triggers chemicals that weaken the influence of the immune system. This, in turn, lessens the body's ability to fight cancer.

Not long ago, a group of scientists started studying the immune systems of men whose wives had breast cancer. After their wives died, it was found that each of the surviving husbands experienced a chemical change in the immune system. The stress of grief, along with the depression and anxiety that frequently accompany bereavement, had influenced the immune system and reduced its ability to fight disease. This may very well explain why surviving spouses so often become ill and die following a mate's death.

Other research has shown that depressed patients have a similar suppression of the immune system. If you get depressed, therefore, you could also be more likely to get sick physically. We once knew only that the mind *could* trigger illness. Now research is beginning to discover *how* this happens as the brain and immune system influence each other.[12]

THE MIND AS A PREVENTER OF DISEASE

As we have seen before, not all minds work alike. Although stress and pressure reduce the influence of the immune system and lead to increased illness in some people, others seem to thrive under stress. These have been called "psychologically hardy, stress-resistant" individuals, and their number may be larger than we once thought. Major setbacks and stressful occupations stir these people on to action. And they rarely get sick in response to pressure.[13]

What is unique about these hardy people? Psychologists at the University of Chicago have discovered that there are three common mental attitudes within the minds of "high-stress/low illness" individuals.

First, there is a positive attitude toward *change and challenge.* These people live challenging lives, are willing to take a few risks, and do what they can to fight boredom. When change comes into their lives, they try to see this as an opportunity for growth, rather than as catastrophe and a reason to quit.

In contrast, the people who fall prone to sickness are those who use avoidance tactics to deal with stress—tactics like watching more TV, drinking too much, taking tranquilizers or other drugs, and sleeping a lot. The researchers described these as "self-defeating tactics" that really don't deal with the cause of the stress. Instead, the stress "remains in the mind unassimilated and unaltered, a likely subject matter for endless rumination and subconscious preoccupation." This continues to drag the person down mentally and makes him or her more prone to illness.[14]

A second attitude of hardy people is *commitment.* Physically healthy individuals are actively involved with life. They take sincere interest in their families, are active in their communities, and believe their work and other activities are interesting, useful, and important.

The value of commitment will come as no surprise to those who are Christians. Since the dawn of Christianity, religious leaders have emphasized the importance of an active commitment to Christ, rather than the casual and periodic nod to religion that seems to characterize so many church-goers today. An "easy-believism" Christianity is not very meaningful or healthy because it lacks real commitment and provides no challenge.[15]

A third characteristic of hardy people is the feeling of being in *control.* This is the belief that we have some influence over our lives, jobs, and families. Such control is not easy to arrange, and when we cannot control our circumstances, it is difficult to convince ourselves that we can. A recent theory maintains that depression often comes to those who feel helpless and unable to control their life circumstances.[16] Apparently, physical illness may come to these people as well.

THE MIND AS A HEALER OF DISEASE

Perhaps there is nothing that makes one feel more out of control than the knowledge that he or she has a terminal illness with little chance of survival.

This was the situation facing Norman Cousins in 1964, when he was diagnosed as having "ankylosing spondylitis"—a disease of the connective tissue. In plain language, the tissue that holds the bones together was disintegrating. "In a sense," Cousins wrote later, "I was becoming unstuck." The doctors gave him one chance in five hundred of recovering—and admitted that even this was optimistic.

As editor of the prestigious *Saturday Review,* Norman Cousins was known both for his sense of humor and for his determination.[17] Until the time of the diagnosis, Cousins had "been more or less disposed to let the doctors worry about my condition. But now I felt a compulsion to get into the act. It seemed clear to me that if I was to be that one in five hundred I had better do something more than be a passive observer."[18]

The patient's subsequent actions are well known. Cousins knew that emotional tension, stress, frustration, and anger could have harmful effects on the body. But what about the positive emotions? Could love, hope, faith, confidence, and a will to live also influence the body's chemistry? Could laughter enhance the immune system's ability to fight the disease? Might there be scientific evidence for the Old Testament statement that "a cheerful heart is good medicine"?[19]

Norman Cousins decided to experiment on himself. He had a lot to gain if his thinking was right; and little to lose if he was wrong. *With the full cooperation of his doctors,* Cousins stopped taking medication—except for large doses of vitamin C. He moved out of the hospital and began his now famous laughter treatment. Whenever he felt pain, instead of calling for morphine, he watched a funny movie on the screen in his room or had the nurse read segments from humor books. "It worked," he wrote in a book describing his experiences. "I made the joyous discovery that ten minutes of genuine belly laughter had an anesthetic effect and would give me at least two hours of pain-free sleep."[20]

When Cousins later wrote about his recovery, he was the first non-physician to ever have an article published in the *New England Journal of Medicine.* After leaving his post at *Saturday Review,* he was invited to join the UCLA Medical School faculty, where he began giving lectures on how attitudes and emotions can both bring on disease and improve prospects for recovery. In a later book, he expressed a concern that people might misinterpret his personal experience and assume incorrectly that people could "hah-hah their way out of all their problems."[21] Cousins has been careful to emphasize the importance of competent medical treatment for serious illness, but he is convinced that of almost equal importance is what he calls "the belief system."

> The belief system represents the unique element in human beings that makes it possible for the human mind to affect the workings of the body. How one responds—intellectually, emotionally or spiritually—to one's problems has a great deal to do with the way the human body functions. One's confidence, or lack of it, in the prospects of recovery from serious illness, affects the chemistry of the body. . . . We must learn never to underestimate the capacity of the human mind and body to regenerate—even when the prospects seem most wretched. . . . What the patient expects to happen . . . can be as potent in touching off biochemical processes as any medication.[22]

These are not merely the unfounded speculations of a literary expert who writes well but has no knowledge of medicine. Cousins is highly sophisticated in his knowledge of physical healing, and there is increasing research evidence to support his conclusion that our minds do influence the body chemistry so that healing follows. The immune system that can be slowed down by stress, probably can also be aroused and stimulated to greater disease-fighting action when the brain gets messages of hope, determination, and humor.[23]

This may explain why placebos so often work to reduce pain and bring healing. The word "placebo" is usually used to describe a pill, injection, or other treatment that contains no medical ingredients but is believed by patients to be genuine medication. Apparently when people believe they have been given something that will bring recovery, the mind can create change in the body chemistry. This chemical change can remove pain, reduce anxiety, and even move the body toward recovery from an illness.[24]

Can any of this explain acupuncture? I have a friend from the Orient who routinely inserts needles into his neck and claims that this reduces muscle tension, brings relaxation, and eliminates back pain. Like most Westerners, I have been skeptical of acupuncture, and I certainly don't accept the traditional Chinese explanation that needle insertions manipulate *ch'i* and bring a balance between the *ying* and *yang* life forces.

Initially, it was assumed that acupuncture was a highly developed kind of placebo—the influence of belief on the body. This theory was challenged with the discovery that acupuncture works in veterinary medicine—with animals who don't know they're supposed to believe in its effectiveness.

More recent conclusions suggest that centuries of experimentation have led the ancient masters of acupuncture to discover those places in the body that can be stimulated to secrete "endorphins": chemicals that are known as the body's "natural pain killers." It appears that similar pain-reducing chemicals can be released both by acupuncture needles, and by the thoughts in a human mind.[25]

A widely heralded theory of pain suggests another answer. Apparently the nervous system can only handle a certain amount of information at a time. When too much information comes along, chemicals in the spinal column stop the signals from being noticed. It's like closing a gate to prevent more sensations from getting to the brain. Researchers are discovering that pain can be dulled if other, stronger stimulations are trying to get the brain's attention at the same time. This may explain why soldiers intensely involved in battle, or athletes who are concentrating on the game, sometimes don't even notice until later that they have been seriously injured. Do acupuncture needles help to relieve pain in a similar way, by creating a distraction and shutting the normal pain gate?[26]

THE MIND AND FAITH HEALING

These findings might also help us understand some faith healing.

Barbara Heinsohn (that's not her real name) was in her early forties when she went to the Philippines with a friend who had multiple sclerosis (MS). They found a psychic surgeon, one of David Oligani's friends, and the lady with MS had three operations. Each time, she felt better and appeared to have improved.

Barbara had not planned to have an operation, but she did have a long-term problem with gallstones, and one night she got in line to see the healer. He operated in the chapel, poking his hands around her abdomen, pushing aside what appeared to be blood, and eventually holding up what he proclaimed to be her gallstones. Barbara was so relieved to have had a painless operation that she gave the healer $300.00 as a gift for his chapel.

Two weeks after her return home, Barbara had a gall bladder attack, followed by "real" surgery that removed thirty stones. And her friend with the multiple sclerosis recognized that all of the former symptoms of her disease returned.

"I'm a fairly level-headed woman," Barbara reported later. "But just being around all those sick people, watching people going into trances and seeing dozens of bare-handed operations with blood and tissue all over, seeing what seemed to be miracles performed every day—all that had gotten to me. They'd made me a believer."[27]

How could Barbara have known that the surgeons are really sleight-of-hand artists? Hidden under their knuckles are both beetlenuts that can be squeezed to produce a red, bloodlike liquid, and tiny objects—sometimes cotton, sugar cubes, or chicken entrails—that can be held up as "bad tissue," then whisked away by an assistant before anyone can take a closer look. When they are desperate enough, and when they are caught up in the emotional excitement of a healing meeting, even educated, intelligent, and level-headed people like Barbara and her friend can be led to believe that healing has taken place. These beliefs trigger the body's natural tranquilizer-chemicals[28] and the person feels better—at least until he or she leaves the healer and gets home. And sometimes, as we have seen, the beliefs can be so strong that the body actually heals itself.

Has all of this explained away divine healing? Many years ago, Bertrand Russell, the British philosopher, argued persuasively that a time would come when science could explain all events in this world and we would no longer need religion, "imaginary supports," or invented "allies in the sky" to account for what we didn't understand.[29] Have we now reached that time in our understanding of faith healing? Can we now dismiss the influence of the supernatural and conclude that healing, including the miracles of Jesus, can be explained by mind-induced chemical reactions?

Such a conclusion would be both premature and, I believe, inaccurate. We now have greater understanding about how the mind works to bring healing, but such understanding does not mean that God is no longer in existence or at work. It is possible that Jesus and the early disciples, as well as more recent faith healers, could have stimulated belief in the minds of sick people and brought healing through natural chemical reactions. For some people, their new religious beliefs may reduce stress and, as a result, lead to the disappearance of stress-produced illness. If we are honest, we also would have to admit that some modern healers, probably well-intentioned, are temporarily relieving symptoms in their meetings but not bringing about as many healings as they claim.[30]

But how do we account for the instant healings in the New Testament, for the resurrection of dead people, and for some modern miracles that appear to have occurred but cannot be explained scientifically? How do we respond to those who once were involved with psychic surgery as participants, and who now maintain that radical changes really do come to people, not because of sleight-of-hand and other deception, but because of occult powers? Science has not eliminated the supernatural or provided answers to these questions. We will turn to them again in a later chapter.[31]

THE MIND AND WELLNESS

With the increasing recognition that the mind can influence the body, a new kind of medicine has been making its appearance within recent years. Unlike traditional medicine, that exists primarily to rid people of disease and physical symptoms, the new medicine goes further. It assumes that many people can *be* well, in that they have no illnesses, but they still do not *feel* well. Medically, there is nothing wrong, but these people are bored with life, drained, unfulfilled, and incomplete.

To help such "patients," the new medicine seeks to create "wellness"—an inner sense of well-being, self-confidence, optimism, serenity, interest in others, and vitality. As defined by one leader in the field, wellness is not a static state. It comes to people who see themselves as growing, changing, maturing persons. "High level wellness means taking good care of your physical self, using your mind constructively, expressing your emotions effectively, being creatively involved with those around you, being concerned about your physical and psychological environment."[32] In clinics throughout the country, doctors who practice the new medicine teach people how to control stress, get over harmful habits, develop more realistic life goals, and learn how to take care of their bodies. Working on the assumption that one's lifestyle is a crucial factor in sickness and health, the wellness doctors help people change attitudes and the way they live.

Stated simply, the new medicine is helping people to change their bodies and improve their health, by changing their ways of thinking. While some have criticized this new approach,[33] it nevertheless rests on an old and proven principle: One good way to change your body is to change your mind.

6
THE
PRESSURED
MIND

Roger Pettit, copilot of Air Florida Flight 90, peered into a
snowstorm as the plane taxied to the runway of Washington's
National Airport. It was late January and many of the pas-
sengers, strapped into their seats and waiting for takeoff, were
looking forward to a mid-winter vacation in the sun. But the
weather in Washington was not cooperating, and neither was the
airplane. The runway was slushy, the Boeing 737 was ice-laden,
and the instrument panel warned of engine problems. Four
times the copilot reported that conditions were "not right" for
takeoff, but the pilot ignored the warnings and decided instead
to coax his airplane into the air.

He failed.

Seconds after takeoff, Flight 90 lost altitude, slammed into the
Fourteenth Street Bridge, crashed through the ice covering the
Potomac River, and sank to the bottom, killing seventy-four
people, including the pilot, the copilot, and four motorists on the
bridge. The next morning, newspapers all over the country
showed dramatic pictures of a few struggling survivors being
pulled from the icy waters by heroic rescuers.

Investigators later concluded that two words could summarize
the major reason for the crash of Flight 90: *human error*. According to one government study, mistakes on the flight deck lead to
70 percent of all air accidents and near-accidents. The potential
for disaster is high when there is miscommunication, noncooperation, poor teamwork between cockpit personnel, or—as

with Flight 90—an unwillingness to heed danger signals. For the people on that 737, human error proved fatal.[1]

Airline industry officials, industrial psychologists, management consultants, and a number of stress experts have confirmed what most of us have long suspected. People don't work efficiently when their minds are distracted by fatigue, personality clashes with co-workers, communication failures, or the pressures of high-stress jobs—like those of pilots or air-traffic controllers. Our number one health problem may not be the cancer or heart attacks that we mentioned in chapter five. The most harmful and widespread health hazard in our society may be stress—the wear and tear that we encounter because of our pressured minds.

THE STRESS OF LIFE

When I was a college freshman, taking my first course in psychology, the professor told us one day about a new and controversial book written by Hans Selye, a medical researcher in Montreal. At that time, no one could have predicted that Selye's book, *The Stress of Life*,[2] would launch an explosion of interest in the causes and management of stress. During the past thirty years, thousands of research studies, books, popular articles, seminars, and college courses have tried to analyze and help people cope with stress.

We human beings spend a lot of time and energy interacting with the world in which we live. Most of us, at times, must meet the pressures that come from unpleasant weather, crowded stores, inefficient and sometimes rude salespeople, snarled traffic, unreasonable co-workers, and impatient or critical family members. Our bodies must fight off viruses and adapt to the punishment that comes from sleeplessness, lack of exercise, and some of the harmful and high-caloric things we put into our stomachs. Even as you read these words, people nearby struggle to cope with physical problems and try to adapt to athletic injuries, hearing loss, arthritis, serious disease, or the physical and emotional trauma of surgery. The death of a loved one, the breakup of an engagement, the loss of a job, the failure to get a promotion, the unfaithfulness of a mate, the arrest of a teenage son—these are among the emotional pressures that people face every day. And in the midst of everything there are fears, insecurities, low self-concepts, feelings of anxiety, discouragements, and loneliness, all accompanied sometimes by spiritual doubt, pessimism, and a loss of hope.

This isn't a very positive picture, but it reminds us of the pressures that are part of being alive. More surprising, perhaps, is the fact that so many people live genuinely happy and productive lives in spite of the obstacles. Selye himself pointed out that a "full life" must involve stress,[3] and in a later book he argued that stress can motivate us, stimulate us to action, add interest to life, and spur us on to greater personal achievement.[4]

The stress-management books rarely focus on the positive side of stress, however. Most people can handle the positive by themselves. But we need help in handling the disruptive pressures of living in what one writer has called our age of haste.[5]

THE AGE OF HASTE

The things that pressure us and the ways in which we react depend on our personalities, interests, desires, past experiences, religious beliefs, and even the place where we live. What puts you under pressure may not bother someone else. The things that create stress for a mother who weeps for her starving children in Central Africa are different from the stresses we face in a land of abundance and overeating. The peer pressures of the teenage years are different from the pressures of middle age or the stresses of being old in a society that values youth, beauty, and vitality.

In Western industrialized nations, however, and especially in the United States and Canada, we have become intensely pressured because of two powerful and suffocating attitudes: tension from lack of time and addiction to affluence. These feed on each other, stifle creativity, rob us of health, prevent leisure, and create minds that increasingly are harried and pushed.

The tyranny of time. We are a time-conscious people. Our lives are controlled by the clock. We hate to waste time and sometimes read books on time management.[6] Many of us fill our schedules to overflowing, rush from activity to activity, perpetually feel hurried and harried, and keep on trying to do more than our limited time allows. Often we complain of being too busy and sometimes there is sadness because we have so little time to relax. Nevertheless, we keep pushing ourselves and seem to believe that busyness is a mark of importance and a must for success.

Dr. Paul Rosch, president of the American Institute of Stress, believes that feeling rushed is one of the major contributors to stress in our society. Many of us never feel caught up, and there's always something that needs to be done.[7] We keep trying to do more, accomplish more, and cram more into less and less time. This simply cannot be done, but we keep trying and feel increasing pressure when we fail to meet our unrealistic goals. Such pressure wears us down physically and mentally. It makes us prime candidates for heart attacks and leaves us more susceptible to a variety of physical and mental illnesses.

While these problems may once have been restricted to business people, professionals, and busy mothers, the harried mindset now extends to people in almost all segments of society. A worker on the assembly line of a General Motors plant describes the problem beautifully. "There's a drinking fountain thirty feet from me, but I never have time for a drink of water," he told a recent interviewer. "There's no time for talking, either. The job is not only fast and hard, but boring. Your mind wants to wander, but you have to keep concentrating. The noise winds you up, drives you to move faster. This job messes with your head." When he gets home, the man is too tense to relax.[8] And if he is like thousands of others, he has a part-time job after work—to supplement his income and add more pressure.

The addiction to affluence. One reason for this time pressure appears to be our widespread desire for material things, our love affair with relaxation, and our struggle to maintain and improve current standards of living—even in times of inflation. As a nation we have come to believe that we "owe it to ourselves" to own expensive stereo and video systems. We "deserve a break," the television commercial tells us, so we go on luxury vacations, buy a variety of labor-saving gadgets, and spend money on recreational possessions—like boats, backyard swimming pools, campers, pool tables, and vacation cottages—that we are too pressured to enjoy and too busy to maintain (sometimes because we are working so hard to meet time payments).

It is easy for any of us to fall into the trap of buying things we don't need, having to pay for repairs when our possessions break down, and feeling under financial pressure to maintain our accustomed standard of living. Sometimes we buy gadgets and then feel guilty because we don't use them. This adds to the pressures of life—especially if the gadgets are video games that stimulate competition. Before long, we find ourselves becoming more and more pressured by the things that are supposed to help us relax.

THE COPING MIND

Since many of our pressures start and grow in the mind, it is logical to assume that coping also must begin with our thinking.

The defensive mind. Freud was one of the first to recognize that our minds don't always cope and handle pressure in logical and efficient ways. Sometimes, for reasons that we still don't understand completely, the mind plays tricks on itself. Perhaps to defend us against anxiety, the mind keeps us from seeing the full impact of our pressures. Others may see how stress is affecting our lives but our minds may keep us from seeing this ourselves.

Generations of psychology students have learned about something called "ego-defense mechanisms." These are ways of thinking that automatically protect our minds from experiencing anxiety and from recognizing danger. As many as eighteen or twenty of these defense mechanisms have been proposed. These include:

- *Denial of reality,* which is the refusal to be aware of threatening topics, to admit weaknesses, to face criticism, to admit danger, or to look at unpleasant sights;
- *Rationalization,* which seeks to find logical and socially approved excuses for one's actions or beliefs;
- *Projection,* otherwise known as the tendency to "pass the buck" and blame others for one's own shortcomings, mistakes, misdeeds, thinking, feelings, and intentions;
- *Emotional insulation,* in which the person becomes emotionally detached from a painful or threatening situation;
- *Repression,* which involves the convenient forgetting of things that would be painful to remember; and
- *Displacement,* which may involve yelling at your kids or slamming a door, when you really are mad at your boss and are too threatened to tell him precisely what you think.

These mental reactions are not necessarily bad. They protect us all from being overwhelmed by pressure. But when the defensive mechanisms keep us from facing reality and stop us from working to remove or reduce pressure, then the defensive mindset is harmful because it prevents us from coping.

The humorous mind. We have already seen that humor contributes to physical health but there is good evidence that a little laughter also helps us handle pressure. People who can't laugh have a more difficult time coping with life.

We cannot assume that all laughter is therapeutic. Some humor, for example, is caustic, hostile, cutting, socially inappropriate, and destructive. That doesn't help very much. Nervous laughter, in contrast, is not aggressive, but often it has nothing to do with anything funny. Instead, the nervous laughter is a cover-up to hide discomfort, embarrassment, or other anxieties. People who are always "clowning around" or wisecracking often are unsure of themselves and may use humor as a way of relating to others, keeping distance from others, and perhaps drawing attention to themselves.

So what makes humor healthy or what makes something funny? To answer questions like these it is necessary to analyze humor, and that isn't easy. Analyzing humor has been compared to dissecting a frog. Both the joke and the frog die in the process.

It appears, however, that we are amused by things that appear unusual, strange, and unexpected. True humor takes the serious things of life, removes the need for logic or inhibitions, and sees old pressures in new, incongruous ways. Cartoons are funny, for example, because they take serious issues and let us see them from an unusual, ridiculous viewpoint. The humorist is amusing because he shows "first, that he is no better than anybody else, and second, that nobody else is [better] either. Comedians are capable of deflating pretentiousness, defying convention, tackling taboos, transforming our anxieties into absurdities,"[9] making serious things look preposterous, and giving us a new perspective on the so-called important things of life. When we laugh, we release tension, let go of inhibitions, express feelings, and relax a little.

Humor only lasts for a minute or two, but it can have long lasting therapeutic effects.[10] It helps people see things in a different perspective and it sometimes builds bonds between people. A young humorist saw this when he wrote a book and sent it to Groucho Marx for evaluation. The hand-written reply came a few days later. "From the moment I picked up your book until I laid it down, I was convulsed with laughter. Someday I intend reading it."

The superstitious mind. Most people know that lucky charms, rabbits' feet, and four-leaf clovers don't do anything to reduce pressure or bring success. Nevertheless, a surprising number of people, including college-educated individuals believe in luck and occasionally use a little magic to reduce anxiety.[11] "It might not do any good," these people reason. "But it can't do any harm, and maybe it will work to bring about what I want."

B. F. Skinner, the famous Harvard psychologist, wrote one of the earliest scientific papers on the psychology of superstition.[12] He watched the pigeons in his laboratory and noticed what they were doing immediately before they were fed. One pigeon, for example, was pecking at the corner of the cage when the food arrived. For some reason, the pigeon associated the pecking with the arrival of the food, and whenever the bird was hungry, it would return to the old pecking behavior. It had associated the pecking with food and worked on the (false but persisting) assumption that the pecking would bring what it wanted.

Skinner concluded that something similar happens with people. The gambler who has a successful day at the races, for example, may continue to wear the same shirt or use the same betting formula in hopes that this will bring success again. The student who studies at a particular spot in the library and then gets an A on a test assumes that the place of study is related in some way to the test grade. This isn't logical, everybody agrees with that, but the superstition persists and the student returns to the same study spot whenever a big test approaches.

Athletes are among the most ardent believers in superstition. As we will see in a later chapter, some players insist on wearing the same socks or other clothing that were worn during a previous success. Others wear neck chains, rub lucky charms, or go through a variety of rituals in the hope that these will improve performance. And the superstitious acts do help, but not because of anything magical. The rituals reduce anxiety and increase confidence so that the athlete plays the game with reduced feelings of pressure.

Sometimes superstition also helps people who are afraid and feel powerless. It has been shown that soldiers often carry protective charms and engage in superstitious actions before they go into combat. All of this helps to calm the pressured mind.[13]

The relaxed mind. Superstition and laughter may help us to feel better, but they don't do anything to solve the problems that cause pressure and anxiety in the first place. To do this, some stress experts suggest that we first must learn how to relax the body. Then we can more calmly think of ways to tackle and solve the problems that are putting us under pressure and causing anxiety.

Many people have heard of the fight-or-flight reaction. When a rabbit is frightened, its heart beats faster, its muscles get tense, and its whole body gets prepared for action—to either fight a danger or to run. The same things happen to people. Stress arouses us physically and mobilizes the body for action. If the stress is only present for a short time, the heightened state of physical arousal helps us meet the challenge and then everything returns to normal.

Problems come when the pressures persist and the body remains in a state of tension. After a period of prolonged physical alertness, the body begins to break down. Ulcers develop, for example, tension headaches appear, blood pressure could rise, or there may be a heart attack or some other tension-produced sickness. While the body is trying to cope, thinking is less efficient and productivity begins to decline. All of this is a spur that pushes some people to work harder. This, in turn, creates more pressure and hastens the coming of physical or mental collapse.

Because it is difficult to think clearly about problem-solving when the body is tense, the relaxation therapies teach us how to unwind physically. Often this can be done simply by getting more rest, exercise, time away from work, and a balanced diet. But stress-management consultants often mention three other ways of unwinding: by relaxation training, by imagination, and by biofeedback.[14]

It has been suggested that *relaxation training* is more difficult and time-consuming than giving people a tranquilizer, but relaxation training undoubtedly can be more healthy and long lasting.[15] According to Herbert Benson, the Harvard researcher who did pioneering work in this area, we need four elements to help us relax: a quiet environment, a passive attitude in which we try to forget our work and worries for a few minutes, a comfortable position, and something to think about—like a word or familiar Bible verse.[16] Then it helps if we can begin with our toes and move up the body, progressively tensing then relaxing each set of muscles. It also can be relaxing to breathe deeply and slowly. And for those times when you can't do your entire sequence of relaxation exercises, take an opportunity for some deep breathing and tensing then relaxing one set of muscles, like those in the hands or feet.[17]

Dr. Benson is careful to stress that exercises like this should not be attempted by people who are taking medication or who have known physical problems, unless the doctor approves.

Using the *imagination* can also be a way to relax. The body often slows down physically when we imagine a happy, relaxing, and pleasant scene. Some manufacturers have even produced cassette tapes that are nothing more than sounds of the surf or of birds chirping in a forest. Listening to these is assumed to be relaxing.[18]

Of greater scientific validity is the current focus on *biofeedback*. For many years it was assumed that we could not voluntarily control the heartbeat, blood pressure, brain wave activity, skin temperature, or other autonomic body functions. Now it appears that the mind can have great control over the body. Biofeedback is both a field of scientific study and a procedure for helping our minds get that control.[19]

In biofeedback, neurophysiological and other biological activities of the body are recorded and presented to the person. For example, the current skin temperature, the heartbeat, or the alpha waves of the brain can be monitored continually and displayed on a screen. The person can attempt to change these readings. If he or she imagined that the room was hot, the skin temperature would rise, and this change would be recorded on the screen. By thinking about a relaxed scene, the brain wave pattern would change.

The excitement over biofeedback and its ability to teach the mind how to control the body led to some furor in the scientific community. As with anything new, there were excessive claims about the power of biofeedback to reduce pressure and control tension. But expensive monitoring equipment made it difficult for biofeedback to be used at home.

More recently, however, portable feedback units have become available, continuing research and professional meetings have clarified what biofeedback can do, training programs have shown counselors how to use the new techniques, and biofeedback has become a standard stress-management technique.

How the Mind Can Handle Pressure

Relaxing the body is only a step toward the handling of pressure. To bring more permanent relief we must try to determine what is creating the pressure, decide if we can make any changes in our pressure-producing circumstances or in our attitudes, and then act on the basis of what we have concluded. All of this sounds simple and logical but, as we have seen, the mind doesn't always act logically when it is pressured.

Most of us can think more clearly if we are relaxed and able to withdraw temporarily from a difficult situation. It also is good to have a friend or counselor who can help us see things more clearly and give encouragement and moral support when we need to take action. Recent studies of counseling have been emphasizing the great importance of "social support systems"—families, church members, and other groups of friends who can be supportive and give practical help whenever we feel pressured.[20]

This surely was part of the strength of the early church. After Christ returned to heaven and the Holy Spirit came to earth, the believers banded together in supportive fellowship and prayer groups.[21] These people lived with danger and economic pressure, but they knew the value of mutual support and sincere prayer.

Perhaps in those early days they also took an honest look at their values. They were not controlled by the tyranny of time and there was no addiction to affluence. On the contrary, they freely shared with one another and accepted each other.

Within recent years there has been a new interest in cognitive therapies. These are approaches to counseling that help people challenge their own thinking and change some of their attitudes. Perfectionistic people, for example, have been challenged to reevaluate their beliefs that everything must be perfect. One counselor asked a lady to list the advantages and disadvantages of being a perfectionist. She could think of only one advantage and six disadvantages, including increased pressure and an inability to relax. The counselor helped her to realize that things didn't have to be perfect to be acceptable, and as a result of this attitude change, her life became more relaxed and her work actually improved.[22] Sometimes it is impossible to change circumstances, but most of us can learn to relax our pressured minds by changing our own attitudes.

USING THE MIND TO APPLY WHAT WE KNOW

I once attended a stress-management seminar and came away with mixed feelings. The instructor was entertaining and the information was good, but I didn't learn anything new. I now know that many people have similar reactions. We know about getting exercise and rest, changing our thinking, taking time to pray and worship, learning to laugh, and building relationships with supportive friends. But too often we ignore what we know and keep living the same old pressured lives. Why?

It may be that some people are overwhelmed by all the stress-management techniques. They throw up their hands in frustration and do nothing to change. Others may rush to make big changes in their lifestyles, only to fail and give up in discouragement. Many of us are impatient and stop trying to change when improvement is not immediate. Think, for example, of how often we give up a diet after the first week.[23] To bring more permanent change, we must use our minds to develop several attitudes.

First, there must be *commitment*—a willingness to change, even if it is inconvenient to do so. Sometimes this only happens when we discover a serious stress-induced illness, or learn from the doctor that "the only person who can reduce your pressure is you."

Then, there must be *patience*. This is rare in our achievement-oriented culture, but we must recognize that lasting change evolves gradually. Think about diets again. Fad diets take off weight quickly, but they rarely keep it off.

Third, we need to *establish priorities*. No one can change everything in life at once. Instead, it is more realistic to list our pressures and then start dealing with them one at a time. Recognize that some things probably never will change and that some battles aren't worth fighting. A lot of pressure is reduced when we accept what can't be changed and focus our efforts where success might be possible.

Optimism also helps. When we expect to succeed, we get much further than when we assume that failure is inevitable.

Then, we need to *seek and accept support*. Decide what support you need. Who can help you, how can others help, and what steps must you take to get the help? For one last time (honest!) let us use dieting as an example. It is easier to stick with a diet when someone is encouraging us than when we try to do it all alone.

Last, and most important, *remember that there is supernatural help available*. Self-control and patience are "fruit of the Spirit," promised to believers who submit their lives to the control of God's Holy Spirit.[24] Jesus prayed in the garden immediately prior to crucifixion and we too can bring our pressures to God in prayer.

Sometimes we pray and ask for peace, but the pressures still remain. Emotional blocks, insecurities, doubts, fears, and other hindrances keep us "uptight," even when we want to relax. God can remove these obstacles to peace. Sometimes he does this through direct answers to prayer, but often he works through the insights that come from a friend or counselor.

When our minds are pressured we can start by asking him to show us the way to peace.[25] We can talk things over with a friend, and we might also ponder the topic of the next chapter: how our minds are influenced by feelings.

7
THE
EMOTIONAL
MIND

Lincolnshire is a quiet community, with expensive homes, manicured lawns, winding streets, and people who keep to themselves. Near the outskirts of town, a plush resort has changed the face of the village, and the erection of several executive office buildings has added both traffic and wealth. But Lincolnshire rarely gets into the newspapers, and the residents don't seem to mind their anonymity.

One crisp evening last winter, a single shot jolted the peace of this community, shattered a window in one of those expensive homes, and left a nineteen-year-old high school graduate dying on the carpet of his girlfriend's living room. Within hours the police had solved the crime and arrested a teenage suspect. The motive for murder was as old as recorded history: *jealousy*.

In big cities, where shootings and murders are frequent, everyone knows that lover's quarrels sometimes erupt in violence. But in little towns like Lincolnshire, the people rarely encounter such aggressive revenge, especially from someone who lived in their neighborhood and went to the nearby high school. There was local interest in the trial and guilty verdict, but the townspeople seemed more inclined to ponder the sadness of a local teenager whose family life was tense and whose mind was depressed, angry, and obsessed with thoughts of revenge.

THE ANALYZED MIND

How would you account for the thinking of that teenager? How do we explain the actions of people who kill others? How do we understand the minds of those who drive dangerously, break the law, explode in violence, attempt suicide, plunge into depression, or withdraw into their own little psychotic worlds? How do we account for our personal feelings of impatience, guilt, irritability, self-hatred, excitement, lust, or failures in self-control? These are the questions that psychologists, cognitive scientists, physiologists, theologians, teachers, and many of the rest of us ask every day. These questions don't have easy answers, and sometimes they lead to heated debate between the experts.

A lot of this debate assumes there can only be one way of explaining how people think and act. Consider religious conversion, for example. The conservative theologian says God is at work, changing the convert's life and bringing a new birth. The sociologist may claim that social pressure is important, especially if the conversion came in response to the urgings of others. The psychologist might argue that the convert has inner needs that can be met by the new faith. And it may be suggested that emotions like fear and guilt also bring about the decision. A neurologist may add that there are changes in the convert's brain waves and physiology that may influence the conversion process.

Which of these is correct?

It could be that they all are. We are *biological* creatures, influenced by heredity and physiology. Humans are *social* creatures who are sensitive to the influence of others. We have *psychological* needs, feelings, insecurities, and past experiences that influence our thoughts and actions. But the Bible states that we are also *spiritual*, created by God, known by him, and living in a universe that is held together by his power.[1]

There is no need for us to say that behavior is "nothing but" the influence of psychology, biology, or supernatural forces. These and other influences can all work together to change our lives and account for our behavior. God may use social influences and psychological needs to change my spiritual life. Depression may come from a mixture of biological and psychological influences. The joy of living may come both from hard work and from God's goodness. Uncontrolled anger may rise from frustration, unclear thinking, and sin. The murder of a teenager may come from a combination of rage, insecurity, social pressure, biological arousal, and insensitivity to God. To get a more complete understanding of the mind and its influence on behavior, we need to look at life from a variety of perspectives.

As a Christian, I believe that God ultimately is in control of the universe and that he created the laws of psychology, sociology, physiology, and every other discipline. But even people who reject God can work in their various fields of study and reach conclusions that help us to understand and analyze minds—even when these same investigators fail to see the divine influence in what they are studying.

THE ANGRY MIND

Anger has been called "the misunderstood emotion"[2]—a feeling that causes confusion and disagreement among psychologists, frustration in readers of self-help books, debate among theologians, and tension in all of us.

Anger gives us a good example of how thinking and emotions go together, like two sides of a coin. It is wrong to assume that thoughts and feelings are unrelated and always competing. Both arise in the mind, and one is not more important than the other. Emotions, as we know, can influence thinking, and thinking in turn can control the way we feel.

Anger is both an emotion and a way of thinking. It is a way of releasing tension and communicating how we feel. It can motivate us to action, pull us down emotionally, stimulate our thinking, or distract us from our work or other activities.

Anger usually begins when some event occurs or some idea enters our thinking. Next, the mind makes an interpretation of the event or idea. This interpretation may convince us that something is unfair, or we may realize that we have been hurt or frustrated. This leads to an emotional response, followed by a reaction to the emotion. See the diagram below:

Event or idea

↓

Interpretation: We find meaning
in the event or idea

↓

Emotion: This is a response
to the interpretation

↓

Reaction to the emotion

As an example, let us assume that you hear of an acquaintance who has been criticizing you behind your back and saying things which are untrue. Learning about this is the "event." You interpret this as being unfair slander on your reputation and this leads to the emotion of anger. It is likely that you will react to this anger in one or more of several common ways.

Anger can be stifled. Sometimes we hold anger in and silently boil. It is well known that this isn't healthy, especially if we stay angry for a long time. Anger arouses the body physiologically and stifled anger can increase the likelihood of ulcers, tension headaches, or other psychologically caused illnesses. As we will see later in the chapter, suppressed anger can also lead to depression.

Anger can be expressed physically. For many years counselors argued that instead of squelching anger, we should express it, get it off our chests, blow off steam, or work it out in sports or other strenuous physical activity.

When I was in college, the student council once bought an old car and a sledge hammer. For one dollar students could slam the car three times. This was promoted as a fund-raiser, but the advertising promised that the sledge-hammer treatment would take away all our hostility after finals. Such an idea has been proposed more seriously in a number of counseling clinics where counselees, especially angry kids, are encouraged to pound punching bags. This is assumed to be better than holding the hostilities within, and it is much better than punching one's brothers and sisters.

Does this activity help people release their anger and get rid of it? It now appears that the answer may be no. Instead of reducing anger, ventilating may stimulate hostility and make it worse. One research study encouraged boys to play with violent toys, kick the furniture, and freely express their "pent-up anger." After doing all this, the boys were found to be more angry than they had been at the beginning.[3] Hollering at your mate or children doesn't clear the air; it clouds it and makes matters worse.[4]

Anger can be talked out. If kicking furniture and yelling are both unhealthy, what about expressing one's anger through a nice quiet talk? Surely that will help us feel better.

Not always, say some recent findings.[5] It is possible that talking about an emotion rehearses it and makes us more angry. The same is true if we sulk silently, continually mull things over to ourselves, write about it in letters and journals, or devise ways of getting revenge through passive aggression. (Passive aggression comes when people deny that they are hurt or angry, but get even or get what they want through backbiting, noncooperation, or other subtle forms of hostility.)

Anger can be understood. For several decades there have been continuing debates about the causes of anger and aggression. We know, for example, that anger has a physical component. It can be aroused by electrically stimulating certain portions of the brain, it can be reduced when these same portions are removed, it can be aroused by changes in body chemistry,[6] and it is sometimes more common in women during the premenstrual week. Several years ago, a man named Charles Whitman climbed the clock tower at the University of Texas and started shooting at people walking across campus. Fourteen people died and thirty-one were wounded before Mr. Whitman himself was killed. An autopsy showed that he had a fast-growing tumor near the amygdala—a tiny almondlike region of the brain that is known to be associated with violence and aggression.

From this, it does not follow that anger is "nothing but" a physiological reaction.[7] As we have seen, our past experiences, learning, and attitudes each have a bearing on how we interpret a situation and on how we react. There is, too, a theological side of anger. When one's anger hurts others, turns to revenge, refuses to forgive, or simmers in bitterness, it is not only harmful psychologically, but according to the Bible, that kind of anger is also sin.[8]

Anger can be handled. Some of the research that analyzes anger also shows how it is best handled. Young boys who played with toy guns and kicked furniture were better able to deal with their anger when they talked it over with another person and understood why others had acted in ways that made them angry (for example, "she was tired," or "he wasn't feeling well"). People whose blood pressure had gone up in response to anger were able to lower their blood pressure through an approach known as *reflection*—waiting until the angry person who insulted them had calmed down and then trying to have a reasonable discussion of the issue.[9]

The angry mind can also be calmed when we:
• decide that we really want to control anger;
• determine that we will not fall into the trap of revenge or continual rumination on the person or situation that made us angry;[10]

- attempt to deal with the hurt and pain that caused the anger in the first place;
- try to develop the art of forgiveness, realizing that for most of us we cannot do this unless we have divine help;
- admit our feelings whenever we are angry;
- try to share our anger objectively and, if possible, with the person who is causing the anger. It helps to use "I" statements ("I feel hurt," "I am angry") instead of making accusations. Resist the temptation to bring up past grievances that are likely to add ammunition to the present complaints;
- listen to the other person, recognizing that he or she might be angry too, and with good reason;
- attempt to get understanding between you and the other person, even though there might not be agreement; and,
- avoid both sinful, harmful reactions to anger and the tendency to ignore the anger in the hope that it will pass.[12]

All of this takes time and is easier to read in a book than to put into practice. Sometimes there will be a need for counseling, but for all Christians it is good to remember that self-control is one of the fruits of the Spirit.[13] Fruit trees grow slowly and so may the mind's ability to control anger. But the evidence is in: It can be done.

The Depressed Mind

Three or four years ago, six teenagers heard a talk about nuclear war and decided to start a letter-writing campaign to the president of the United States. Over 8,000 letters were delivered to the White House, most written by teenagers, but some coming from children as young as six or seven. "Dear Mr. President," one of these began. "I am ten years old. I think nuclear war is bad because many innocent people will die. The world could even be destroyed. I don't want to die. I don't want my family to die. I want to live and grow up. Please stop nuclear bombs."[14]

According to research by two child psychiatrists,[15] many children are uneasy about the future, scared of nuclear war, and afraid that they may never grow up. A Carnegie Foundation report discovered that some college students have similar fears. Many have lost faith in the future[16] and are living by a philosophy that says, "Let us take life easy, eat, drink, and be merry, because life won't last much longer."[17] On the surface many people act happy and unconcerned, but behind the façade there are minds filled with fear that is mixed with anger and a lot of depression.

Some very famous people struggled with emotions like these, long before anyone had heard of nuclear war. Rousseau, Dostoevsky, Queen Victoria, Lincoln, Tchaikovsky, and even Freud, grappled with depression. In biblical times, Moses, Saul, Jeremiah, Elijah, and David were all depressed, and more modern theological giants—Martin Luther, Charles Spurgeon, Hudson Taylor, and C. S. Lewis, for example—could be added to the list. Many of us who are more contemporary and less famous are also included in the company of those who struggle with depression. Sometimes, the depressed mind is also angry and fearful, but not always.

Most of us are familiar with the sadness that characterizes depressed people. There is no joy in living and often the mind is filled with thoughts of guilt, self-condemnation, hopelessness, fear, loneliness, lethargy, and anger. The deeply depressed person has little interest in life, may have difficulty sleeping, often feels empty or worthless, and sometimes thinks about suicide. In reflecting on his experiences as a patient in a psychiatric hospital, one pastor wrote that it is "impossible for those who have never been depressed to fully understand the deep, perplexing pain that depression causes."[18]

Some causes of depression. What causes minds to be depressed? Hundreds of research reports have tried to answer that question. The findings show that depression can arise from a variety of sources.

There are, for example, the biological issues. Most experts seem to agree that at least some people have an inherited tendency (professionals might call this a "genetic predisposition") to be depressed. For much depression, especially that which is severe, there are also chemical changes in the brain. These may be produced by psychological stresses, they may come from biochemical malfunctions in the brain, or they may result from improper diet, low blood sugar, or a lack of sleep. Antidepressant drugs, or the older treatments such as shock therapy, work to alter the chemical activity in the brain and bring relief.[19]

But the causes of depression are not limited to biology. There is evidence that depression can arise from guilt and involvement in sin, from feelings of inferiority, from unrealistic ambition, and from something that Nietzsche called "the melancholia of everything completed"—a realization that one has reached all of life's goals. More commonly mentioned is the depression that comes from loss, helplessness, and anger.

Everyone knows that depression frequently follows the *loss* of a loved one through death, but we can also become depressed when we lose a home, lose a job, lose the closeness of a child or friend who moves away, lose our health, or face the loss of our self-esteem. Moving, retirement, the breakup of a marriage, and even the loss of purpose in life can all bring on depression, and so can the belief that we have lost something even when we haven't.

Frequently these actual losses—and losses that are feared, anticipated, or imagined—leave us feeling helpless. Even when there is no loss, it appears that *helplessness* itself can be an important cause of depression. When a person feels that nothing can be done to solve a problem or to change a situation, it is easy to give up hope, to stop trying to make things better, and to slide into despair.[20]

More widely held is Freud's view that depression comes *when people are angry* with others but refuse to see or admit that the anger exists. Instead of facing anger and trying to deal with it, these people hold it within, get angry with themselves, and are overwhelmed with depression. Many writers have criticized this theory and argue that it has no real basis in fact,[21] but others, I suspect, are like me. Whenever I feel "down" I ask, "What is making me angry and what can I do about it?" Often that is the first step toward change.

Some ways of coping with depression. Most psychologists, I suspect, have at least one whole shelf of books that deal with the topic of depression. Some of these talk about the mind; others do not. Some describe complicated theories, while others are more practical. There are books for counselors, self-help books, and several volumes on theology and depression.

I respect many of the people who write these books. Some of them are my friends, and most have a sincere desire to instruct counselors, help depressed people, and encourage their families. It is distressing, however to find books that tell people to snap out of depression, to stop sinning (this advice is based on the assumption that all depression results from sin), to make the choice to be happy, or to apply some self-help formula that is "guaranteed to work." As we have seen, depressed minds are formed from a variety of forces and the treatment of depression can be as complicated as the causes.

It is helpful to start by admitting honestly that one is depressed and then looking at the possible causes of the depression. Since we can't always see these ourselves, the perspective of a friend or professional counselor can help. When there is loss, helplessness, or anger, it helps to face these and to ponder ways of going on in spite of life's difficulties. When there is sin and guilt, confession to God is essential, and it is often useful, as well, to confess to another human being.[22] Try to see the present situation from God's point of view, recognizing his sovereignty and asking in prayer for his help. Sometimes we can change our environments—take on a new job, for example, or change residences. And it is wise to ponder whether one's diet or physical condition might be a problem. If the depression persists, a good physical examination would be wise. Antidepressant drugs, taken under the control of a physician, can also be helpful. This is especially true when such drug use is supplemented by counseling that attempts to find the depression's cause and that helps people deal more effectively with the pressures and demands of life.

None of this is easy, and sometimes it takes a long time for recovery to be complete. Almost always, the road to recovery is filled with potholes that bring stumbling and periodic slips back into the depressed state. But it is important for depressed people to remember that most get better—especially when there is counseling and the support of friends.[23]

THE LIBERATED MIND

There are many myths about emotion. Sometimes we think, for example, that women are more likely to get depressed than men, but that isn't necessarily true. Some people still believe in stoicism, the ancient but erroneous belief that emotion isn't good for us and that feelings should be squelched and never expressed. In some places the view persists that if we give in to emotions, we risk losing control of ourselves and respect from others. Others like to give unbridled expression to their feelings, sometimes to the embarrassment of their friends.

It is more liberating to realize that emotions are a part of being human. Even though feeling may be the most poorly understood of all the mental functions,[24] we know that life is richer because we can both think and feel. Envy, guilt, confusion, hatred, disappointment, and anxiety may complicate our lives and sometimes cloud our minds, but think how empty we would be without excitement, joy, love, hope, humor, anticipation, and the pleasure of enjoying beauty or intimacy.

Psychologists, and others who study the mind, sometimes give so much attention to the negative emotions that they forget the good feelings. As we have seen in earlier chapters, the biblical writers didn't make that mistake. The apostle Paul was in jail when he wrote to encourage the Philippians. He wrote about joy, peace, and freedom from anxiety. Then he told them to let their minds dwell on whatever is true, noble, right, pure, lovely, admirable, excellent, and worthy of praise.[25] Would this be possible without both thought and feeling?

The envious mind. Paul's writings show that he was very familiar with the Old Testament. It is likely, therefore, that he was familiar with an interesting psalm written by a cymbal player named Asaph.[26] Apparently the man was having a struggle that most of us have faced—why do good things happen to bad people, and bad things happen to good people?

The followers of God were having problems when Asaph wrote the seventy-third psalm, but for everyone else, things were going so well that the writer felt some envy.

> I was envious of the prosperity of the proud and wicked. Yes, all through life their road is smooth! (They never have any pains.) They grow sleek and fat. They aren't always in trouble and plagued with problems like everyone else, so their pride sparkles like a jeweled necklace and their clothing is woven of cruelty! These fat cats have everything their hearts could ever wish for! They scoff at God and threaten his people. How proudly they speak! They boast against the very heavens, and their words strut through the earth.
>
> And so God's people are dismayed and confused, and drink it all in. "Does God realize what is going on?" they ask. "Look at these men of arrogance; they never have to lift a finger—theirs is a life of ease; and all the time their riches multiply."[27]

In contrast to this happy picture, the writer struggles with trouble and woe.[28] Perhaps it would be accurate to conclude that his mind was filled with anger and depression, along with his confusion and envy.

The enlightened mind. Then, suddenly, there is a shift in thinking. His mind shifts away from the successes of godless people and from his own plight. He begins to think about others and his mind turns to God.

When we see things from our own narrow point of view, it is easy to be envious and discouraged, but from God's perspective things look different. These envied people are on a slippery path, the psalm writer concludes. He calls himself "stupid and ignorant" for thinking that God overlooks the problems in this world and will not bring justice.[29] Asaph's mind concludes that God is just, fair, and concerned about the injustice in this world. When we believe that, envy fades, and there is less reason for despair, depression, and unhealthy anger.[30] And there is cause for encouragement.

The encouraged mind. Simply stated, the Bible shows that God loves us, sticks with us, and guides us both in this life and into the next. He strengthens us and ultimately will bring justice to this world.[31]

Recently I heard the true story of Ray Winfield. In 1955, while he was away at work, a freak storm swept through the Poconos where his wife and children were camping. Twelve people, all members of the same church, were swept away—some never to be seen again. Ray Winfield lost his whole family.

For weeks he walked around in a daze of grief and confusion. Reading the Bible was almost a meaningless habit, until one day he came to Psalm 73:26. "My health fails," he read. "My spirits droop, yet God remains! He is the strength of my heart; he is mine forever!"

Almost immediately Ray Winfield felt the weight of despair begin to lift. He began to experience the truth of an old adage: Earth has no sorrow that heaven cannot heal.

It may not be possible, and it certainly isn't desirable to discuss the emotional mind in a purely rational way. Our minds think, but they also give rise to feelings—including the irrational feelings that led a teenager in Lincolnshire to commit murder.

Sometimes the emotional mind leads to depression, anger, and the emotions we have discussed in this chapter. And sometimes the mind is so overwhelmed that it leads people to think and act in ways that others call abnormal, psychotic, and sometimes "crazy." It is to this troubled kind of thinking that we now turn our attention.

8
THE
TROUBLED
MIND

There are times when I wonder about my sanity. It seems that I have a lot of neurotic ideas, personal hangups, and inner insecurities. I struggle with my self-concept and have questions about my own competence. Sometimes, I get depressed, misinterpret what other people say, and reach conclusions that I know are irrational.

If I thought these ideas were unique to me, I certainly wouldn't share them, especially in a book. I have reached the conclusion, however, that almost all of us wonder, at least on occasion, about our own mental health. Periodically, most "normal" people feel depressed, intensely angry, fearful, and inclined to withdraw from others. We worry about our problems, wonder if we can do our work, think we might be bordering on instability, and may even toy with the idea of suicide.

There are many stories about the insecurities of nursing students who arrive for their training on the psychiatric ward. "It was mysterious and a bit foreboding," one nurse wrote in describing her own experience. On the first day,

we took a tour of the place and received our key to the locked wards. The key was important. It was the concrete division between *them* and *us*. Whenever you doubted your own sanity you could look at the key and tell yourself, "I'm okay."

We needed that reminder, because during our psych nursing experience the dividing line between the mentally ill and the "normal people" became fuzzier and fuzzier. Often we suspected that we really belonged on the other side of that fuzzy line, and we feared being found out.[1]

It is probably true that most people feel uncomfortable when they think about mental illness. We wonder why people "go insane" and feel a little nervous when we read that emotional problems are very common. We don't know how to respond when a friend is deeply depressed, intensely anxious, or admitted to a psychiatric hospital. We may joke about people who are "crazy" and laugh at stories about psychiatrists, but we recognize our own insecurities and tend to stand bewildered when we think about troubled minds.

None of this is new. Throughout recorded history abnormal behavior has been viewed with fear and sometimes squelched with incredible cruelty. In medieval times, for example, people were starved, beaten, burned, cut, immersed in freezing water, confined in coffinlike cages, and otherwise tortured, all in an attempt to make the body so unpleasant that the madness-producing evil spirits would leave. More humane treatment was first proposed less than two centuries ago but the idea met with considerable resistance. Even today, patients in some mental hospitals are treated with disrespect and insensitivity.[2]

It is not easy to understand troubled minds, to accurately diagnose psychiatric problems, and to determine the best way of helping those whose thinking is irrational, distraught, or depressed. New biological discoveries and psychological approaches to therapy do not always live up to the claims of their discoverers, but great progress is being made, nevertheless. At last, we are beginning to understand some causes and effective ways of dealing with mental problems.

THE ANXIOUS MIND

At the core of much troubled thinking is the issue of anxiety— that vague feeling of tension and apprehension about things which might happen. Sometimes this anxiety appears to be irrational, and there is no apparent reason for any fear.

Easier to understand is the anxiety that appears when we are faced with potential problems or dangers that everyone can recognize. The hospitalized patient feels anxious on the night before surgery, knowing that the next day could bring pain, serious body damage, bad news about one's condition, and perhaps even death. The uncertainty about hospital procedures and one's possible reaction to the surgery bring further concern.[3] Anxiety of a similar kind could be seen in the soldier who is about to enter battle, the high school sophomore who is scheduled to speak at a student assembly, or the new employee who is very insecure about the first day at work.

Several years ago some psychologists decided to study anxiety in a group of paratroopers. Think of your reaction to the idea of stepping out of a plane in midair and falling a few hundred feet before your parachute opens—unless it doesn't work! As you might have guessed, the novices felt tremendous anxiety when the plane took off, but those who had made a hundred or more jumps took the whole thing in stride and found the experience exhilarating. These experienced jumpers knew what to expect, sensed less danger, and had a lot less fear.[4]

Freud never studied people jumping out of airplanes, but he did talk to many anxious people and his views on anxiety have been widely accepted, even by those who disregard many of his other ideas.[5] Freud recognized that it is normal to be anxious when we are faced with real danger. Sometimes, however, anxiety is neurotic and concerned more with inner shame or guilt than with external threat. The anxious person is ashamed of what he or she has done in the past, and there may be embarrassing thoughts about one's lusts or desires. For some there is a fear of being discovered, of losing self-control, or of being ridiculed and ostracized.

In practice, it is difficult to distinguish normal anxiety from neurotic. And it should not be assumed that one of these is better, or worse, than the other. Anxiety of both kinds can alert us to real danger—and protect us from foolish, harmful, and immoral actions.

But anxiety can also make us so vigilant that we become jumpy and even paranoid. Anxious people often have a great and persisting need for reassurance, and sometimes there is an inability to relax. Occasionally, I see this in students who are constantly uptight, worried about grades, afraid of failure, and so tense that they are unable to sleep. Their anxiety comes from the pressures outside and the expectations that they put on themselves.

In this age of continual change and constant media exposure, it is easy to be overwhelmed by the demands that call for action and by the information that relentlessly pounds our senses. Some can cope better than others, but given enough stressful input, any of us would be overwhelmed by the anxiety and collapse under the pressure.

THE DISTRESSED MIND

This pressure can create great distress. Hans Selye, the famous stress researcher whose work was discussed earlier, has defined distress as any kind of activity, pressure, or stress that is harmful, damaging, or unpleasant.[6] When our minds are distressed, we don't always think clearly or logically, we sometimes act impulsively or irrationally, and we may feel overwhelmed by emotions such as anxiety, depression, or futility.

Professional counselors are interested in these symptoms of the troubled mind because they often give a clue about what is causing the distress. It is naive and unrealistic to assume that all mental disorder is caused by only one or two influences—such as chemical imbalances, unconscious impulses, or personal sin. There are perhaps hundreds of pressures and other distressing influences that work together, or alone, to disrupt feelings, influence behavior, and create troubled thinking.

There are, for example, *biological causes* of mental illness. Research is continuing to uncover the diversity of ways in which biochemical influences, genetics, nutritional imbalances, glandular malfunctioning, brain damage, and numerous diseases can trigger anxiety, depression, and other symptoms of mental illness.[7] The professional journals are filled with stories of people like the man who was normally a loving father and husband, but who erupted at times into violent anger. He would beat his wife and daughter without provocation and seemed to be showing no signs of change despite several months of counseling. One night, he came home from work with five flavors of ice cream for the family to splurge on after dinner. It was a pleasant evening, but within hours the man was violent again. Suddenly it dawned on the wife that these explosions always occurred after her husband had eaten ice cream. Laboratory tests revealed a rare allergy to milk. When dairy products were removed from his diet, the violence and "mental illness" disappeared.[8]

It would be simplistic and wrong to assume, however, that troubled minds only result from physical illness or from the body's malfunctioning. Even when we are in good health or have a normally functioning brain, we can be overwhelmed by the *psychological pressures* of life. Fear of failure, the lingering influence of traumatic past experiences, continual family tension, social ineptness, inadequate learning, job demands, overwhelming guilt—these are among the pressures that can stretch our minds to the breaking point.

In moving through life, we are always making decisions. Frequently, these decisions are made in reaction to events or in response to demands that come from other people. Without giving much thought to what our minds are doing, we make our decisions by looking at the available facts and acting as logically as we can.

But sometimes there are too many facts pushing our minds and we become confused. Sometimes, because of limited knowledge or experience, we don't understand the facts. Sometimes, our attention is distracted so we miss some of the facts. People who panic in fires, for example, know how to reach an exit, but an awareness of danger distracts their thinking. Sometimes, like when a football player grabs the ball and runs in the wrong direction, we misinterpret the facts and act in ways that make sense at the time, but later are seen to be unwise or foolish.

Troubled minds are often minds that don't have all the facts straight but are trying, in the best way they can, to avoid harm and to cope with life's demands and pressures. If the outsider can try to see things from the distressed person's point of view, strange behavior and "irrational" thinking often begin to make sense.

No mind is an island, however. We live in communities and societies, and, at times, our distress has *social causes* that interact with the psychological. The stresses of war, economic depression, unemployment, poverty, racial or sexual injustice, or even the pressure to keep up social appearances can all create stress and distorted thinking.

Then there is the issue of *sin*. Christian counselors have written about this for decades, but the writings of a psychologist named O. Hobart Mowrer and a famous psychiatrist, Karl Menninger, have directed professional attention to the moral basis of mental illness.[9]

In his own career, Mowrer so distinguished himself that he was elected president of the American Psychological Association, partially in recognition of his research on learning. But Mowrer also struggled with depression and his problems were so overwhelming that he could not attend his own presidential installation. Later he wrote that hours of psychoanalysis had not helped because the therapy never reached the real core of the problem—guilt over wrongs that he had done. In a book that raised a lot of controversy, Mowrer argued that many personal problems come from sin and the failure to find forgiveness.

To my knowledge, Mowrer did not believe in God. The theory defined sin as some action that wronged another human being. People were encouraged to confess to other humans and to make atonement on a human level.

Menninger, in contrast, seemed more open to theological issues. He defined sin as "transgression of the law of God; disobedience of the divine will; moral failure," and failure to do as one ought toward one's fellow man.[10] His book, like Mowrer's, was a call for psychiatry and psychology to return to a consideration of moral standards and personal responsibility. Here were appeals for greater emphasis on sin and forgiveness.

This, of course, is a theme that frequently appears in the Bible. According to the Scriptures, we have all sinned, and we all need to experience God's forgiveness. When we confess our sin to God, he forgives. When we acknowledge that Jesus Christ is Lord, he makes changes in our lives and promises that we will have eternal life. While all sin is ultimately against God and must be confessed to him, the Bible also teaches that whenever we wrong a fellow human being, it is good to confess our sins to each other.[11]

In one sense, all mental illness is the result of sin—the sin that entered the world centuries ago and has created problems ever since. But we cannot conclude, logically or on the basis of Bible study, that mental illness always results from personal sin, and neither can we assume that sin in an individual's life always leads to a troubled mind. Such a view is too simplistic. Sometimes a person sins and subsequently is overwhelmed by guilt and troubled thinking. But in other cases, mental problems arise from the physical, psychological, and social pressures that come even to those who seek to avoid deliberate sin and who try to walk in ways that please God.

THE COUNSELED MIND

Freud's famous system of psychoanalysis was a highly complex, long-term approach to relieving the distress of troubled minds. Freud assumed that problems and anxiety came from irrational forces, unconscious motivation, sexual and aggressive impulses, inner conflicts, and the lingering effects of early childhood experiences—all of which were assumed to be buried in the mind. Analysis was to involve the long process of uncovering these hidden forces and bringing them to conscious awareness where they could be handled.

The treatment of troubled minds has come a long way since the time of Freud. Many of his insightful ideas are still widely accepted, and there are many therapists who work within a psychoanalytic framework. But modern treatment also involves physical examinations and biochemical treatment; attempts to change environments and to reduce social pressures; the teaching of social skills; the stimulating of encouragement and support from friends or relatives; the reliance on prayer and other religious influences; and the use of counseling.

It is difficult to count the number of counseling approaches that currently are used to understand and help troubled minds. Each approach is held with enthusiasm by at least a few therapists, each seems to be at least mildly helpful, and it appears that each fails with some people.[12] Observers have noticed that each of these therapies is also based on a set of assumptions about human nature and the way people change.[13]

The "moral models" of helping assume that people are responsible both for the problems that come into their lives and for the solutions. The therapists motivate people to face problems realistically and to find ways to change. The Reality Therapy (RT) of William Glasser, the Rational-Emotive Therapy (RET) proposed by Albert Ellis, Carl Rogers' person-centered therapy, and the more recent Gestalt therapies are examples of this approach.

"Compensatory models" is the name given to approaches such as behavior therapy or transactional analysis. Here, the therapist assumes that human beings are shaped by forces beyond their control. The counselee is not responsible for the coming of the problem, but he or she must take responsibility to solve the problem, with the counselor's help. Reverend Jesse Jackson has forcefully presented this idea to black audiences with his repeated assertion that "you are not responsible for being down, but you are responsible for getting up."

The "medical models" assume that people are not responsible for their problems or for the solutions. The troubled mind needs to be treated by an expert who gives medication, guidance, and sometimes advice, with or without the patient's active cooperation. This is closely related to the "enlightenment model" that says people are responsible for their problems but not for the solutions. Many of the highly structured programs for treating drug addicts, criminals, juvenile delinquents, or people with eating disorders fall within this category.

Which of these is best? Which is right? These questions lead to endless debate. Most counselors reach conclusions based on their own personal preferences. Some Christian counselors try to decide on the basis of Bible study, but even here there is disagreement. A few have submitted these questions to research studies, but research on the effectiveness of counseling is among the most difficult to do with precision. It appears that the effectiveness of any approach depends on the personality and sensitivity of the counselor, the motivation of the counselee, and the nature of the problem. And there is evidence to suggest that in spite of exaggerated claims of success, the approaches are about equally effective.[14]

What, then, does one do when the mind is troubled? Most of us begin by talking to our friends, or to the hairdressers, neighbors, or others in the community who give informal counseling every day.[15] If things don't get better, it would be wise to have a good physical examination, and then try to find a counselor who is sensitive, professionally trained, and alert to spiritual issues. Watch out for people who call themselves counselors but who have no training and are unwilling to discuss their qualifications. Such people are often sincere and sometimes they can help, but frequently they do more harm than good.

THE BALANCED MIND

It is difficult to define mental health. Everyone knows that it isn't healthy to withdraw into a world of continual fantasy and neither is it healthy to be constantly depressed, violent, or obsessed with thoughts of suicide. But is it healthy to be joking all the time, overly religious, a workaholic, or a perfectionist? And since most of us have emotional ups and downs, is it possible to always have a stable, balanced mind?

These are the kinds of issues that concern mental health experts. Most would agree that the mentally healthy person is able to cope with daily problems, get along with other people, control emotions, accept responsibilities, and not get bogged down with inner conflicts. In addition, it is widely agreed that well-adjusted people have at least some sense of self-esteem, an ability to love and be loved, a recognition of one's own uniqueness, sensitivity to others, an acceptance of the fact that other people are different, and a capacity to think about and plan for the future.

Psychiatrist O. Quentin Hyder has proposed that Jesus was the most mentally balanced person who ever lived. He had a good sense of self-esteem, a concern for others, and an ability to meet the demands of daily living. He had a clear sense of right and wrong, a commitment to serving God, an ability to relate to people, and a stability that enabled him to remain calm and controlled under stress.[16]

All of this can leave us mortals feeling pretty incompetent. But it is wise to remember that most of us get along pretty well even though no person is perfect, and no mind is completely free from anxiety, distress, and trouble. Part of the process of growth is to become more stable and balanced in our thinking. This is possible, as we can see by looking at the case history of a young man who was surrounded by people with troubled minds, but who kept his own sanity and left a powerful mark on the world.

A SOUND MIND

In the Middle East, there once lived a king who went mad. He became like an animal, lived in the fields, was unkempt and probably wasn't rational. His plight was especially pathetic because the king had once lived in great splendor and he knew beforehand that the madness was coming.

The king's name was Nebuchadnezzar. At the height of his power, he led a successful attack on Jerusalem, destroyed the city, plundered all its wealth, and brought large numbers of captives to serve the Chaldeans in Babylon.

One of the captives was a young Jewish man named Daniel. The king had told his associate to find a few "strong, healthy, good-looking" young men who "have read widely in many fields, are well-informed, alert, sensible, and have enough poise to look good around the palace."[17] Daniel was one of the people who was chosen for this royal service.

It is clear that Daniel was physically healthy. He refused to eat the king's rich food, lived instead on a simpler, more balanced diet, and even looked healthy and well-nourished.[18] He was intellectually alert and well educated,[19] and there is abundant evidence that he was a man of prayer who was deeply committed to obeying God.[20]

Someone has suggested that people with stable minds are at peace with God, at peace with themselves, and at peace with society. Daniel was well-adjusted in all three areas. He was not afraid to talk about his beliefs[21] and he worshiped God openly and without wavering, even when the king had promised death to anyone who continued to pray.[22] As a person, he seemed to have inner confidence, doubtless because of his trust in God, and he refused to manipulate people, to gossip, or to let others be hurt.[23] As an employee, Daniel was beyond reproach in terms of his honesty, integrity, and effectiveness.[24]

King Nebuchadnezzar, in contrast, was proud, ruthless, self-centered, pleasure-seeking, and disinterested in God. At times, he was given messages from heaven, and when crises arose, the king listened. But he quickly went back to his old ways, and appeared to be intimidated by his nobles and government officials. King Nebuchadnezzar had a confused, unstable mind, in contrast to the stability of Daniel. Perhaps it isn't surprising that the king went mad. In time, his sanity returned and he gave honor to God, but when the king died, his successors continued in the old ways. The contrast between Daniel and his unstable monarchs was striking.

What accounts for the difference? Daniel's physical condition, intellectual competence, and personal integrity undoubtedly were significant. The most notable difference between Daniel and the kings, however, lay in Daniel's faith.

Faith is not something that undercuts mental health. It is not belief unfounded on fact.[25] Faith is believing something for which there is a lot of evidence but no absolute proof. It is impossible, for example, to prove that God exists, but the evidence for this is strong, much stronger than the evidence for God's nonexistence. According to the Bible, faith gives us hope and the confident assurance that what we do not see, does in fact exist.[26]

Daniel had this faith and it gave him stability. Paul had it too. The *King James Bible* quotes the apostle as saying that God has not "given us the spirit of fear; but of power, and of love, and of sound mind."[27] More modern translations use slightly different terms, but the message is the same: God gives us freedom from fear (internal security), spiritual power, love (the ability to relate to others), and self-discipline (the ability to control ourselves).

On the corner of my desk, tucked under a paper weight, there is an old yellow envelope that I can look at whenever I sit down to write. Sometime, two or three years ago, I wrote six words on the envelope: Spiritual wisdom, power, guidance, and stability. This is what I pray for almost daily. The Holy Spirit gives us wisdom, power, guidance, and mental stability. Reliance on that divine provision is the major way to control a potentially troubled mind.

9
THE
MATURE
MIND

Hanging on the wall of the Louvre in Paris is a famous portrait commonly known as "Whistler's Mother." The elderly lady had not intended to have her portrait painted, but when a model failed to show up one day, Mrs. Whistler demurely and patiently sat while her son worked on the canvas. When the painting was shown at the Royal Academy, Whistler simply titled it an "Arrangement in Grey and Black."

Many people have heard of Whistler's mother, but few are aware of Whistler's temper. The famous mother was Scottish, born in the Hebrides, and later married to a graduate of West Point. For a time they lived in Massachusetts, where their son was born, but in 1843 the family moved to Russia where Whistler's father had been invited to direct the construction of a railroad. When they returned to the United States, the young James Whistler entered West Point where, for the next three years, he accumulated a string of demerits and was in constant conflict with the superintendent, a man named Robert E. Lee. Dismissed before graduation, Whistler eventually went to Paris where he studied art and lived a Bohemian lifestyle, before settling in London.

Whistler was known for his piercing wit and fiery personality. He complained that people didn't appreciate his paintings and once sued a critic who had accused the artist of "flinging a pot of paint in the public's face." He constantly criticized the British, sometimes dressed outlandishly, quarreled frequently, and even mistreated his subjects. "You can't call that a great work of art," one man protested after sitting for a portrait. "Perhaps not," Whistler replied, "but then you can't call yourself a great work of nature."[1]

The pages of history are filled with examples of people, like Whistler, who are talented artists, musicians, composers, orators, scholars, scientists, or statesmen but who are personally immature, self-centered, bombastic, and unable to get along with people. In our times, we hear periodically about leaders of nations who cannot control their tempers, spiritual leaders who cannot control their sexual urges, and business executives who can run giant corporations but can't maintain stability in their own families. Some of the public figures whom we most admire appear to have brilliant minds when they do their work but very immature minds when they relate to others or try to control themselves.

THE MATURING MIND

According to one dictionary definition, maturity is a state of perfection, full development, and completeness. It is an ideal, a state of mind that no human ever achieves completely. For this reason, it is better to think that we each have matur*ing* minds, rather than minds that have reached maturity. Sometimes people's minds mature along with their bodies, but often individuals who mature physically can be like Whistler, very immature in terms of their thinking and sensitivity to others.

Over thirty years ago, Harry Overstreet wrote *The Mature Mind*. The popular book swept through twenty printings and alerted people to the importance of developing personal and emotional maturity.[2] Later, the same author challenged the idea that maturity comes to those who follow the directive "Know Thyself." Too often, Overstreet concluded, the attempt to know ourselves leads to confusion, self-centered brooding, and morbid introspection. He suggested, instead, that maturity comes as we move away from excessive self-analysis and adventure forth to build interpersonal relationships. The greatest maturity comes to those who search out and "find the things, people, ideas, and cultural and other environmental forces" that can shape minds.[3]

More recently, psychologists have written about maturity using words that sound similar to the mental stability discussed in the previous chapter.[4] According to these analyses, as we grow toward mental maturity, we develop:

- a more realistic view of ourselves. This means that we can see our strengths and weaknesses without overestimating either. We can laugh at ourselves and evaluate ourselves accurately.
- an ability to accept ourselves and others. This does not mean that we like everything we see in ourselves or others and neither does it mean that we don't try to improve. Instead, we accept the fact that everyone, ourselves included, has fears, desires, hopes, and sometimes misperceptions that can create tension and misunderstanding.
- an ability to live in the present but to have long-range goals. Some people live in the past; others think only of the present or spend their lives dreaming of the future. Maturing people honestly face their present circumstances, but try to plan realistically and flexibly for the future. These people don't drift through life. They set personal goals and make life plans, but they try to avoid rigidity. They live in accordance with their goals without letting their goals control them.
- a set of values and moral standards. Maturing people have a sense of what is right and wrong. Unlike the child or sociopath who is completely self-centered, the more mature individual has a concern for others and lives by ethics and values that exist for the good of everyone.
- an interest in life and a determination to develop our interests and abilities. "The immature person is trying to protect or defend himself from life, the world, others, and himself as well, while the mature person is involved in the tasks of life."[5] People with maturing minds do not withdraw from life. Even in old age they are learning, growing, and trying to develop their potentialities.

The self-actualized mind. Abraham Maslow was a famous psychologist who once wrote a college textbook on abnormal behavior.[6] The experience left Maslow wondering if we focus too much attention on troubled minds, and don't give enough thought to healthy, maturing human beings.

This led Maslow to look for what he called "self-actualized" people. Most of these people, he concluded, are at least sixty years of age. They are not static, but even in their later years they still are moving toward maturity. Some successful talented people, like Van Gogh, Wagner, and probably Whistler, were never self-actualized, but others were outstanding examples. Maslow's list included Abraham Lincoln, Albert Einstein, Eleanor Roosevelt, Albert Schweitzer, George Washington Carver, Pablo Casals, Martin Buber, Ralph Waldo Emerson, and Jane

Adams. These were "superior specimens" of humanity, people whose maturity was reflected in a number of outstanding characteristics.

According to Maslow's research, self-actualized people tend to show: the ability to judge others accurately, a clear notion of right and wrong, creativity, a dedication to some work or duty, courage and a willingness to risk making mistakes, a relative freedom from internal conflict and personal problems, an ability to respect and enjoy people, a healthy self-respect, an ability to make decisions even when faced with opposition, self-discipline, an ability to form deep relationships, a commitment to marriage, belief in a meaningful universe, an ability to enjoy sex even in later life, a willingness to be constructively critical, a relative freedom from fear and uncertainty, and a joy in living.[7] Self-actualizing people never tire of life. They "enjoy life in general and in practically all its aspects, while most other people enjoy only stray moments of triumph, of achievement or of . . . peak experience."[8]

THE PERFECTIONISTIC MIND

If you are like me, you probably read the above paragraph and wondered how well you fit. Although most of us fall far short of these high standards of maturity, we still can accept these as goals toward which maturing minds move.

Sometimes, however, people get the idea that they must be perfect to be mature or to be acceptable. In our society we admire quality (perhaps because we see it so seldom), and we teach our children that self-worth and good performance go together. The child begins to assume that mistakes will not be accepted, and soon he or she becomes anxious and self-condemning when it isn't possible to reach perfection.

The perfectionistic mind develops what has been called "all-or-nothing" thinking. "If I don't get an A on the test, I am a total failure," someone might conclude, "If I don't give a perfect speech, I am incompetent as a speaker." Such thinking leads people to strive for goals that are difficult if not impossible to attain.

Often the perfectionist dwells on self-critical ideas that lead to low self-esteem. The mind is filled with "should statements." "I should never make a mistake," the person thinks, "I should always do exercises," "I should never let myself skip my prayer time."

The higher one's standards, and the greater one's need to be perfect, the more frustrated the person becomes in trying to reach his or her overly ambitious goals. When one is constantly thinking about perfection, the mind is distracted so that it concentrates less on one's work or musical performance. This leads to a lower quality of performance—the very thing that the perfectionist fears.

Often perfectionists know that their thinking is irrational, but a lowering of one's standards leads to feelings of tension and anxiety. Perhaps it isn't surprising that one expert in this area has concluded that perfectionists are vulnerable to depression, obsessive-compulsive disorders, and anxiety neuroses.[9]

How, then, can we develop maturing minds and move toward self-actualization, without getting bogged down in the mire of perfectionism? The answer is found in a consideration of the idea of excellence.

THE EXCELLENT MIND

Thomas Peters and Robert Waterman are management experts whose work has taken them around the world, observing and consulting with business organizations. It didn't take these men long to discover that some corporations—IBM, Proctor and Gamble, 3M, Hewlett-Packard, Disney, Delta Airlines, Eastman Kodak, Marriott, Dow Chemical, and McDonald's, for example—have characteristics that enable them to stand head and shoulders above their peers. These companies maintain close contact with their customers, respect their rank and file workers, and try to encourage innovation. They are America's best-run companies, Peters and Waterman wrote in a highly acclaimed book that remained for over a year on the best-seller lists. They are corporations characterized by excellence.[10]

When Lyndon Johnson was president of the United States, he had one Republican in his cabinet, a man who was also a psychologist. John W. Gardner believed that businesses, individuals, and societies could never hope to achieve real success unless they set high standards and worked to achieve their goals. In short, we must strive for excellence.

"Some people have greatness thrust upon them," Gardner wrote. "Very few have excellence thrust upon them. They achieve it. They do not achieve it unwittingly, by 'doin' what comes naturally'; and they don't stumble into it in the course of amusing themselves. All excellence involves discipline and tenacity of purpose."[11]

What is this excellence? What are its characteristics? To answer these questions, let us begin by considering what excellence is not.

What excellence is not. It should come as no surprise to conclude that excellence is *not* the same as perfection. While some people try to be perfect, no human being can attain that goal. Perfectionism, as we have seen, ultimately leads to frustration, discouragement, and guilt.

Excellence does *not* necessarily involve competition. Everybody can strive for excellence, without trying to "beat out" others. We each have skills, abilities, and interests that can be developed. It is possible that we all can be excellent, and still able to support and cooperate with one another.

Excellence does *not* have to apply equally to every area of our lives. Over my desk, as a constant reminder, there hangs an ornate little frame enclosing one word. The word, printed in white on a black background, is "Excellence." I strive for this in my work, including my writing. I want to be an excellent husband and father, an excellent psychologist, and an excellent speaker. But I have no aspirations to be an excellent cook, mechanic, athlete, or salesperson. These are not my areas of expertise or special interest. We can only be excellent in some areas of life.

Excellence is *not* limited to high-status occupations. Gardner writes that we must "learn to honor excellence (indeed to *demand* it) in every socially accepted human activity, however humble the activity, and to scorn shoddiness, however exalted the activity."[12]

It should be added that excellence is *not* limited to our vocations. We can strive for excellence in our hobbies, child rearing, and spiritual growth.

Finally, excellence is *not* the same as worldly success. It is possible to be successful in this world without being excellent, and it is possible to achieve excellence without being acclaimed as successful.

The meaning of excellence. Excellence is a mindset, a way of thinking, that involves at least six attitudes. The excellent mind is characterized by:

- *Effort.* We cannot be lazy and excellent too. "Every truly worthwhile achievement of excellence has a price tag," according to Ted Engstrom. "The question you must answer for yourself is, How much am I willing to pay in hard work, patience, sacrifice, and endurance to be a person of excellence? Your answer is important, because the cost is great."[13]

• *A commitment to goals.* Some of these goals may be clear and well-defined; some may be more vague. Nevertheless, the decision to seek a goal and the determination to persevere are important traits for any person who wants to develop excellence and be successful.[14]

John Naber, the swimmer, won five gold medals at the 1976 Olympic Games in Montreal. He was praised by the press, cheered by the crowds, and acclaimed by his countrymen. But a few weeks after the Olympics he plunged into a deep depression. Later he realized that this came because he had attained his goals and no longer had anything to aim for. When he found new goals, the depression lifted. In contrast, the speed skater Eric Heiden had no post-Olympic depression. After winning several gold medals, he turned his attention to another goal, that of becoming a surgeon like his father.[15]

• *Flexibility.* It is difficult to attain excellence if we are rigid and afraid to move.
• *Discipline.* Excellence rarely comes to people who are undisciplined and easily distracted.
• *Persistence.* This only is seen in people who believe in what they are doing and are convinced that their goals are worth achieving. This is true even when there is failure. On the road to excellence, all people make mistakes.
• *Balance.* Some people are so committed to excellence in one area of their lives that they ignore everything else. It is difficult to attain excellence in our vocations, for example, if we ignore our families, fail to take care of our bodies, pay no attention to colleagues, or overlook our spiritual lives.

A biblical view of excellence. The New Testament Book of *James* was probably written by the brother of Jesus and, originally, may have been a sermon.[16] It is one of the most practical books in all of the Bible. The word "excellence" is never mentioned, but the entire book stresses the importance of quality living.

Chapter three, for example, reminds teachers that they have a special obligation to be careful how they teach and influence others. Then we are given several marks of excellence.

First, excellence means that we are careful what we say. The tongue is a small part of the body, but it can do tremendous damage, sometimes in a very short time. Who among us has not

said something, perhaps in anger, and wished later that we had
kept quiet? Such outbursts, like the words of encouragement
that also come from our mouths, arise in our minds. When the
mind is filled with sour thoughts, it is unlikely that our words will
be very sweet.[17]

Second, excellence means that we are careful how we act.
James encourages his readers to live lives that are characterized
by goodness, humility, and gentleness.[18] How easy it is to be
rude and inconsiderate, with our families, with people in our
communities, and even with our colleagues at work.

Recently I attended a conference where I met several business
friends. It was interesting to notice how some of them were
dressed, and how they interacted with others. I try not to judge
people by the way they dress, but it was difficult for me to believe
that the sloppy dressers would be careful business people. It was
easy, too, to wonder if the people who radiated a seemingly
superficial charm might also be insincere in business dealings.
The old adage probably still is true: Actions can speak louder
than words.

Every counseling student knows that good counselors must
first of all be genuine, warm, and sincerely interested in others.
Perhaps these traits are also marks of excellence.

Third, excellence means that we are careful how we think. In
our culture, we admire drive, enthusiasm, and hard work. That
is how we get ahead, and many would agree that these are characteristics of excellence.

But sometimes that drive leads to bitterness and insensitive
boasting. Twice, in one short paragraph, the Bible warns against
the dangers of envy and selfish ambition. These are even described as coming from the devil.[19]

As we build our careers, most of us accept three basic myths:
• Only some people can be successful.
• People who are successful have wealth, power, prestige,
  and/or independence.
• Success is tied with self-worth: only the people who succeed
  are worth anything in our society.

None of these ideas is supported by the biblical writers. This is
part of the "worldly wisdom" which James criticizes and Jesus
challenged.[20] Minds that are caught in the web of selfish ambition can never attain excellence.

Fourth, excellence means that we are aware of spiritual values.
James writes about being peace-loving, pure, considerate, mer-

ciful, impartial, sincere, and known for good deeds.[21] This is a list that echoes the writings of both Paul and Peter.[22]

The biblical writers do not imply, however, that we should simply be aware of these characteristics. They are to be developed in our lives both through conscious effort and through a dependence on the Holy Spirit, who gives believers the strength and wisdom to move toward excellence.

Fifth, excellence means that we are intent on getting along with others.[23] Quarreling, manipulating people, coveting, wallowing in our own self-centered desires—each of these is condemned, along with a mindset that tries to build friendships with the world, even though this will put us at odds with God.

In contrast, we are called to submit to the divine will and to work at becoming peacemakers. None of this comes naturally. Perhaps that is one reason why excellence is rare. It involves effort and discipline.

Not long ago, the circus visited our community and the local papers lauded the performance of Gunther Gebel-Williams. At each performance, this man steps into a cage with tigers and lions, puts them through fifteen or twenty crowd-pleasing tricks, then turns his attention to the bears, performing horses, elephants, and smaller animals that are part of other circus acts. His whole family travels with the circus, and each is involved with animals. They work fifteen-hour days and spend eleven months of every year on the road. The family Rolls Royce usually stays in the garage at home, because nobody is there to drive it.

Why would anyone enjoy such a life? There are only brief periods of stardom, but many hours of hard, patient, sometimes dangerous, and often frustrating work. The animals need attention and months of careful training. The performers can't take days off and they have to be on time for work.

But there is a sense of satisfaction that comes in striving for excellence. "I perform for only one reason," Gebel-Williams said in a recent interview, "so I'll be able to train animals."[24]

THE SPIRITUAL MIND

Few of us will ever strive for excellence in the circus, but everyone can work toward excellence and maturing—toward satisfaction—in his or her spiritual life.

Not long ago, two private foundations financed a project in

which representatives from the nursing profession could meet together to study the spiritual dimensions of mental health. The task force was interested both in mental illness, and in the ways that religious beliefs could help create healthy, maturing minds.

These mental health experts knew that religious beliefs can have an enormous positive influence on the mind, but beliefs also can get distorted and create confusion. The spiritually mature mind avoids unrealistic, extreme thinking, and develops a "balanced" perspective in at least six areas.[25]

Sin and guilt. The spiritually mature mind recognizes that everybody sins, but knows that we each can and will be forgiven if we confess to Christ and daily experience his pardon and restoration.[26]

Unhealthy thinking goes to one of two extremes. Sometimes it ignores sin, pays no attention to right or wrong, and lives under the illusion that one has reached a state of sinless perfection. At the other extreme are people who have become so preoccupied with sin that they are perpetually self-condemning, overwhelmed by feelings of guilt, and convinced that their sins are unpardonable.

Freedom and restraint. Healthy people have a mixture of creativity, spontaneity, and enthusiasm, combined with discipline and self-control. Unhealthy people either throw away all the rules and live lives characterized by licentiousness and lack of responsibility, or they drift to the extreme of rigidity, legalism, and an oppressive need to work harder at pleasing God or atoning for their guilt.

God's control. The spiritually mature mind recognizes that the God who is sovereign and in control also gives us freedom to make decisions and to act responsibly. In contrast, the spiritually unhealthy person either concludes that "there is no God, so everything depends on me" or assumes that God is a genie who does whatever we want, whenever we ask. This view was stated concisely by a young man who announced, "I don't need to make any plans for my future. Whatever happens, God will fix it up for me."

Self-estimate. According to the nurses' task force, this is a core issue in mental health. It is healthy to recognize one's weaknesses but to know, at the same time, that we also are God's creatures— unique, valuable, loved, worthwhile, and gifted. We don't need to be perfect to get God's favor or to be worthwhile as people. The spiritually and mentally healthy mind determines to do the best job possible, without the compulsion to strive for perfectionism. Sometimes we will succeed in reaching our standards and sometimes we won't, but that is part of being human.[27]

The unhealthy mind moves instead to grandiosity and the belief that one is always right and capable of doing things without help. Or there is the opposite reaction of intense self-condemnation, often accepted with the belief that it is somehow honoring to God to think that one is despicable and the worst example of God's creation.

The idea of suffering. The healthy mind accepts suffering as part of the human condition, faces it realistically, and draws both on God's strength and on the support of others who can help us face the pressures of life. The spiritually unhealthy mind either seeks suffering (on the assumption that self-inflicted and other human misery pleases God and "breaks us" so that we can serve better), or blithely and unrealistically assumes that God will prevent suffering and always remove it if only we have enough faith.

Relationships. Healthy, spiritually mature people seek to build good relationships with others, without squelching one's own identity. In contrast are those who either ignore and withdraw from people so that they become loners, or become so enmeshed with others and dependent on others that the person loses his or her individual identity.

It is interesting to ponder why people move away from spiritually healthy thinking and toward these unhealthy extremes. In some cases, the extremes appear to come because of personal stresses, individually distorted thinking, or the experiences of growing up in homes where biblical values and teachings are not known or practiced. At other times, it seems that sincere, dedicated people reach faulty and unhealthy theological conclusions because they, or their spiritual leaders, have ignored or misinterpreted the Bible's teaching.

A CONCLUDING OBSERVATION

Some of history's most famous people, including many creative minds, have been immature and mentally unhealthy. We have already mentioned Whistler and several others. It is true that the "world would be an incomparably poorer place without the legacy of immature personalities such as these."[28]

But it also is true that when minds are maturing, spiritually and/or psychologically, they are better able to show the clear, intelligent thinking and creativity that we will be discussing in the next three chapters.

Most of us would agree, I suspect, with the conclusion of a thoughtful British theologian. "Perhaps maturity can be achieved through simple innocence and unworldliness," he wrote. "But, it is more likely that those who seek ethical purity by withdrawal from the world and from exposure to temptation can attain that goal largely at the cost of developing a full human maturity. Involvement with the rough and tumble of the world, in which one can take risks, can be hurt, and can make mistakes, is for most people the means by which maturity is gained. Sin is not a route to maturity, but it is in a sinful world that development in maturity has to occur."[29]

10
THE
THINKING
MIND

"Arthur, how much is 6,427 times 4,234?"

Without hesitation the handsome eight-year-old turned to the psychologist and gave the answer, "27,211,918." His voice was stilted and his face showed little expression, but his answer was right, as always.

Thirteen-year-old Iris was more active and inclined to squirm. "Tell me," the same psychologist asked, "in 1998, which months will have the seventh on a Wednesday." Still squirming and without pausing, Iris shot back her answer: "January and October."

Arthur and Iris are among more than five hundred children who have been studied at the Institute for Child Behavior Research in San Diego. Each possesses one or more extraordinary abilities—in areas such as mathematics, music, electronics, or memory. Some can give instant answers about the calendar—knowing, for example, which day of the week is 22 October 1934. Another, at age three, could take apart and correctly reassemble appliances such as radios and vacuum cleaners. One has the ability to memorize and repeat television credits after only one viewing. But there is one way in which all of these children are the same. Each is mentally retarded.

Textbook writers call them "idiot savants." Most are normal-looking children who have difficulty relating to others, great problems in communication, low overall IQ's, an inability to do regular school work, and at least one talent that surpasses the capabilities of even the most brilliant people.[1] The experts are less sure how the minds of these unusual people work.

One theory suggests that there may be brain damage in the left temporal lobe (see Figure 2–1) or in the reticular formation (Figure 2–2). This damage, or some other malfunction, may interfere with the chemistry of the brain and give these people an ability to concentrate in one or two areas, with great intensity and with little distraction. Unlike the normal brain that attends to a variety of things and can comprehend what it encounters, the savant's brain focuses its concentration in narrow areas and has little comprehension of what it encounters. A few of these children recover and are able to function normally, but most spend their lives in institutions for the mentally retarded.

THE MINDLESS MIND

In attempting to understand these "gifted-retarded" people, some cognitive scientists have looked for clues that could help us understand how normal minds work. It has been found, for example, that people with exceptionally good memories are sometimes able to concentrate well and to absorb large numbers of facts, but their reasoning abilities are poorer. Nietzsche once remarked that "many a man fails to become a thinker for the sole reason that his memory is too good."[2] Somewhat like the idiot savants, these normal people who can concentrate well and re- member much are less able to reason. In contrast, there is the absent-minded professor who may reason well but forget much.

At times, we all forget and each of us fails to reason carefully. Recently, a New York tire company mailed discount coupons to 20,000 homes each month for a period of eight months. The coupons were dated and valid only for the month in which they were mailed. One of the coupons promised to give a vehicle inspection for $1.99, instead of for the regular $3.00 price. In the fourth mailing, however, the printer made a mistake and the coupon price was $2.99—a one penny saving. When researchers compared the number of car inspections before, during and after the error, it was found that the coupons attracted as many new customers when they read $2.99 as they did during the other months. Why, it was wondered, would people go out of their way to redeem a coupon that essentially saved them nothing?[3]

Some have suggested that the answer is "mindless thinking." If we paid attention to every stimulation that came to the mind, we would be overwhelmed. To avoid this, we focus our critical thinking on novel situations and handle the rest automatically— without giving them much thought. When something is very familiar, like driving the same route to work every morning, or when we encounter some fact that doesn't concern us very much, we react mindlessly. Store managers are well aware that items marked "sale" and placed near the check-out counter sell well, even when there is no reduction in price. Everybody knows that coupons are supposed to give discounts so the car owners didn't pay any attention to the misprint that gave only a one-cent reduction.

At times, we each do things in a routine manner so we can think about something else. Mindlessness, however, occurs when we appear to be paying attention to what we are doing— like clipping a coupon and making an appointment to take the car in for an inspection—but in fact we are not really thinking. Sometimes this can have serious results.

It has been suggested, for example, that mindlessness may actually shorten one's life. In old age homes, the elderly people who were encouraged to engage in mindful activities—like making decisions or taking care of plants—lived longer than those whose way of thinking was more mindless. Cancer patients who hear their diagnosis sometimes mindlessly assume that recovery is unlikely, so they are less inclined to obey doctor's orders or to fight the disease.[4] All of this leads to the fascinating question of how active minds think and are able to solve problems, without being mindless.

THE ACTIVE MIND

Recently, I heard a radio announcer trying to convince his listeners that every modern business person needs a car phone. "Don't waste valuable time sitting in traffic while your competitors are doing business and making sales," the announcement urged. "With a phone in your car you can increase business and build profits."

You can also increase the likelihood of accidents. The radio announcer didn't mention that the mind has difficulty attending to two ideas at once, especially if the activities involve similar parts of the brain. It is not difficult to listen to music and read a book at the same time. Different parts of the brain are involved. But it is much harder to concentrate on driving and telephoning at the same time. In one study, drivers were tested while they talked on the phone and drove in simulators. In 47 percent of the tests, drivers who were talking on the phone tried to drive the car through spaces that were too small. It is fortunate that the tests were not done on the highway.[5]

We *can* learn to do two similar things at once, however. One study required people to read short stories and to write dictation at the same time. At first the concentration and performance were both poor, but soon the subjects learned to do both well.[6] (I suspect I am not the only one who has learned to read a book or magazine whenever I watch television.) And in time, we can learn to drive and to talk at the same time. How can this be possible?

Again we find ourselves dealing with biology. A large part of the human brain consists of "association cortex"—portions of the parietal and frontal lobes that have no direct connection to the muscles and sense organs. Instead, the association cortex neurons are connected to each other and since humans have more association cortex than any other animal, it is assumed that this is what enables people to ponder ideas, to plan for the future, to function with a high level of intelligence, and to think with words and sentences.

Only humans have the intelligence to invent and use language symbols. Right now you are looking at a series of black marks on white paper. The black marks convey a message. You comprehend because you know how to read and understand words. How did you learn this?

That question is still being answered by people who are specialists in "neurolinguistics." Clearly human language has something to do with our ability to hear, and reading is connected with the ability to see or to feel braille symbols. But how do we learn the meaning of symbols or master grammatical principles and the complexities of a foreign language? It appears that repetition enlarges the dendrite tips of the neurons in the brain. This change lets information pass more quickly from one part of the brain to another. The physical changes, especially those in the association cortex, are at the basis of learning.

In learning a language, certain parts of the brain become of special importance. There is, for example, a region of the temporal lobe known as Wernicke's area. It is there that we perceive language. Elsewhere, there are areas for producing speech, storing memories, interpreting gestures,[7] and recognizing faces.

Phrenology and the mind. Could it be assumed that we can map out the brain so that we know where every aspect of thinking takes place? In the late eighteenth and early nineteenth century, people tried to produce such maps through what they called "the science of phrenology." This was a belief that "mental faculties" like loyalty, devotion, modesty, or aggression, could each be localized on the surface of the skull. Phrenologists produced detailed maps of the brain and sometimes would run their hands over people's heads and give personality readings.

We now know that these maps were mostly wrong. There is no scientific basis for this old idea that the shape of the skull gives a clue to one's personality or intelligence. We do know the location of motor and visual areas of the brain, however, and we know both where speech is centered and where some memories are stored. Nevertheless, it is not yet possible to find specific regions of the brain to account for learning, thinking, or personality differences. Each brain is a little different, and as surgical probes have shown, no two are exactly alike. They don't even reason alike.

The problem-solving mind. Teachers and motivational speakers sometimes give formulas to help people reason and solve problems. One recent book has argued, for example, that there are seven steps to solving problems and making decisions. We should pray, asking for divine wisdom; identify the causes of the problem or what really has to be done; establish specific objectives or priorities; generate a list of the ways that you could proceed; select the most logical alternative; test this out and see if it works (if it doesn't, go back and try something else); then implement the final plan.[8]

Formulas like this can be helpful, but they assume that problem solving is logical and orderly. This isn't always true. Novices sometimes analyze problems on a step-by-step basis, but when people become experienced—people such as medical specialists, well-established counselors, business executives, and experienced plumbers or other tradespeople—they often skip the careful reasoning and make a guess about a diagnosis or possible solution to a problem. Often the guess is right. Once they learn the basics of logic and become experienced in a field of expertise, these competent people appear to be able to sift through the data in their brains and reach accurate conclusions.

One of the most frustrating courses I ever took was entitled "Rorschach Interpretation." The Rorschach, as you may remember, is the famous ink-blot test. People are shown pictures of ink blots and are asked to tell what they see in the ink-blot designs. The theory of their designer, Hermann Rorschach, was that people would reveal things about their minds as they looked at the ink blots and reported what they saw.

My professor had an uncanny ability to interpret Rorschach responses. One day, for example, a student gave the test to a man who had recently attempted suicide. As the man's responses were read to the class, the teacher interrupted and said, "This man is seriously contemplating suicide." All of us were greatly impressed at our instructor's ability, but we were frustrated both because none of us could make such interpretations and because the teacher couldn't tell us how he did it. His explanation that it must be "intuition" didn't help.

What may help is an understanding of how experts and novices differ. The expert has a large background of knowledge from which to draw information. He or she has the ability to see things in perspective and because of past experience pieces of information somehow are more easily linked together. Without the earlier study, training, and experience, the later intuition would never be possible.[9]

Many professional schools, such as those that train lawyers or business people, use the case-study method of training. Students analyze and discuss hundreds of specific problem cases, all on the assumption that in time the graduate will be able to "know what works and what does not." Apparently there is truth in the old idea that if you want to be a good physician, musician, writer, mother, counselor, preacher, pilot, or carpenter, you have to work at it for a while and eventually things will "click," so that you intuitively know what to do. For most fields of study, it may be that ten or more years could pass before things really click. And expertise in one area doesn't automatically carry over to some other area.

THE REMEMBERING MIND

Sometimes a person's behavior depends less on training or past experience and more on what one expects to happen. It is widely assumed, for example, that the drinking of alcohol can make people more aggressive and less inhibited sexually. But does this actually happen?

To find out, two psychologists at the University of Washington did a series of experiments in which some people consumed alcoholic drinks (vodka mixed with tonic water) and others got nonalcoholic tonic water.[10] Previous research had shown that if both drinks are chilled and a squirt of lime juice is added, it is difficult to determine which has the alcohol. Most of the experimental subjects, therefore, didn't know what they were drinking. All of them were then given a series of psychological tests to measure such things as mood, anxiety level, sexual arousal, and the tendency to be aggressive.

The results are similar to those obtained in a variety of other studies. When people think they are consuming alcohol, their behavior changes whether or not there is any liquor in their drinks. This has been called the think-drink effect. People act like they expect alcohol will make them act, even after drinking water that they thought was mixed with vodka. One man acted intoxicated, stumbled around the room, and tried to make a date with the female research assistant. He excused his behavior by saying that he had had a few drinks. I wonder if anyone told him that his drinks didn't contain any alcohol?

It should not be assumed from this that the drinker's behavior is "all in the mind." Alcohol consumption does make a number of differences. In terms of motor behavior, like the ability to drive a car, the alcohol does adversely influence drinkers more than many realize. And researchers have found that alcohol, marijuana, and other drugs can hinder one's ability to remember. There is also good evidence that on the morning after, drinkers who consume large quantities of alcohol really can't remember what they said or did at the cocktail party the night before.

The stages of memory. In a variety of laboratories, researchers are trying to unravel the mysteries of memory. Most currently agree that there are at least two stages to the forming of memories.[11]

Whenever the sense organs are stimulated they send electrical charges into the brain and on down the neuron pathways. If we don't pay attention to these stimulations, they fizzle out, usually within a few seconds. This is why they are called "short-term memories." Sometimes we can keep them alive for a longer time. Most people, for example, can remember a telephone number long enough to dial it, but unless the number is of special importance, it disappears quickly. Students can sometimes cram enough facts into their brains to pass a test, but then the information seems to disappear forever.

Some memories, however, do not fade. When short-term memories are mulled over, little growths appear at the synapses—those bridges between neurons. These growths remain as "long-term memories," even after the initial stimulation is gone.

Someone has likened this to the influence of little streams of water running down a hillside. When the water stops, the little streams disappear. But if the water runs long enough, a small channel is cut out of the hillside and becomes a permanent memory of the water's original presence. In a similar way, long-term memories are created out of short-term memories if these keep flowing long enough.[12]

Why do some short-term memories fade while others become transferred into long-term memories? Part of the answer may lie in the brain's "gatekeepers"—portions of the brain (primarily the hippocampus) that appear to weed out unimportant ideas or experiences and allow only some impressions to reach the cortex where they become long-term memories and are stored. Alcohol apparently blocks the gates and prevents new long-term memories from being formed, at least while the alcohol is present. That is why the drinker may not be able to remember what happened at the previous evening's party.[13] Some antibiotics may also interfere with the forming of long-term memories. And emotions play a role as well.

Whenever we are emotionally aroused, there are chemical changes in the body, including the brain. Sometimes these chemical reactions stimulate long-term memory but at other times— when you have an accident, for example—the brain gets an electrical shock that wipes out the short-term memories and prevents them from forming long-term memories. This is why people often cannot remember the events that came immediately before an accident. And witnesses to crimes are sometimes so traumatized that they can't remember details of the event when police question them later.

It has been known for many years that people and animals learn and form long-term memories better when they are in stimulating and enriched environments. The stimulated brain has more of the chemicals that are needed to change the neurons and help us form new memories.[14] It becomes important, therefore, to keep people active at all ages—especially when they are young children who sometimes get ignored, or old people who may have little stimulation if they live alone or in boring nursing home environments.

THE FORGETFUL MIND

"Millions of neurons, each retaining its own memory, would constitute the brain's long-term memory. The altered neurons constitute a network of memory as sensitive as a spider's web: touching one strand of the web, or activating one or two neurons in the network, triggers all of the others. That's why hearing just a couple of notes can call up an entire score, a complete performance and the memory of the evening when it all happened."[15]

But what happens if your mind seems less like a spider's web and more like a sieve? Why do we have trouble remembering?

Sometimes there are physical reasons for memory failure. Brain damage, for example, sometimes destroys the memory neurons. Stroke victims who spend hours relearning lost skills, are really forming new neural connections. For others, chemical changes may prevent the long-term memories from being formed or retrieved.

For most of us, it seems likely that memories get distorted over time and sometimes are embellished by our imaginations. Sometimes, therefore, people "remember" things that didn't really occur or forget details that are too painful to remember. Freud wrote about these memory failures many years ago, and more recent cognitive scientists have observed that some kinds of amnesia have no known physical basis. Psychologically, some events are just too painful to remember.[16]

What do you do about déjà vu? One unusual but very common type of memory experience is what we know as "déjà vu." The words are French and can be translated "already seen." Assume, for example, that you are on vacation, perhaps standing in a store that you have never visited before. Suddenly you have the mysterious sensation that you have lived this instant previously. Some have called this evidence of reincarnation and others have wondered if it is ESP. Since déjà vu experiences often precede epileptic seizures and since the experience is common in brain-damaged patients, some have assumed that this is evidence of some neurons misfiring because of a malfunction.

There is a simpler and perhaps more accurate explanation, at least for people whose brains are functioning normally. At times, something in the environment triggers a group of neurons in the brain. This arouses vivid memories from the past, memories that are so similar to the present situation that we think we have "been here before" even when we have not.

Of more practical importance to most of us is understanding how we can get our memories to improve.

Improving memory. Can you memorize the following list of numbers? How long would it take?

1 4 9 2 1 7 7 6 1 8 6 5 1 9 4 5 1 9 6 3 1 9 8 4

It is difficult to memorize a list of this length since most people can only keep about seven digits in mind at a time. I suspect, however, that some readers noticed that the above numbers are a string of dates: when Columbus discovered America (1492), America became independent (1776), Lincoln was shot (1865), the Second World War ended (1945), and Kennedy was assassinated (1963). The 1984 refers to George Orwell's famous book. Now try to repeat the list.

Some idiot savants can perform amazing feats of memory because they have trained their minds to concentrate and resist distraction. In similar ways, the rest of us can use gimmicks to boost recollection. Do you remember "thirty days hath September"? When I was in the Navy we had to learn that the port side of the ship was the left side and that it always showed a red light. So we remembered that "*port* is *red* and should be *left* alone." When I was in grade school I had trouble spelling "arithmetic" until I learned "*a* red *i*ndian *t*hought *h*e *m*ight *e*at *t*obacco *i*n *c*hurch."

These mnemonic devices help us remember because they are meaningful. They help explain the performances by memory experts who appear on television, and it appears that some memory-triggering devices are involved in the ability of actors and singers to memorize exceptionally long scripts. In their best-selling book on memory, Harry Lorayne and Jerry Lucas declare that "all memory, whether trained or untrained, is based on association."[17] When ideas and images can be tied together in some meaningful sequence "memory chain," or when thoughts are associated with something that is easier to remember (like associating a string of numbers with historical dates), then memory improves. We also remember better when we really want to remember, and when we use a little repetition. Next time you meet someone whose name you don't want to forget, try using the name two or three times in your conversation.

A few people in this world—one report[18] says about 1 percent of the population—appear to have photographic memories, but most of us struggle to recall what we want to remember. Perhaps we can take some comfort in the well-known case of a Russian man who seemed to remember everything. The poor fellow lived a life of chaos because his thinking was overloaded with facts that he could not forget. Some forgetting can be a real benefit—so long as we don't forget too much.

THE CHOOSING MIND

Philosopher Karl R. Popper has proposed that our minds have to contend with three worlds. World 1 is the physical world of external reality. World 2 is the subjective world of inner experience that each of us carries in our brains. World 3 is the world of objective knowledge that has been acquired by civilizations for centuries and now is growing at a stupendous rate. Each of these worlds can influence individuals, but right now we are having a special challenge in trying to cope with an explosion of data in World 3. No person can master everything, but societies must be sure that every part of World 3 is mastered by at least a few people. And within each generation there must be scientists, scholars, and artists who can rediscover, reorganize, and expand World 3.[19]

The existence of our three worlds, and the smallness of finite human minds, means that for each of us there are books that will never be read, ideas that will never be encountered, and experiences that will never be had. We are only on this earth for a few years, and because of our limited time and intelligence, we have to make choices about what we will do and think.[20]

For many years, psychologists, theologians, and philosophers have talked about the will. The behaviorists and many psychoanalysts de-emphasized free will and assumed that most, if not all, of our behavior was predetermined. Now we are beginning to return to the idea that people must make choices. Some will be foolish and harmful. Some will be rushed and made without careful reflection. Most will reflect our values and beliefs. Many will come in response to social pressure but some will be made independently. Much of education, psychotherapy, spiritual training, and values clarification must focus on helping people choose from the mass of available information or alternatives and make wise, responsible choices.

For the Christian, it is sobering to ponder the implications of World 3, but comforting to realize that God, and only God, knows all things. He can guide us in our learning and choice making. He can direct our education and thinking. And he can help us develop the intelligent minds that we consider next.

11
THE
INTELLIGENT
MIND

In 1904, the school officials in France had a problem—there were too many children in the Paris schools. The poor students were holding back the good ones, and the bright youngsters were so bored they amused themselves by creating havoc for their frustrated teachers. After a long debate, the school board decided that the slower-learning children would have to be removed from the regular classrooms and put into special schools. This would make class sizes smaller and enable the quality of education to improve.

But how would they decide which students to remove? The officials didn't want to ask the teachers. They might be reluctant to say that a student was dull if he or she was friendly, well-behaved, or from a good family. And the temptation would be great to conclude that all troublemakers were really stupid and best put in someone else's class. To avoid such bias, the French educators wanted an objective test that would identify the genuinely dull students.

Could such a test be devised? To find an answer, the school board turned to a psychologist named Alfred Binet. Working with a colleague, Binet designed the first intelligence test and was the first person to use the term "intelligence quotient," or IQ. Soon there were revisions, translations, and variations of the original test. Many enthusiastically concluded that intelligence testing was psychology's greatest achievement. Children and adults were tested all over the world, and the scientific journals exploded with articles about the nature and measurement of intelligence.

There was one young man, however, who looked at this excitement from a different perspective. An employee of the Binet Laboratory in Paris, he had been hired to develop tests of reasoning. In trying these on children of different ages, he found that the wrong answers could be as interesting as the correct ones. The man tested some of these ideas at home with his own children, and eventually he concluded that mental reasoning goes through stages. Younger children, he proposed, think much differently than children who are older. Before long the man resigned from his position at the Binet laboratory, returned to his hometown to continue the research, and began writing some of the hundreds of articles and books that would flow from his productive life. In time, this man became more famous than Binet, his former employer. The man's name was Jean Piaget.

The intelligent mind. Even since Piaget's death in 1980, his work has been debated, praised, condemned, and expanded by others. Some have bypassed Piaget and worked instead to develop and use a variety of more modern intelligence and other psychological tests, even though the testing movement has been attacked by scientists, educators, journalists,[1] and government officials. Some have focused their efforts on trying to find the biological basis of intelligence; others have studied both child prodigies and the mentally retarded in an effort to understand unusual types of intelligence; and some have studied how language acquisition is related to intelligence. Although it may not seem to have much relevance to our daily behavior, there have also been heated debates about whether we need language to think. Some say words and symbols are the basis of intelligence; others argue that we think without words.[2] And in the years that have passed since Alfred Binet first came to the rescue of those Paris schools, scientists have continued to debate what we even mean by an intelligent mind.

EXTREMES OF INTELLIGENCE

Mental retardation is a vague term that traditionally has referred to people with IQ's of 70 or below. (An IQ of 100 is assumed to be average.) Some retarded people are so limited in their mental capacities that they can hardly talk and have no ability to care for themselves. Much more common are the mildly retarded who may have trouble in school, but who can hold simple jobs and get along in society, pretty much by themselves. While the causes of retardation continue to be debated, most experts agree that low intelligence can come from physical influences—such as brain damage, disease, or genetic inheritance; from environmental influences—such as limited stimulation especially during the early years; or from a combination of both heredity and environment.

At one time, retarded people were put in institutions and left to fend for themselves, but more recently there have been increasing efforts to educate the retarded. It has even been argued—probably with unjustified optimism—that there are "no limits to learning,"[3] and that all of us can be more intelligent than we are now. Based on this belief, the forward-looking government of Venezuela has created a cabinet-level post for the "Development of Human Intelligence." As you might guess, educators from around the world are watching with great interest to see if and how the Venezuelan experiment will work.

The prodigy's mind. In the meantime, mind-watchers continue to encounter examples of gifted people who are at the high end of mental ability scales. They exist today, some perhaps as capable as the eight-year-old Austrian boy whose father brought him to England in 1764 to take part in the twenty-sixth birthday celebration of King George III.

According to one writer, the streets of London were crowded with "visitors, jugglers, puppet shows, and pickpockets."[4] Glittering balls were held on the warm June evenings, and at the Great Room in Spring Garden, the little Austrian boy and his twelve-year-old sister were on display as "prodigies of nature." Together they played the organ and harpsichord to the delight and amazement of everyone who heard them.

The boy was already a celebrity throughout Europe. He had performed before emperors and kings, had composed highly acclaimed chamber music, and was about to write his first three symphonies. Long before he reached adulthood, Wolfgang Amadeus Mozart was on the way to establishing himself as a great composer.

How did Mozart do this? How did Felix Mendelssohn or Franz Shubert compose so much great music while they were still very young? What has led others to become outstanding writers, scientists, mathematicians, and people of extraordinary achievement even before they reach adulthood?

Often these child prodigies come from unusually capable family backgrounds. Most are first-born, many are male, and most come from very stimulating environments. According to psychologist David Feldman, prodigies are people who perform at or near the level of professionals even while they are very young. To do this, all of the things that make a brilliant youngster must "coincide at exactly the right time, in exactly the right place, under exactly the right conditions. There has to be a cultural preparation and an appreciative audience."[5]

As they grow older, these children also realize that they are different. Some live lonely lives, trying to cope with their intelligence, their peers, and their overawed teachers. Some try to hide their unusual abilities, and a few "burn out" and lose interest in being brilliant by the time they reach their teenage years. Others—like Yehudi Menuhin, the contemporary violinist, and mathematician Norbert Wiener—were child prodigies who went on to live highly productive lives.[6]

Most of us, of course, are neither retarded nor gifted prodigies. We have learned what experts and laypeople both agree to be the three basics of intelligence: the ability to understand and use words and symbols (this enables us to speak, read, and write), the ability to solve practical problems, and the ability to get along in social situations.[7] These characteristics are not always measured by intelligence tests, but that may not be bad. Some experts are now convinced that the tests, and the resulting IQ scores, aren't even good indicators of intelligence.

MULTIPLE INTELLIGENCE

Popular magazines and Sunday newspapers often print "mind puzzles," sometimes taken from intelligence tests and occasionally presented as a way to measure one's own intelligence. Try the following questions, for example. (The answers are in the back of the book with the footnotes.)

1. How would you plant a total of ten trees in five rows of four trees each?

2. Water lilies double in area every twenty-four hours. At the beginning of the summer there is only one water lily on the lake. It takes sixty days for the lake to become covered with water lilies. On what day will the lake be half covered?

3. You are given six toothpicks of equal length. Arrange them to make four equilateral triangles, the sides of which are one stick long.

4. Two train stations are fifty miles apart. At 2:00 P.M. one Saturday afternoon two trains start toward each other, one from each station. Just as the trains pull out of the stations, a bird springs into

the air in front of the first train and flies ahead to the front of the second train. When the bird reaches the second train it turns back and flies toward the first train. The bird continues to do this until the trains meet. If both trains travel at the rate of twenty-five miles per hour and the bird flies at one hundred miles per hour, how many miles will the bird have flown before the trains meet?

5. How many animals did Moses take into the Ark?[8]

The first and third of these questions tend to test one's ability to solve spatial problems, while the other three are more concerned with reasoning ability. To solve them correctly you would have to read them carefully, ignore data that isn't important, and get rid of some assumptions. For example, the toothpick problem can only be solved when one abandons the idea that the toothpicks all have to be flat on the table.

Tests like these can be challenging, and often they are able to predict how well a person will do in school. But do they test intelligence? Researchers like Dr. Howard Gardner of Harvard would say no.

In a highly acclaimed but controversial book, Gardner has proposed that intelligence tests and mind puzzles have been unfair to many people. The tests, and those who construct them, have assumed that intelligence is primarily concerned with linguistic-verbal abilities. This assumption, says Gardner, is too narrow. In his book, *Frames of Mind*,[9] he proposes, instead, that there are multiple intelligences, each residing in specified parts of the brain, each developing more or less independently of the others, and each able to be trained.

Although he presents this theory in a tentative fashion, Gardner suggests that there are at least seven intelligences: linguistic (dealing primarily with words and language), musical, logical-mathematical, spatial, bodily-kinesthetic (having to do with physical skills including dance, acting, and athletics), and two groups of personal intelligences, one of which concerns inner self-awareness and the other involving the interpersonal skills needed for dealing with others. No one person has all of these intelligences in equal amounts; we each have more of some and less of others. But all can be developed, especially if the education process begins early in life.

Individual cultures decide which one or two of the intelligences is most important, and people who have those intelligences are considered "smart." In our society, for example, we value linguistic and logical-mathematical intelligences. Our intelligence tests focus on these areas, and so do the curricula of our educational institutions. People with high spatial intelligence, or those with outstanding bodily-kinesthetic intelligence, rarely do well on IQ tests, nor do they perform well on the school assignments that are part of our linguistic-verbal society.

According to Gardner, this theory says a lot about how we educate people. In our culture, both schooling and testing favor people with verbal-reasoning intelligence and leave the rest of the population at a distinct disadvantage. We waste much human potential because we focus on linguistic and logical intelligence, conclude that people who lack these are "dumb" or "stupid," and throw them on "society's scrap heap."[10] Much wiser, says Gardner, would be an educational policy that abandons intelligence tests (since these measure only linguistic and verbal aspects of intelligence), attempts to discover abilities early in life, and educates people in all seven areas of intelligence.

LEARNING AND INTELLIGENCE

Most of us, I suspect, got a clear message from our experiences at school. We learned that "smart kids get good grades and that stupid kids don't do well at school." Our parents and teachers urged us to study harder—all on the assumption that success in school and in life both depend on one's ability to excel in verbal knowledge and linguistic skills. The idea even persists in graduate schools where students learn, even today, that success as a doctor, preacher, counselor, or other professional, will only come to those who are able to memorize and remember great numbers of facts.

As a teacher of counseling students, I have noticed that some people can have a good intellectual understanding of counseling theories or techniques, but still be incompetent as practicing counselors. Physicians can get high grades in medical school examinations but be poor surgeons. Seminary students, and some of their professors, can debate theology with great skill but know little about being sensitive to people, walking with God, or relating their systematic Christianity to real life.

From this, it does not follow that factual learning should be abandoned or de-emphasized. Everybody needs to know facts and to possess verbal abilities, especially in a society like ours where the chief business commodity is no longer assumed to be agricultural products or the productions of industry. Ours has become an "information society"[11] where most people are involved in the production and distribution of facts and ideas. Even as we focus on the other intelligences, it would seem that we must continue to give special attention to the verbal-linguistic ones. This raises the issue of learning and the mind.

Superlearning. Not long ago, I was in Central America where I shared with some friends that my wife and I were trying to learn Spanish. "You need to use superlearning," one of my Guatemalan friends suggested. "It will make a great difference in the speed and efficiency of the way you learn."

Shortly after returning home, I decided to investigate superlearning. Based on the oft-quoted but rarely documented idea that we use only ten percent of our brain power, superlearning suggests that we need to develop our "potential quotient"—the ability to learn faster and remember more.[12] The process begins when we learn to relax.

Many years ago a Russian count was having trouble relaxing and getting to sleep. Finally he summoned a servant and told him to get Johann Goldberg, a skilled harpsichordist who was able to play music that Johann Sebastian Bach had written especially for the count. As Goldberg played, the count relaxed and eventually fell asleep. Whenever the insomnia returned, the count summoned Goldberg and eventually the musician was installed in a nearby room so he could be available upon request. So pleased was the count that he rewarded Bach with a lavish gift of gold, and the music became known as the "Goldberg Variations" in honor of the obliging harpsichordist.[13]

Some of Bach's music—like that of Vivaldi, Teleman, Corelli, Handel, and other baroque composers—has a beat that tends to parallel the human pulse rate. These slow, or *largo* movements, have been found to calm both the body and the mind. When this happens, learning is much more efficient and memory is greatly improved.

Consider, for example, the basic formula of superlearning. After getting in a relaxed position, the learners tell themselves that they are about to enjoy their learning, and then they start the music. After a few ten- to fifteen-minute practice sessions, it is relatively easy to breathe in harmony with the music. Then the learning begins in eight-second intervals.

First, you breathe in for two seconds.

Then, in four seconds you repeat some piece of information, such as a Spanish phrase: "*Hace mal tiempo*—the weather is bad."

Then breathe out for two seconds, and repeat the process with new information.

The theory assumes that such pacing gives the mind time to turn short-term memories into long-term memories with great efficiency and with minimum distraction. And there is increasing evidence, both from studies in North America and Europe, but especially from work in the Soviet bloc countries, that superlearning does, in fact, work. Advocates argue that superlearning can help one learn large numbers of facts, Bible verses, lengthy lyrics, material from scripts, or the subject matter for a test—all to the beat of Bach's Goldberg variations or similar music.

The superlearning idea might even help your houseplants. A California researcher named Dorothy Retallack wrote a book several years ago in which she claimed that plants were healthier and greener when grown in the presence of baroque music.[14] You may be interested in knowing that country-western music had no influence on plant growth, jazz helped a little, but when plants heard rock music all day, they shriveled and died. Parents of teenagers could make all kinds of interpretations from this interesting fact!

Regardless of one's musical tastes, however, it appears that learning, and the development of some kinds of intelligences, can be influenced by the environment in which the mind works.

ARTIFICIAL INTELLIGENCE

To understand learning and the intelligent mind more completely, some cognitive scientists have recently been trying to duplicate human intelligence on the computer. Their work, known broadly as the study of artificial intelligence (usually abbreviated AI), is progressing with such momentum that no book can hope to give an up-to-date survey of what is happening.

Everyone knows that the computer has already revolutionized our ways of storing, processing, and retrieving information. With the right software and modems, my little desk computer can give me instantaneous contact with almost anything I need to know. Computers have transformed business, medicine, and the Internal Revenue Service, but they also are changing the church,[15] and the practice of counseling and psychotherapy.[16]

According to futurist Alvin Toffler, computers can enrich our environments and ultimately make us more intelligent.[17] But could computers also take over and eventually get so big and powerful that they outrun our abilities to understand and control them? Could they so control our lives that we lose the ability to think or to cope whenever the power fails or the computer shuts down?[18] Marvin Minsky, a computer scientist and AI authority from MIT, has suggested that machines in the foreseeable future might reach the human level of intelligence, begin to educate themselves, move to the genius level, and develop immense power, creativity, and even emotions. "If we are lucky," Minsky suggests, "they might even decide to keep us as pets."[19]

With all of this speculation, it is helpful to consider what computers can and cannot do, especially when they are compared to the human mind.[20]

The superior computer. In many respects, computers are superior to the human mind. The computer can remember more, figure out in seconds what it may take the mind months to calculate, and do it all with precision and accuracy. As we have seen, all of this is revolutionizing our society.

But computers can't form beliefs, become aware of themselves, develop loyalties or moral values, laugh and experience humor, appreciate art or music, make ethical decisions, or play with ideas. Even though they have been programmed to do certain kinds of therapy, computers cannot show care and compassion. They are magnificent tools for processing and even generating information, but they cannot decide whether a person should be forgiven, a decision is right, or a criminal should be put in jail. In short, it appears that the computer's greatest ability is in the speed and accuracy of what it does rather than in the quality of its "thinking."

The superior mind. The human mind does make many mistakes and people do differ in intellectual abilities. Nevertheless, the mind is able to pick up information from the environment in ways that no computer can match. And surprising as it may seem, the mind is better able to recognize objects and to make sense of events within the environment.

Much of the AI research has attempted to re-create the intelligent mind's ability to deal with real-world objects. If the computer knows that a table has a top and four legs, it would be able to recognize this figure:

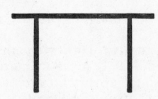

But it might have difficulty or be unable to recognize these:

If it knows the shape of the letter Q, it would recognize this:

Q

But it probably would not be able to recognize the following as the same letter.

QQ ℐ℩℩Q

Similarly, a computer could "read" these words:

THE DOG

But it would have difficulty making sense of other, more distorted words, such as these:

THE DOG

THE DOG

dog

dog

Consider the following two questions: (1) What is Ronald Reagan's zip code? (2) What is George Washington's zip code?

The programmed computer would search through its files of information to answer the questions. It would find the answer to the first question and conclude that there was no answer on file for the second. The human mind would know immediately, however, that there was no need to search for an answer to the second question because it is absurd. Washington is dead. He never had a zip code, and he doesn't have one now. At present, even intelligent computers cannot make that kind of initial evaluation, although work is continuing to program computers so they can process information more like humans.[21]

The modern computer is not a good example of how the mind works, because the computer circuits are basically linear. The computer works quickly, but it deals with information in serial fashion, with one decision made after another. In contrast, the brain's neurons are linked with thousands of other neurons and the information can fan out via millions of channels at the same time. AI research cannot simulate such complexity, at least now, and it seems that because of its many parallel pathways, the brain will continue to be able to think with a complexity that the computer will never match.

None of this is meant to criticize the computer or to play down the remarkable work of those who are working to develop artificial intelligence. This is an exciting and potentially very useful area of research. But even the most advanced AI capabilities are crude when compared to the human mind.

"It will be a long time before any AI system can perceive and interpret scenes in the natural world with even a fraction of our competence," Morton Hunt has concluded. "The human mind, in terms of the space it needs, the cost of keeping it running, and the scope of its accomplishments, is still a vastly more efficient knowledge processor than the most advanced computer in existence or on the drawing boards."[22]

ULTIMATE INTELLIGENCE

All of this gives us reason to ponder and stand in awe of the One who created our human brains with their various intelligences. Even with computers, we cannot begin to comprehend the complexity of the human brain. And even with all our brain power, no human being can even approach an understanding or appreciation of the knowledge, wisdom, and power of God.

A. W. Tozer summarized this long before computers were widely known or used.

> That God is omniscient is not only taught in the Scriptures, it must be inferred also from all else. . . .
>
> God knows instantly and effortlessly all matter and all matters, all mind and every mind, all spirit and all spirits, all being and every being, all creaturehood and all creatures, every plurality and all pluralities, all law and every law, all relations, all causes, all thoughts, all mysteries, all enigmas, all feelings, all desires, every unuttered secret, all thrones and dominions, all personalities, all things visible and invisible in heaven and in earth, motion, space, time, life, death, good, evil, heaven, and hell.
>
> Because God knows all things perfectly, He knows . . . all things equally well. He never discovers anything, He is never surprised, never amazed. He never wonders about anything. . . .[23]

In all of our thinking about the mind and intelligence, it is good to remember wise King Solomon's conclusion that "The reverence and fear of God are basic to all wisdom. Knowing God results in every other kind of understanding."[24] God is the source and personification of ultimate intelligence and wisdom.

With the writer of Romans, we can sing: "Oh, the depth of the riches and wisdom and knowledge of God! How unsearchable his judgments, and his paths beyond tracing out! Who has known the mind of the Lord? . . . For from him and through him and to him are all things. To him be the glory forever! Amen."[25]

12
THE
CREATIVE
MIND

Some Japanese names have become well known in our language since the second World War. Almost everyone has heard about Toyota, Atari, Fugica, Yamaha, and Sony—all names of quality Japanese products—but do you recognize the name Suzuki?

Almost fifty years ago, a young violinist named Shinichi Suzuki devised a creative program to train young musicians. For several years, no one heard of this in the West, but then we began to see pictures of child violinists, some as young as seven or eight, dressed impeccably, standing in rows on a concert stage, playing the music of Mozart and Vivaldi with enthusiasm, precision, and accuracy. Educators in the West began to talk with excitement about the "Suzuki method" and many went to see for themselves at the Suzuki Talent Education Center in Matsumoto, Japan.[1]

The observers found that the Suzuki method begins training very early. During the first year of life, infants are exposed to recordings of great music. Near the time of their first birthdays, the children start hearing frequent recordings of the twenty short songs that will be part of their early training. At about age two they begin attending a group where children and their mothers play games and do exercises. Interest in playing the violin is carefully aroused and before long each child gets a personal instrument. The mother's active involvement and enthusiasm is crucial. She learns how to motivate the child, and most are expected to spend at least two hours daily in practice and work on the lessons.

The Suzuki teachers emphasize the fine points of music, but their goal in training is much broader. They want to build character, and music is seen as a means to that end. By starting early, they develop the child's competence when the brain is still in a plastic stage of development. And there is constant emphasis on the crucial importance of a strong parent-child bond.

Observers have noticed, however, that the program has some disadvantages. Since the children learn to play by ear, many have difficulty when they later try to read music. Learning by imitation creates magnificent performances, but often the musicians have a rigid style and a "difficult-to-alter" manner of performance. Although 5 percent of Suzuki children become professional musicians and some become accomplished adult performers, most have learned to play music in a stereotyped way and almost none displays any inclination toward composing. "The transition from skilled performance to original composition is difficult to make in any case," one observer has written,[2] and it may be that the Suzuki method makes this transition "nearly impossible."

But is it possible to teach creativity and to develop creative minds? These questions concern music teachers and others who work with young people; but within recent years the instilling of creativity has also been of increasing concern to leaders in the competitive world of business and industry.

MOLDING THE CREATIVE MIND

Roger von Oech has been described as the resident creativity guru of California's Silicon Valley.[3] A specialist in computer sciences and the history of ideas, von Oech conducts expensive and highly innovative "Creative Think" seminars for executives of Apple, Arco, GTE, GE, Sears, Xerox, and other corporate giants.

Creativity, he believes, involves thinking in new ways. It comes to people who can let their imaginations wander as they contemplate a problem, who can temporarily forget about being practical, and who discard the idea that there can be only one way of doing things. Creative ideas are assumed to come most often to people who have a playful attitude, who are not afraid to look foolish, and who are willing to take risks or try nontraditional ways of doing things.

The experts do not all agree that creativity can be taught in seminars or in books,[4] but this has not stopped dozens of consulting firms, and their clients, from developing workshops, designing manuals, and establishing creativity learning centers. The selling of creativity seminars for management has become a big business,[5] and courses in creativity are becoming more common in business colleges.

Most of these programs assume that everybody can be creative. They reject the idea that creativity is an inborn trait, possessed by only a few fortunate individuals. Many would agree with the conclusion, presented many years ago,[6] that creative and inventive minds can be developed in anyone who goes through four phases. First, there is *preparation* during which the problem is investigated thoroughly. Then, there is an inactive period of *incubation*, followed at some later time by an *illumination* in which solutions seem to come from nowhere and pop into the mind.[7] The fourth state, *verification*, involves a careful elaboration and confirmation of the new insight.

More recent research suggests that creativity isn't always that organized. Creative minds work in a variety of ways, depending on the nature of the problem. The creation of music, for example, may differ from the creating of a new scientific formula. New architectural designs, new college courses, new ways of stimulating sales, new theories of personality, or new ways of conducting a worship service might each involve creativity. A person who is creative in one of these areas may not be very creative in another. What, then, can we say for sure about creative minds?

ANALYZING THE CREATIVE MIND

In the late 1860s, two inventors with creative minds developed a "writing machine" and persuaded a gun manufacturer named E. Remington to manufacture the first commercially produced "type-writer." For reasons that are still debated, the letters were arranged in what we now call the "QWERTY" keyboard (named after the order of the first six letters on the top row of the typewriter, under the numbers). Later, it was found that other letter arrangements are more efficient, but most typewriters and almost all typists know the "QWERTY" arrangement, so it seems unlikely that a change will ever occur.

If you know how to type, can you draw a keyboard from memory and label each of the keys? Can you describe how you type, or quickly report which finger hits the "x"? These questions illustrate a problem that cognitive scientists face when they investigate skills and cognitions. Often people do things rapidly and efficiently without giving much thought to what they are doing. It is faster for most of us to type than it is to draw a picture of the keyboard or to describe how we move our fingers.[8] It is easier for creative artists to do their work than it is for these same artists to describe what they are doing. Sometimes, the analysis even interferes with performance. Try thinking about how you type, or start showing somebody what you do when you type, and your typing speed is likely to drop.

To study creativity, therefore, scientists have tried to design creativity tests (many of these now appear to be of debatable validity), have watched creative masters as they work, and have analyzed the notebooks and creations of great musicians, artists, and inventors. Rutgers professor Howard Gruber, for example, spent ten years studying the creativity of Charles Darwin[9] and currently is preparing a detailed book on the creativity of Jean Piaget. Such analyzers must be careful not to dissect creativity so much that it dies. But when analyses are carefully made, they give us fresh insights into the nature of creative minds.

Is there a creative personality? As we have seen, most researchers are reluctant to claim that a creative personality exists. Tchaikovsky, for example, was timid and self-doubting, but Wagner was bold, conceited, and domineering. Byron was promiscuous and hypersexual, but Tennyson was a faithful husband. Newton was intolerant and contentious; Einstein was a mild-mannered and simple man.[10] Darwin was active and involved with people; Marie Curie was much quieter and less social.

Nevertheless, creative people do appear to have some things in common. Almost all are independent and somewhat nonconformist in their ideas—although not always in their lifestyles. All are knowledgeable about their fields, deeply committed to their work (many are workaholics), flexible in their thinking, goal-directed in their lives, daring in their willingness to take risks or try something new, and active in their imaginations. Many resemble jugglers who can keep a number of ideas in mind at the same time but are able to engage in "bracketing"—the ability to put other issues aside for a while (to bracket them) while they concentrate on a problem that needs to be solved.[11]

A little help from heuristics. Does all of this mean that only some people will be creative and that creativity seminars are a waste of time and money? Not necessarily. It is well known that some people, the Beethovens and Einsteins for example, tend to be more creative than others, even without training. Nevertheless, it appears that almost everyone can benefit from what has come to be known as "heuristics." A heuristic is a gimmick or other way of thinking that often helps people solve problems and reach creative solutions. Creativity seminars teach heuristics such as the following:

- *Environmental conditions influence creativity.* Many people are most creative when they are free from distractions, well rested, and unstimulated by drugs or alcohol. No support has been found for the idea that hallucination-producing drugs lead to greater creativity. Neither is it always best for creative people to work in isolation. Sometimes aloneness *is* helpful, but at times there is value to interacting with people. Perhaps you remember the famous story of Archimedes who was given the problem of finding how much gold was in the king's crown. The insight is supposed to have come while the famous Greek philosopher was soaking in a public bath. When he got his insight, he jumped to his feet and went streaking naked through the streets, repeatedly shouting "Eureka!" which in Greek means "I have found it!"

- *Knowledge has a crucial influence on creativity.* God created the world out of nothing, but we who are his creatures must be steeped in knowledge of an area before we can hope to experience creativity. Great music is not composed by people who know nothing about harmony and cadence. Great medical insights do not come to bricklayers or mathematicians. It is only when we are highly knowledgeable about a field that creative ideas appear. Pasteur said it well: "Chance favors a prepared mind."[12]

- *Unusual thinking influences creativity.* Brainstorming can be helpful, at times, because it involves a temporary suspension of critical judgment and encourages people to think of "crazy ideas" and improbable solutions. Sometimes these lead to practical and creative insights.

    Other kinds of unusual thinking include the use of analogies. When he thought of the human ear as being something like a telephone receiver, Alexander Graham Bell made progress in his invention of the telephone. Sometimes it is helpful to pretend that you are a little elf, somehow getting right inside your problem. It is reported, for example, that Einstein once spent time fantasizing that he was riding along a light beam.

There can also be value in using different words to think about our work. When Xerox executives stopped thinking of themselves as manufacturers of copy machines, and assumed instead that they were in the "automated office business," creativity and subsequent sales jumped substantially. In contrast, many railroads have collapsed because the company leaders never got beyond railroading so they could see themselves, instead, as being in the transportation business.[13] Thinking creatively often means thinking imaginatively, and thinking big.

• *Formulas can influence creativity.* I once taught a course for college freshmen about how to survive in academia. In preparing for the course, I found something called the SQ3R study method. The plan included five steps: *survey* the problem or chapter to get an overview of the issues, raise *questions* about the topics, *read* the material carefully, then go over it again and attempt to *recite* the essence of the material, and finally *review* the material by going over it once more.

Does this study plan work? For some people and for some material it probably is helpful, but it could also be stifling. The same could be said for creativity formulas, such as the preparation-incubation-illumination-verification suggestion that was mentioned earlier. If these help, use them. But when they are more of a hindrance than a help, they should be abandoned.

• *Premature closure influences creativity.* In a highly practical book on creativity, Harvard researcher D. N. Perkins suggests that many creative efforts fail because of "premature closure." This is the tendency to reach a conclusion too quickly, before all possible alternatives and possibilities have been considered.[14] Creative people look at problems from a variety of angles before they start working on practical solutions.

I once read that Thomas Edison was criticized because he wasted so much time and energy doing experiments that were not necessary. The critic was a Yugoslavian born scientist named Nikola Tesla who was also an inventor. During his lifetime Tesla created over seven hundred inventions, including high-frequency voltage, the neon and fluorescent lights, basic electric motors, and remote-control devices. He believed that a lot of things could be worked out in the mind before they were tried out in practice.[15] Tesla was one creative person who avoided premature closure.

OBSERVING THE CREATIVE MIND

When I was a young college professor, my wife and I were invited to travel with the college choir on a tour of little towns in northern Minnesota and Wisconsin. The trip took place in mid-winter and some of the concerts were in small churches where the warm and friendly people had braved sub-zero temperatures to be present. After the concerts, most evenings, we would be taken to someone's home where we drank coffee and talked, sometimes far into the night.

These late conversations had a profound influence on me. I began to realize, for the first time, that many people struggle alone with intense problems. I learned that there were pastors and other church leaders who had almost no training in counseling, but were dealing daily with people who had serious emotional difficulties. It was shortly after that choir tour that I began to write, hoping that in some small way I could share my training in psychology with those who had little knowledge of my field. At first I had difficulty finding a publisher, but soon I was launched on what would become a new career—writing.

In those early years, I never read writers' magazines and wasn't even aware that books about writing existed. Almost by accident, I stumbled on articles about writing and was caught off guard by statements like this:

> The art of writing is immensely more difficult than the beginning writer may at first believe. . . . Good writing involves the operation of many mental processes at once. . . . No human activity I know of takes more time than writing: it's highly unusual for anyone to become a successful writer if he cannot put in several hours every day at his typewriter.[16]

If we could observe the minds of creative people, I suspect many would show this kind of dedication. At the beginning, there often is a desire to be famous, wealthy, or influential, but as creative people get more involved in their work, it appears that many become increasingly motivated by the drive to improve quality and to strive for excellence. Some become like Tchekhov who wrote that writers must "once and for all give up being worried about successes and failures. Don't let that concern you. It's your duty to go on working steadily day by day, quite quietly, to be prepared for mistakes, which are inevitable, and for failures."[17]

The art of a modern writer. Madeleine L'Engle, prize-winning novelist and writer in residence at the Cathedral of St. John the

Divine in New York, would agree with Tchekhov's analysis. She also considers writing to be a creative art.

According to L'Engle, each work of art has a life of its own. It exists out in space somewhere, and the artist's task is to put the symphony, painting, or story into tangible form. "I believe," she wrote in a book describing her own creative work, "that each work of art, whether it is a work of great genius, or something very small, comes to the artist and says, 'Here I am. Enflesh me. Give birth to me.'"[18] When I first read these words, I found the idea to be strange and mystical.

But L'Engle's conclusions aren't as unusual or as rare as they may seem. Many other creative people have reported similar experiences. Novelist John Gardner, for example, believes that he almost goes into a trance when he writes, seems to be "taken over by a muse," and is surprised later at how the ideas have come together on the paper.[19] Is such a strange experience the work of some supernatural influence? With Christians, is this the Holy Spirit at work? Is such creativity the result of some spontaneous activity of the brain's right hemisphere? Is this some strange aspect of creativity that can never be explained?

However we answer, it appears that these experiences are most seen in people who have a dedication to their creative tasks. L'Engle writes every day whether she feels like it or not. She likens her craft to prayer. "It's not a matter of feeling like it, or waiting . . . [until] I feel inspired," she told a recent interviewer. "Both in work and in prayer, inspiration comes during rather than before."[20]

It was careful reflection, and not momentary inspiration, that led me to resign my tenure and leave my full-time teaching position not long ago. I didn't want to lose contact with students (I still teach part time), but I needed more time for writing. I wanted to refine my communication skills, improve my creativity, and serve God more effectively through writing. I had come to the assumption that no growing person is ever completely satisfied with his or her work. The push to do better is what keeps us going. And from what I can gather, based on my informal observations of creative people in a variety of fields, that drive and struggle for quality is part of what makes minds creative.

UNDERSTANDING THE CREATIVE MIND

Dick Hayes and Linda Flower are researchers at Carnegie-Mellon University, who have undertaken some of the most boring work imaginable. They have asked creative people to say what is going through their minds as they think about their creations. Then, by reading and analyzing these reports, the researchers have attempted to gain some understanding of what goes on in creative minds when they are active.[21] We still don't know with certainty how creative ideas are formed; this still is one of the most difficult problems in cognitive science. But some things are becoming clear.[22]

We know, for example, that creative acts begin with study, fact gathering, and conscious efforts to create or to find solutions.

Then there is a time of fatigue, frustration, or distraction by other things. For a while the creative issue seems to be forgotten, but it appears that the mind continues to keep working, without our conscious awareness. Perhaps some short-term memories are cast aside during this period. Maybe the ideas fan out simultaneously through the brain where, free from distractions or the controls of directed thinking, the electrical impulses are able to form new associations. Sometimes these then pop into awareness as new insights that "dawn on us." None of this happens if the mind hasn't been fed first with conscious ideas, and often it doesn't happen at all until we are able to pull away from the problem for a while and focus our conscious attention on something else.

Once the insights appear, either dramatically or slowly, the creative person can get on with the task of creating, or testing the validity of one's insights.

It seems probable that Picasso will go down in history as the twentieth century's most famous artist. His creations were sometimes diverse and complicated, like the famous painting *Guernica*. But at other times Picasso's work was very simple. "Once I drew like Raphael," he said near the end of his life, "but it has taken me a whole lifetime to learn how to draw like children."[23] Without meaning to condemn Raphael, it appears that Picasso recognized that there is a unique freedom and lighthearted creativity in the line drawings of children.

In many respects, creativity comes most freely to those who can shed some of their intellectual inhibitions and think in simple, childlike ways. Perhaps this was in the mind of Jesus when he called a little child to stand beside him while he spoke to his followers. "I tell you the truth," he said. "Unless you change and become like little children, you will never enter the kingdom of heaven. Therefore, whoever humbles himself like this child is the greatest in the kingdom of heaven."[24]

COPING WITH THE CREATIVE MIND

Philip Yancey is a creative writer whose work has brought him into contact with a number of Christian musicians, artists, and authors. Many of these are dedicated people who have come to Christ "as little children" and have had careers characterized by great creativity and accomplishment. But Yancey notes that these creative people are not all the same.

"I lump them into two sets," he writes, "Christian entertainers and Christian servants." The Christian entertainers are those musicians, actors, writers, speakers, and comedians who fill our periodicals, dominate our seminars, and appear on our television screens. They have fame, prestige, and money, but many also have deep longings and self-doubts. It isn't easy to live a Christian life in the limelight, before an audience.

In contrast, the Christian servants are rarely in the spotlight. They toil unnoticed in remote places. They live among the rejects of society and work for low pay, long hours, and no applause. Their talents and skills are given to the poor and uneducated. Yet somehow, in the process of losing their lives, they have found them and attained rewards that the famous never experience.[25]

Even if we assume that all people can become more creative than they are now, it seems clear that some individuals have special creative abilities. These people, with creative minds, have been given much. In turn, society (and the God who created us) expects much in return.[26] Like all gifted people, they have a responsibility to use their creative abilities in ways that serve others. And those who are acclaimed as artists, preachers, and entertainers need our prayers lest their creativity causes them to fall into destructive pride and self-sufficiency.

These thoughts about creativity, and about coping with our own creations, lead us to consider some of the most common and fascinating creations of all: our own imaginations and dreams. It is to these issues that we turn our attention in the next two chapters.

13
THE
IMAGINATIVE
MIND

Several years ago, a sixty-one-year-old man entered the office of a young physician named Carl Simonton. The patient had an advanced form of throat cancer. He was very weak, weighed only 98 pounds, could barely swallow his own saliva, and was having difficulty breathing.

The patient's doctors had almost given up hope. Some thought that treatment would only make the man worse, but Dr. Simonton, a trained specialist in "radiation oncology"—the treatment of tumors—decided to try something new. Along with the radiation therapy, the doctor began teaching his patient how to relax and to use "mental imagery" in fighting the disease.

The man was instructed to set aside three, fifteen-minute "imaging" times every day. Sitting quietly, he was to relax by concentrating on the muscles in his body, starting with his head and going to his feet, telling each muscle group to relax. Then he was to picture himself in a pleasant, quiet place—sitting by a stream, on a beach, or any place that he would find relaxing.

In this relaxed state of mind, the patient was then asked to imagine what his cancer was like. He was to think of the radiation therapy as an onslaught of millions of tiny energy bullets that would hit all of the cells, both healthy and cancerous, but destroy only the weaker, "confused" cancer cells. Then the man would imagine that the body's white cells would come swarming in, pick up the dead and dying cancer cells, and flush them out of the body through the kidneys and liver. Finally, the patient was to visualize the cancer growth as decreasing in size and his health returning to normal. After each fifteen-minute exercise, the patient was free to go about his other activities, until the next imaging period.

Even Dr. Simonton was amazed at what happened next. The man showed almost no negative reaction to the radiation treatment. Before long he was able to eat again. He gained strength and weight, and the cancer disappeared—completely. Radiation therapy, accompanied by mental imagery, had cured the disease. The doctor called this "exciting and frightening," and the patient was so enthused that he decided to apply the mental imagery technique to alleviate his arthritis and to improve his sex life. He had been impotent for over twenty years, but the approach enabled him to gain full sexual activity after only a few weeks of imagery.[1]

The mental imagery technique was tried on other patients and found to be so successful that the doctor eventually moved away from radiation therapy and developed his own, more mental, cancer-treatment approach. Convinced that cancer often comes to people who have been resentful, depressed, self-pitying, disappointed, and with low self-esteem, Dr. Simonton and his psychotherapist wife began teaching patients to have "healing visualizations." As we have already seen, stress tends to suppress the immune system and make the body more vulnerable to diseases, like cancer. To change this, the Simontons now teach people how to relax by using mental images. Then, the patients use their imaginations to picture the cancer cells being defeated, murdered, and carried away.

MENTAL IMAGERY

As you might imagine, the Simonton approach to imagination and cancer has been highly criticized. One psychiatrist has called it a "cruel hoax" that leads desperately ill people to think they can get rid of serious illness by reducing stress and stimulating their imaginations. Others have pointed out that there is no solid research evidence to show a link between stress and cancer. And critics have been quick to note that there is no carefully done research to prove that the "imaging" treatment is really effective.[2]

Even the critics recognize, however, that imagination has a powerful influence, not only on our health, but also on our attitudes and daily lives. Over a century ago, Sir Francis Galton attempted to study mental images scientifically, and for a while the infant field of psychology continued the work. Then, in 1913, behaviorism made its debut and mental images were dismissed as being of no importance. Europeans, like Carl Jung, continued to study images, but on this side of the Atlantic researchers and counselors turned their attention to other things.

Now all of this is changing. There is a new popularity to the study of fantasy, the mind's images, visualization, imagination, or what more often is simply called "mental imagery."[3] There are college courses in mental imagery, professional journals and newsletters,[4] a variety of books and popular publications, annual conferences, and a professional organization known as the International Imagery Association.

The meaning of imagery. Simply defined, an image is a mental representation of something that is not actually present.[5] Mental imagery involves bringing images to mind and holding them there while they are examined or pondered. Most of these mental images are visual pictures. If you are asked to count the number of windows in your house, for example, you probably will form a mental picture of the house and "walk around, in your mind," counting the windows. But there can also be images of sounds (you can imagine the voice of someone you know well), smells (can you imagine the smell of some favorite food?), and other sensations.

Because of our ability to form mental images, life is probably much more interesting than it would be otherwise. We can imagine faraway places, get more involved in novels, "relive" pleasant events from the past, and experience images of people whom we know. But images do more than make life interesting. Some experts maintain that images stimulate creativity, help us solve problems, keep mentally balanced, release the "hidden powers of the mind," change behavior, stimulate spiritual growth and—if Dr. Simonton and many others are right—cure disease.

MENTAL IMAGERY AND SICKNESS

Historical documents have shown that mental imagery is one of the world's oldest healing techniques. Among the ancient Egyptians, Hermes concluded that the mind caused disease and that it was best treated if patients could form vivid images of a healing god. This idea was picked up by the Babylonians and

Greeks who each built healing temples where diseased pilgrims could come to be healed through dream interpretation. Many years later, a Renaissance physician named Paracelsus proposed that the mind and imagination can both produce disease and cure it.

Modern physicians remained skeptical, but periodically there was scientific evidence to back up the mental imagery viewpoint. In one pioneering project, for example, investigators worked with fifty-two peptic ulcer patients who were all receiving medical and dietary treatment. Thirty-two of the patients were also taught to imagine pleasant experiences whenever they felt anxious. After all fifty-two patients had been treated, dietary restrictions were lifted. Within the next three years, only one of the thirty-two-person visualization group had ulcers redevelop, but among the twenty who had not heard about mental images, eighteen had their old symptoms return.[7]

The natural mind. More recently, following the drug excesses of the 1960s, a young physician named Andrew Weil published a thought-provoking and controversial book. *The Natural Mind*[8] dealt mostly with drug use, but the author built many of his conclusions on the assumption that "all illness is psychosomatic. . . . The causes always lie within the realm of the mind."[9]

Consider boils, for example. According to Weil, the staphylococci that cause boils are always present on the skin. Most of the time there is a mutual balance between the germs and the skin, but at times, because of "changes in consciousness," the balance breaks down and the boils appear. Since the illness is assumed to come as a result of the mind, Weil proposes that it must ultimately be treated in the same way—perhaps even using mental imagery.

Is it possible that the Old Testament account of Job is an example of this theory? Under extreme duress, Job developed boils. These only lifted when his mind was pointed heavenward and he was able to "see" God with his eyes.[10] Job's despair lifted and his pain disappeared.

Mental imagery and pain. Pain, it has been found, tends to be reduced when people are able to distract themselves with mental images. In one experiment, people were asked to immerse their hands in freezing cold water and keep them there until they could stand the discomfort no longer. Some people pulled their hands out in less than a minute, but others lasted for up to five minutes. Those who withstood the discomfort longest were people whose minds focused on pleasant subjects, such as sitting in the sun or warming their hands over a blazing fire in the hearth of a ski lodge.[11]

Experiments like this have shown that mental imagery can control discomfort in the laboratory, but can visualization help in the real life management of pain? Some evidence suggests the answer is yes.[12] Mental imagery has been used to help people deal with the discomfort of childbirth and surgery. Dental patients report less discomfort and pain when they try to forget the dentist's drill and imagine themselves walking through a lush meadow or swimming in a clear blue lake.[13] Perhaps more practical is the recognition that stereo music can distract the patient and reduce pain while the dentist works on the teeth.

There still are many questions about whether mental images can reduce chronic pain. Better established is the conclusion that imagery works more effectively when pain is anticipated (as in surgery, for example), than when it comes unexpectedly. When people can learn to relax, focus their attention elsewhere, or sometimes picture the hurting body part as "a lump of clay that isn't really a part of me," then the pain is reduced. Some have suggested that the feats of Indian fakirs, who walk on hot coals or push needles through their bodies, may be evidence of the mind's ability to direct attention away from pain so that it isn't noticed.

All of this has contributed to the rise of holistic medicine—an approach that focuses on the mental and spiritual aspects of illness, as well as on the physical. Behavioral medicine and health psychology are related fields, dedicated to studying how the mind-body relationship can reduce pain and cure illness. The consideration of mental imagery is one, somewhat small, part of these new fields of science.[14]

MENTAL IMAGERY AND EVERYDAY LIFE

Everybody has had the experience of being in a boring meeting, or listening to a dull speech or sermon. We may try to stay awake or to look interested, but our minds keep wandering. Since it isn't always possible or wise to walk out of a dull meeting, at times we all "walk out mentally" by creating more stimulating and interesting mental images. School children often withdraw into such fantasy thinking. It keeps them from getting bored and from paying attention to their teachers. Under other circumstances (perhaps in faculty meetings), the teachers create boredom-reducing images of their own.

Many people have come to think that such imagining is always bad. Certainly such thinking can be harmful if it keeps people from facing reality or distracts them from being effective in their work. But there can also be positive uses of mental imagery.

Some enthusiasts have suggested, for example, that mental imagery can help us relax, overcome fears and bad habits, expand self-awareness, build confidence, increase learning effectiveness, overcome insomnia, eliminate bad moods, help with decision making, improve athletic ability, build better relationships with others, heighten appreciation for literature and art, prepare for the future, and help people adjust to old age.[15] In later pages we will consider the use of mental images in psychotherapy, stress management, and sports, but at this point let us consider four other areas where mental imagery might have a positive influence on everyday living.

Dieting. Many people have discovered that diets, especially fad diets, don't work very well. The discipline of self-control too frequently gives way to the pleasures of eating, often preceded by the mental games that let us "give in—just this once."

The mental imagery approach to dieting can take two directions. Sometimes, people are encouraged to think of a "negative image" whenever they are tempted to eat. Think of what you will look like if you continue to add weight. Pretend that chocolate is really poison that will damage your system, or imagine that calories will clog up the arteries and stuff ugly globules of fat under your skin.

In contrast, there is the positive approach that encourages dieters to think of themselves as slim and to work on the assumption that they will become what they expect to become.

Recently, I decided to try this approach. As a middle-aged man, I am determined to keep from getting a protruding stomach—but I have a tendency to eat too many snacks and not get enough exercise, especially when I am working on a book. To help with my dieting, therefore, I thought of a friend who has a flat stomach. Whenever I am tempted to snack between meals or to load up on calories, I imagine what my friend would do in a similar situation. He would not eat. This imaging has helped me keep control of my weight and stick with my exercise program, even when I am tempted to quit.

Learning. Some educators have given attention to the use of images in helping people learn.[16] For many years, teachers of English literature and history have enlivened their classes by encouraging students to imagine what it would be like to live in the past, or to be a character in a novel. More recently, students have been taught to use mental imagery to relax, so they can eliminate distractions and concentrate more effectively on their learning. By imagining how counselees must feel, counseling students can gain increased understanding of depression, grief, psychosis, homosexuality, or other issues. Students in professional schools can be encouraged to imagine how their classroom learning may be applied to real life situations.

Confidence-building. Dr. Arnold Lazarus is a psychologist who specializes in treating people through mental imagery. When his counselees report that they are afraid of applying for a job, too insecure to ask for a raise, unable to assert themselves when others mistreat them, or uncomfortable around people, Dr. Lazarus helps these people form mental images of what could happen in these situations.

He calls this "goal-rehearsal." Assume, for example, that you want to ask your boss for a favor, but are afraid to do so. Imagine the different ways that your employer could react. How would you respond in each situation? Imagine yourself getting what you request. "If you repeatedly and conscientiously picture yourself achieving a goal," Lazarus writes, "your chances of actual success will be greatly enhanced."[17] Prepared by this technique, many people have been able to assert themselves, approach the boss, and handle whatever reaction comes.

Insomnia. It has been estimated that over half of all adults have occasional problems with sleeping, and perhaps 15 percent have chronic problems getting to sleep. The market for sleeping pills has grown significantly within the past few years.

Most of us realize that counting sheep doesn't help us get to sleep, but other images can be more effective. The goal is to stop thinking of images that are arousing, imagine that your body is relaxed and in a place where you feel perfectly safe, and picture something that is not too stimulating but that might require some mental activity—like counting backwards by sevens, "daydreaming" about some sport that you are involved in, or trying to recite Psalm 100.

With a little ingenuity, you can probably develop some imagery techniques of your own. Applied to a variety of situations, they might help you cope more effectively with life. And if some people are right, imagery might also help with your spiritual growth.

MENTAL IMAGERY AND RELIGION

Henri Nouwen is a Catholic priest whose insightful spiritual journals have stimulated and encouraged many readers. In one of his recent books, Nouwen wrote about mental images and pondered how such images can mold our thinking and influence our actions. The things we see on television, for example, can affect us profoundly. The movies we watch and the things we read can have enormous impact on our physical, mental, and emotional well-being.

All of this is important, says Nouwen, because the images in our minds have spiritual implications. Some images can so distract us that prayer and meditation become almost impossible. In contrast, mental images about God can help us to know him better, to pray more intimately, and to become more like him.[18]

Some of Nouwen's Catholic forefathers reached similar conclusions. In his *Introduction to the Devout Life*, Francis de Sales wrote that imagination "confines the mind" during periods of meditation and prevents one's thinking from rambling. Ignatius of Loyola encouraged his readers to use all five senses in trying to experience the Gospel events.[19]

A more contemporary writer, and a Protestant, has proposed that intellectual study of the Bible should be accompanied by meditation. This involves "internalizing and personalizing" the passage by imagining that we are present with Jesus or the biblical writers. Using all our senses, we should try to see what the scene was like. Then try to smell the sea, hear the sermon, feel the hot sun, experience the hunger in the stomach, taste the salt in the air, and reach out to touch the hem of Christ's garment.[20]

In what some reviewers have called the most controversial passage in his book, Richard Foster suggests that readers periodically imagine a scene in which the "spiritual body" takes leave of the physical body, floats up into God's presence in heaven, feels the "warm presence of the eternal Creator," and listens to instructions that might come from the Lord.[21]

The healing of memories. A different kind of religious imagery was made popular several years ago when Jimmy Carter was president of the United States. His sister, the late Ruth Carter Stapleton, wrote two widely read books that described the process of healing memories.[22] The approach did not originate with Mrs. Stapleton, but she introduced it to many who were impressed by her obvious warmth and sincerity.

The healing of memories is an approach to helping people. It begins with the assumption that many present problems arise from traumatic "dark and painful memories" that are buried in "the deep mind, that region which carefully records and stores every experience of life." These memories are not always conscious, but they can influence our current behavior and make life unhappy.

Counselors help people find these deep memories, face them, and commit them to Christ in prayer so that he can bring healing, love, and forgiveness in place of fear, hurt, and feelings of rejection. Sometimes people are asked to visualize painful situations from the past or to imagine a difficult personal relationship. Then they imagine Christ coming into the situation to bring healing and to remove feelings of bitterness, envy, disappointment, or hurt.

Critics have noted the Freudian elements in this approach, have accused Mrs. Stapleton of theological and psychological naiveté, and have charged that the healing of memories is a simplistic approach to problem solving.[23] Others have noted, however, that there is value in facing past memories and asking Christ to remove the destructive attitudes and emotions associated with them. By reliving difficult and painful situations in the imagination, and by picturing Jesus being present to heal and guide, there can be personal growth and a new courage to handle problems.

KEEPING MENTAL IMAGERY IN PERSPECTIVE

It has been reported that Albert Einstein once said, "Imagination is more important than knowledge."[24] Not everyone would agree. There can be little doubt about the power and benefits that come from an imaginative mind, but unbridled mental imagery can also be dangerous and destructive. Surely, if we are to be kept from harm and error, imagination must be balanced with knowledge and sometimes with plain common sense.

The physical benefits and dangers of mental imagery. Thomas Sydenham, a seventeenth-century physician, once stated that "the arrival of a good clown exercises more beneficial influence upon the health of a town than twenty asses laden with drugs." A lot of people would agree, at least in theory. But in practice most of us prefer to treat our illnesses with medications. To some extent the medical profession can be blamed for our over-dependence on drugs, but we who keep demanding prescriptions must share a good part of the responsibility.

It is encouraging, therefore, to find physicians who continue to emphasize the healing value of optimism, hope, the will to live, positive images, and even the antics of a good clown. Used in conjunction with established medical practices, these mental attitudes can have a powerful and important effect in bringing recovery.

There is danger, however, in assuming that mental images are all we need, that having a good laugh or a vivid imagination can solve all our physical problems. Medical researchers aren't much impressed with testimonials about the effectiveness of mental imagery. They want hard-core facts and because these are lacking, the researchers have not responded enthusiastically to the imagery approaches to treatment.

Next time I get sick, I'll go to the doctor, listen to his advice, and probably take medications if he prescribes any. I'll also try to supplement that treatment with prayer, hope, optimism, and as much humor as I can muster. And you can be sure that I'll also use a little mental imagery. That can't do any harm, if it is used along with good medical treatment—and it is likely to do a lot of good.

The psychological benefits and dangers of mental imagery. As we have seen, there is mounting evidence that the use of imagery can help people reduce anxiety, handle depression, increase skills, eliminate fears, break bad habits, and cope with a variety of personal problems. In the years ahead, a number of new "imagery-therapies" are likely to appear, and it is probable that these will be helpful.

We must recognize, however, that imagery can also have a harmful side. John Wilkes Booth, the man who shot Lincoln, carried two elaborate images in his mind. One pictured him as a highly acclaimed, successful actor; in the other, he saw himself as the "hero" who would bring victory to the South by assassinating the president. Since he was never able to succeed as an actor, Booth acted out his other fantasy—and changed the course of history. In more recent times Sirhan Sirhan, the man who shot Robert Kennedy, kept a diary to record his mental images of what the assassination scene would be like. Frequent newspaper reports remind us that innumerable other crimes are rehearsed mentally before they are enacted in reality.

Mental images can be harmful when they lead us to act in ways that hurt ourselves and others, or when they cause us to believe things that are not true, not realistic, and not supported by fact. Ponder these statements, for example. "Once I get married, my problems will be over." "I am smart enough to break the law without getting caught." "If I pray hard enough, my cancer is certain to go away." "My fiance is an alcoholic, but he'll stop drinking once we get married." "If I have enough faith, I can do whatever I want." "Anybody, including me, can become a millionaire." Each of these is a way of thinking that could lead to disappointment, frustration, and failure.

It is possible to know when mental images are becoming harmful.[25] Images that dwell on violence, blood, and hurting others, for example, are clearly unhealthy. It can be psychologically dangerous to so identify with some other human being—such as a popular entertainer, athletic hero, or political figure—that you think of yourself as being that other person. It is not healthy to set goals so high that you are certain to fail, in spite of your fantasies and expectations. It is also harmful if your imagination becomes so powerful and your fantasy world becomes so pleasant that you can't concentrate on your daily tasks in the real world. A friend can often help you decide if your mental images are unhealthy. And when mental images—especially highly unrealistic images—begin to dominate your life, it is wise to seek professional counseling help.

The spiritual benefits and dangers of mental imagery. Several years ago, a psychologist proposed that some people have "propositional minds." These are primarily verbal, rational, and controlled by the brain's left hemisphere. Others have "appositional minds" that tend to be nonverbal, emotional, and controlled by the right hemisphere.[26] This has led some Christian writers to wonder if there might be two types of Christians: "word" Christians who are intellectual and verbal, and "spirit" Christians who tend to be more emotional and visceral.[27] The former group emphasizes the intellectual aspects of Christianity and encourages others to *think* in a more Christlike way, while the latter group stresses the feelings that come with following Christ and encourages others to *visualize* in a more Christlike way.

This intriguing theory may help to account for some individual differences among believers and may indicate why people in each of the groups aren't always able to understand or appreciate those who take a different approach to their faith. Theological scholars, for example, can't always appreciate the approach of a Ruth Stapleton, but some of her followers, in turn, are unimpressed by the intellectual debates of the Bible scholars.

It is true, of course, that biblical Christianity includes both facts and feelings—and either of these can be taken to the extreme. It can be helpful to visualize the presence of Christ in our lives.[28] The Bible tells us to taste and see that the Lord is good.[29] We are reminded that we have a friend who sticks closer than a brother,[30] and we know that the Holy Spirit lives inside believers and gives guidance. To picture all of this is healthy and contributes to spiritual growth.

Problems come when we let our mental images take us into realms of thinking that are inconsistent with the verbal teachings of the Bible. I know a lady, for example, who believes that God guides through the "pearls of wisdom" which, supposedly, are dropped into her mind. She makes no attempt to see if these pearls are consistent with the Scriptures, and as a result she is controlled by her own vivid imagination. For this person, mental imagery has become more harmful than helpful. It has the danger of leading a sincere believer astray and into theological error.

Let us not assume, therefore, that imagination is more important—or less important—than knowledge. When biblical knowledge and human imagination are put together, our minds can expand to greater levels of productivity, problem solving, and creativity.

One of the mind's most creative and fascinating features is its ability to produce dreams. Do dreams reveal anything about the mind? Are daydreams any more—or less—significant than the dreams we have at night? If we ever hope to understand our magnificent minds, we have to know something about the mind's incredible ability to dream.

14
THE
DREAMING
MIND

Sometime ago, a woman wrote to Abigail Van Buren, the newspaper columnist, and reported a strange and recurring problem. "I am seventy-four years old," the lady wrote, "and I keep dreaming that I'm pregnant." Realistically, she signed the letter, "Impossible Dream."

The columnist suggested that the woman had a "fertile imagination," but this response brought howls of protest from "Dear Abby" readers.

"Your reply . . . was less than adequate and even flippant," one person protested. "Nature does not waste time with impossible dreams. This lady's dream of pregnancy definitely has a possible meaning. I suggest that it meant she still has potential for growth in a new area of her life." The protester signed the letter "Beautiful Dreamer."

Another reader suggested that the seventy-four-year-old lady should see her doctor immediately, because the dream surely indicated that something like a tumor was growing inside. One reader suggested that the dreamer was unconsciously longing for romance, but another interpretation concluded that the woman "obviously" was about to give birth to a unique, valuable, or creative idea.

Less creative was the suggestion that the dream came because of something the woman ate. And another wrote "Pregnant at seventy-four! That was no dream, lady, that was a nightmare!"

The meaning of nightmares, dreams, fantasies, and visions

has concerned people since the dawn of recorded history. The British Museum contains papyri with dream interpretations written in Egyptian hieroglyphics, centuries before the birth of Christ. Dreams were known to be of importance in the ancient Oriental, Babylonian, and Greek cultures. The Bible is filled with references to dreams, philosophers and theologians have written volumes about dream interpretation, and dream research currently occupies the attention of perhaps hundreds of cognitive scientists.

Some of their reports and books surround me as I begin this chapter. Many of the conclusions are interesting, but sometimes it seems that the experts are not much different than the people who wrote to "Dear Abby." It is easy to agree with Marcus Tullius Cicero, an illustrious Roman orator, who once proclaimed that dream interpretation is sheer superstition—the evidence of conjecture that comes from the minds of people who have turned their "intellectual energies . . . into endless imbecilities."[1]

SLEEP AND DREAMS

If Cicero could be alive today, however, he would discover that while there still are disagreements about the meaning of dreams, scientists have made significant advances in dream research, especially during the twentieth century. Sigmund Freud published his significant work, *The Interpretation of Dreams,* in 1900, and soon the psychiatric world was engulfed with debate and excitement over the psychoanalytic idea that dreams are really wish fulfillments and a "royal road" to understanding the unconscious. Carl Jung, and others who were influenced by Freud, analyzed thousands of dreams and wrote creative accounts of their significance and meaning.

But perhaps a more significant advance in understanding the dreaming mind occurred at the University of Chicago in 1952. A graduate student named Eugene Aserinsky was trying to study the physiology of sleep, but he thought that something must be wrong with his equipment when it reported that sleepers had periods of rapid eye movements as they slept through the night. At the time, most people assumed that the eyes remained at rest during sleep, but when Aserinsky took a closer look, he found that the eyes really did move.

The discoverer of rapid eye movements (usually abbreviated REM's) went into more traditional scientific work, but two of his colleagues, Nathaniel Kleitman and William Dement, began a detailed study of REM sleep. Since then, several thousand volunteers have come to sleep laboratories, been wired to recording devices, and allowed themselves to be awakened and questioned whenever REM's appear. The results of these studies have revolutionized our understanding of sleep and the dreaming mind.

When you go to sleep tonight and your body relaxes, there may be one of those sudden muscle spasms that sometimes shakes the whole bed and wakes you up. There is nothing abnormal about this and soon you will enter the deepest stage of sleep. At that time, your brain waves will slow down, your heart rate and body temperature will drop, and your breathing will grow deeper.

After an hour or so you will come out of this deep sleep and eventually move into REM sleep. At that time, your muscles may become somewhat paralyzed, the neurons in your brain will become more active, and you will start to dream. Almost all of these dreams will be forgotten by morning, but if someone awakens you during one of the periods of REM, it is almost certain that you will report that you have been dreaming.

Figure 14-1 shows how the brain works while we rest. As you can see, we have several sleeping cycles during the night, and about every ninety to one hundred minutes, we experience REM

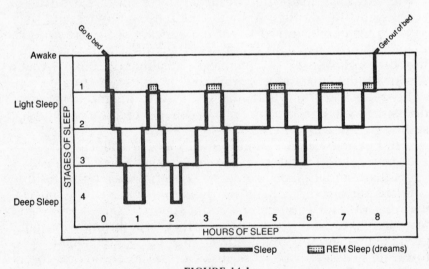

FIGURE 14-1
The Sleep Cycle.
Rapid Eye Movement (REM) sleep, the time when
we dream, occurs four or five times each night

sleep. For most adults, REM sleep with its dreams lasts for one and a half to two hours every night. And the closer we get to morning, the more dreaming and REM sleep we experience.

Facts about dreams. Scientific studies of this cycle have taught us much about the dreaming mind. It is now known, for example, that the brain is active all night. Although REM sleep has vivid and sometimes bizarre imagery, there is also cognitive activity during times of non-REM sleep. At those times, the mental activity is more logical, coherent, and verbal.

It is now widely known that everyone dreams, every night, although the amount of time spent in dreaming decreases slightly as we grow older. Most of our dreams are in color, often our dreams include smell, hearing, or the sense of taste, and apparently dreams consume about the same amount of time that a similar action would take in waking life.

What happens if we don't dream during a period of sleep? To find out, several studies have involved waking laboratory volunteers whenever REM sleep appears. This interruption in sleep has stopped their dreaming, and when it was done for several consecutive days, psychotic-like symptoms sometimes appeared. Later, when the volunteers were allowed to sleep again without interruption, there was a "catch-up" period during which they had prolonged times of REM activity.

Some researchers have found that schizophrenics, and other severely mentally ill people, have shorter periods of REM sleep, but usually these people also have more times of fantasy thinking, including hallucinations, when they are awake.[2] Such findings have led some to wonder if dreams and REM sleep might serve a useful purpose in helping us keep stable minds.

This leads to the questions of why we dream and where dreams come from. Several theories have been proposed to answer these questions.

REASONS FOR DREAMS

Kilton Stewart was an anthropologist who published an exciting paper following a visit to the rain forests of Central Malaysia.[3] Stewart reported that he had found a phenomenal group of people known as the Senoi tribe. These "isolated jungle folk" were described as being free from violent crime, armed conflict, stress, and most chronic mental or physical ailments. Their lifestyles were idyllic and peaceful, according to Stewart, because families gathered every morning to discuss dreams over breakfast. Children learned from their elders how to recall dreams, to value them, and even to change dream content.

A creative American psychologist soon published a book advocating the use of Senoi methods in our culture,[4] and a respected dream researcher proposed that maybe we could be free of tension if we could learn to handle dreams like the Senoi.[5] Buoyed by enthusiasm over these reports, the editors of *Human Behavior* magazine hired a team of cameramen and sent them to Malaysia to make a documentary of the revolutionary dream-control methods. To their amazement the photographers discovered that the Senoi was a dying culture, already suffering from disease, fear of evil spirits, crop failures, and the harmful influence of local politics. They weren't even much interested in dreams and didn't seem to be aware of their popularity in America. It didn't take long for glowing reports about the Senoi to drop out of popular books and dream seminars.[6]

But the influence of dreams on mental health continues to interest more traditional researchers. Many have been impressed with Freud's view that dreams provide a safety valve to let powerful unconscious wishes escape. The wishes are assumed to be disguised as "dream symbols" so the dreamer is not overwhelmed by anxiety. Jung agreed that dreams reveal information from the unconscious, and he developed detailed theories to show how dreaming can help restore psychological balance. One of his contemporaries, Alfred Adler, thought that dreaming was more a reflection of one's current goals, struggles, and attempts to solve life problems. Erich Fromm, Fritz Perls, and a host of lesser known therapists proposed their own theories, and each made dream interpretation and dream discussion a part of therapy.

Even people with different theories agree that dreams help us work through problems and maintain stability, but there is disagreement about how that happens. Since infants and children dream more than adults, some have concluded that dreams provide stimulation for brain development. Another view is that REM sleep involves the sorting out and physiological reorganization of memories. Evidence for this comes from the observation that the amount of REM sleep often increases following intense daytime stress experiences or after vigorous periods of learning.[7]

Much more controversial is a recent theory by two British biologists, one of whom is a Nobel prize winner.[8] They conclude that the brain needs to be turned off from sensory stimulation at times, and that false and nonsensical memories need to be "damped down" or erased from the brain. The electrical firings of neurons that come with REM sleep are assumed to clear the brain of useless connections. The dreams that come with REM sleep are assumed to result from spontaneous neuron firings. Such dreams are assumed to have no meaning, and according to this novel theory, they are best forgotten.

But few people today want to forget their dreams. It is widely assumed that dreams have meaning and that it can be helpful and therapeutic to remember what happens in our dreaming minds.

INTERPRETING DREAMS

Laura was one of my students. Bright and energetic, she contacted me shortly after discovering that I was planning to write a chapter on the dreaming mind.

"It was the most amazing religious experience that I have ever had," she began, when we met to discuss her dream. "I was nineteen, home from college for the summer, and completely frustrated because I needed a summer job but couldn't find one." She had been searching, eight hours a day, for four weeks, but nothing had turned up.

In desperation, one night Laura turned to God, lay prostrate on the floor, confessed her self-centered attitudes, and told God that she was having intellectual doubts about her faith. She pleaded with God, first, to show himself to her that summer, and second, to give her any kind of a job. "I will take what you want," she prayed. "But please use it to stretch my faith."

That night Laura had a vivid dream. She was walking down a dusty road and came into a ghost town. The scene was very graphic. She could feel the breeze in her face, smell the air, and see the details of the unused jail, sheriff's office, saloon, and crumbling gravestones in what appeared to be a mock cemetery. So impressive was the scene that Laura rushed into the kitchen when she awoke, described the dream in detail to her family, and asked if they had ever visited such a site. She was greeted with blank stares. Nobody recognized the details of Laura's dream, and nobody could understand why she found the dream to be so vivid.

Even while they were discussing this, the telephone rang and a lady asked if Laura would like to work as a camp counselor. "I had never applied to the camp or even heard of it," Laura said in telling of her experiences, but ninety minutes later she was driving to Rodeo Ranch for an interview.

"I couldn't believe what I saw," she reported to me. "I stepped out of the car and into my dream. The street, the buildings, the gravestones—everything was identical to the ghost town I had experienced so clearly. Even the dust, smells, and breeze were the same as I had described to my family. I suddenly felt that God was answering my prayer of the night before and soon I began what was to be an incredible summer. Never have I felt such spiritual power or seen God work in so many marvelous ways."

Five years after this experience, when Laura described these events to me, she offered a tentative evaluation of why the dream had occurred. "Rodeo Ranch was a difficult place to work. The salary was low—only $700.00 for the entire summer. The conditions were incredibly filthy, primitive, and unsanitary. The camp was a ranch, filled with horses, and I have a great fear of horses. Without that dream I would never have taken the job, and I probably wouldn't have stayed all summer. But because of the dream, I assumed that God had given me assurance that he could provide for my needs, that he could be trusted, and that he could use such unusual circumstances to teach me some needed spiritual lessons."9

Have you ever had a vivid dream in which you sense that God is speaking or trying to teach something? One recent writer has suggested that dreams are messages from God, the most intimate point of contact that we have with God, and the place where we determine his personal will for us. If you have a problem and are struggling with an issue, says this writer, you can ask God for a dream and then sleep confidently, knowing that God will visit you that night with an answer.10 Another writer has proposed that "unless we have a real interest in hearing from God, we will not bother to seek to understand our dreams . . . . Dreams give us an opportunity to understand ourselves better so that we can find our fulfillment in God. This is only for those whose desire for God is deep, not superficial."11

Statements such as these are built on the recognition that God clearly has spoken to many people in dreams. The Bible is filled with examples of people who have been warned, led, taught, guided, and encouraged through dreams. One doesn't have to be a Bible scholar to remember the dreams of Jacob, Joseph, or the wise men who were warned by God in a dream. The entire Book of Daniel is about a man who had a God-given ability to understand and interpret dreams, and the New Testament gives examples of God leading Mary and Joseph, Paul, Peter, and others through dreams and visions. The last Book of the Bible, Revelation, is the record of a revelation given, perhaps in the form of a dream, to the apostle John.

The Bible gives no hint, however, that such dreams came to everyone, every night. Instead, they appear to have been somewhat rare, and often centered on issues of national or unusual spiritual importance. In the New Testament, for example, the word "dream" appears only seven times. Once this is in a quotation from the Old Testament[12] and the other six references, all in the Book of Matthew, concern the life of Jesus Christ.[13] At times the biblical dreams were hidden in symbolism, but often they were clear messages from God. And they came to people who did not have the Bible, God's written revelation. The writer of Hebrews makes the interesting statement that "long ago God spoke in many different ways to our fathers through the prophets (in visions, dreams, and even face to face), telling them little by little about his plans. But now in these days he has spoken to us through his Son."[14]

It would be presumptuous for anyone to proclaim that God no longer speaks to people through their dreams. Clearly he has spoken through dreams in the past and there is nothing in the Bible to state that he will never do that again. I am willing to conclude that he still does lead through dreams, but probably with less frequency than some modern dream analysts might assume. Because we have the Bible, we now are less dependent on dreams than were our spiritual forefathers. No dream is from God if its content contradicts the Scripture, and surely no dream can tell us much about God's will if interpreters cannot agree on what a given dream means. God may still speak to me through dreams, but I suspect he more often leads in other, clearer ways.

What, then, do dreams mean? When he wrote about dreams several years ago, Erich Fromm titled his book *The Forgotten Language*.[15] More recently, a contemporary researcher named David Foulkes has titled one of his books *A Grammar of Dreams*.[16] Both of these men assume that dreams are a language. Such dream language has images rather than sounds, and like all languages must be studied and learned. The process of decoding dream language began with Freud and has had many translators since, but as we saw near the beginning of this chapter, the interpretations are often confused and sometimes contradictory.

It probably is true that dreams mean different things to different people. For that reason, it is difficult to know exactly what, if anything, is meant when a seventy-four-year-old woman dreams that she is pregnant.

One recent writer, psychologist Abraham Schmitt, has suggested that the emotions in a dream may be more significant than the content and symbols. Whenever we wake, he suggests, it is best to meditate on the dream, try to bring it back to awareness, and summarize its content by either making notes or speaking into a cassette recorder. Make special note of the emotions that were felt, Schmitt suggests, and then try to connect the dream to real life events so the meaning of the dream can be determined. Critics argue that this method lets the dreamer make the dream mean whatever he or she wants it to mean. Schmitt replies that if one deliberately plays back the dream, "it will be clear that there is only one meaning, and it will be the right one."[17] I doubt that the critics will be satisfied with this answer. It *does* appear that much dream "interpretation" really does reflect the interpreter's biases. It is not easy to be sure that an interpretation is correct, so one interpretation often seems to be as good as another. Is it possible that the interpretations of that seventy-four-year-old lady's dream may say more about the interpreters, than they say about the lady or her dream?

Some have suggested that dreams can predict what will occur in the future, but sometimes the dream causes what will happen. When a person dreams of a coming accident, for example, he or she may be more anxious because of this and less careful in driving. The dream, then, could indirectly cause an accident.

Then there is the issue of forgetting and remembering. Most of us have hundreds of dreams that don't "come true" in real life. These are forgotten. What we do remember is the occasional dream that may be followed by an event similar to the dream. These dreams are often remembered and we assume the dream predicted the future. What we fail to see is that the dream and the real life event may have had no connection, and we overlook the much more frequent experience of dreams that are not connected with anything in real life.

Nevertheless, there are some things that we do know. It is clear, for example, that past experiences and present stimulations do appear in dreams. Bladder pressure, the sound of a siren, or the experience of being too cold can each become part of the dream's content. It is known, too, that dreams are often influenced by events that take place immediately before we go to sleep. Exciting or stimulating events of an evening commonly are relived in dreams. If we go to bed hungry, we often dream of food. Fears, worries, and inferiorities that bother us during the day frequently creep into our dreams at night. But do dreams have other meanings or do they stimulate creativity?

Creative dreams. People who make a habit of jotting down their dreams as soon as they awake, often find that the jottings are surprising. One poet dreamed that she had produced the greatest and most profound poem of all time. She dreamed that it would make her famous and in the night she wrote the masterpiece on a pad near the bed. The next morning she read her words:

Hogamus Higamus, Men are Polygamous;
Higamus Hogamus, Women Monogamous.[18]

In her own study of dreams, Christian writer Kathryn Lindskoog reported a personal creation that she wrote after awaking from a dream:

Some people chew tobacco-stuff;
I don't, 'cause I'm not up to snuff.[19]

In contrast, there are those whose dreams have led to significant discoveries. Elias Howe, for example, had long been frustrated over his failure to perfect the sewing machine. One night he dreamed of being captured by savages who were planning to kill him with their spears. As the spears slowly rose and began to descend, Howe noticed that each spear had an eye-shaped hole in the tip. Suddenly he realized that his sewing machine needles could also have their eyes near the point. He awakened immediately, jumped out of bed, dashed to his laboratory, and solved his problem of making the sewing machine work.

Equally famous, perhaps, is the example of Friedrich August von Kekule, whose dream in 1865 led to what has been called one of the most brilliant discoveries in organic chemistry. Kekule dreamed that atoms were dancing before his eyes, but eventually they formed a line and became snakelike. When one of the snakes grabbed its own tail, the dreamer suddenly realized that molecules form rings. He awoke "as if by a flash of lightning" and hurried off to test his new discovery.

The encyclopedias are filled with reports of other inventors, authors, musicians, and artists whose dreams have led to creative work. Robert Louis Stevenson turned a dream into *Dr. Jekyll and Mr. Hyde*. Goethe, Edgar Allan Poe, Voltaire, Danté, Shelley, and Tolstoy used dream material in their works, and so did musicians such as Mozart, Robert Schumann, and Saint-Saëns.[20] Some observers have suggested that such advances are "creative leaps of the well-prepared mind." They may come when a person is asleep, but they are equally likely to appear whenever the creative person is awake but with a wandering mind or with logical, rational thinking suspended temporarily.

FANTASY AND DREAMS

Is it possible that fantasy, daydreams, talking to ourselves, and similar daytime thoughts are as important to mental health as the dreams we have at night? Research by Dr. Steven Starker of Oregon Health Sciences University has led him to reach this conclusion:[21] Our minds have different "fantasy styles," Starker maintains, and sometimes these are seen both in daydreams and in dreams at night. Some people, for example, have a "conflict style" of fantasy, characterized by guilt, negative emotions, and nightmares. Others have an "anxious style," and some have a "positive style" in which their day-and-night fantasies are more pleasant, vivid, and optimistic.

It is well known that psychiatric patients sometimes withdraw into unhealthy worlds of fantasy. Professional counselors often attempt to interpret such fantasies and mental assumptions, using them as clues to understanding the patient's problems. From this it does not follow, however, that daydreaming is always unhealthy or dangerous to mental health. On the contrary, as we have seen, people with rich fantasy lives sometimes are better able to cope with stress, resist disease, and think creatively. Some research suggests that daydreamers are better communicators, less likely to be aggressive, and better able to cope with boredom.[22] Starker even suggests that the study, understanding, and development of fantasy thought may be the royal road to physical and mental health.

The fascinating area of dreams and fantasies leads us into the realm of those strange mind experiences that commonly are known as "altered states of consciousness." These altered states raise questions about what happens to the mind when it is under hypnosis. That is the theme of the next chapter.

15
THE
HYPNOTIC
MIND

Franz Anton Mesmer was the talk of Paris in the 1780s. In spite of his training as a physician, he held the unorthodox view that a mysterious magnetic power permeates the universe and resides in human bodies. Treatment of disease, he proposed, could best be done by using magnetic forces from the environment to restore the patient's "magnetic equilibrium." Such views put Mesmer into conflict with the medical profession in his native Vienna, but laypeople were intrigued with the theory. When the doctor moved to France, his reputation preceded him and soon patients were flocking to experience magnetic treatments.

It wasn't easy to treat so many people on a one-to-one basis, so Mesmer developed a group technique. As many as thirty people would come at a time and sit around a large wooden tub known as a "baquet." The baquet was filled with water, ground glass, iron filings, and long metal rods that extended from the tub and were grabbed at one end by the patients. According to Mesmer, the magnetic fluid in the baquet somehow came to the people through the rods and led to all kinds of physical cures.

Mesmer did what he could to make the healing sessions impressive and emotionally powerful. Soft music played in the background. The room was dimly lit and thickly draped. Mesmer himself demanded silence when he entered the room. Often he wore a long flowing lilac silk robe, and walked about, touching the afflicted body parts with a long iron wand and making magnetic "mesmeric passes" as he waved his free hand through the air.

A few people had no response to this dramatic treatment, but many thought they felt forces moving through their bodies, and some went into prolonged convulsions. These involved jerking of the body, apparent dreaminess or stupor, and sometimes piercing cries. Mesmer's followers called this experience "the crisis" and claimed that it brought great healing.

But King Louis XVI wasn't so easily convinced and undoubtedly His Majesty's interest in Mesmer was sparked by secret reports that some mesmerites had radical political ideas. To investigate, the king appointed a Royal Commission and declared that it would be chaired by the American ambassador to France, a man named Benjamin Franklin.

The commissioners went to work with enthusiasm, conducting experiments and interviewing Mesmer's patients. After careful study, it was concluded that body magnetism did not exist, that the baquet fluid had no power, and that convulsions and proclaimed cures came as a result of the creative imagination of Mesmer and his highly suggestible followers. Shortly after the report was issued, Mesmer left France and the mesmerites went underground, but a half-century later mesmerism reemerged in a more sophisticated form and with a new name—hypnosis.

THE UNCONSCIOUS MIND

Early in his career, and before the theory of psychoanalysis was developed, Freud spent a prolonged time in Paris studying hypnosis under the great masters of the time, Pierre Janet and Jean Charcot. He concluded that hypnotism wasn't necessary as a treatment technique, but the Paris experience apparently did much to influence his thinking about the mind.

According to Freud, the mind is like an iceberg in which the smaller visible part is the region of consciousness, and the larger invisible mass, below the surface, is the area of the unconscious. Freud believed that the unconscious is filled with urges, impulses, passions, hidden memories, repressed ideas, and feelings that seek to exert control over our actions and conscious thoughts. To understand the mind, Freud thought that we had to know more about the nature and influence of the unconscious. That was the purpose of psychoanalysis. It was developed as a theory of personality and as a method of treatment devoted, first, to discovering and understanding unconscious influences, and second, to helping patients face and deal with these influences.

But is there such a thing as the unconscious mind? How does this differ from the conscious mind? Is it true that we cannot "achieve a real understanding of the mind without confronting the problem of consciousness"?[1] Such questions are difficult to answer physiologically, and philosophers have debated them for decades without reaching clear conclusions. Consciousness cannot be observed scientifically, and it is difficult if not impossible for any one person to know with certainty what is going on in the conscious mind of another.

Perhaps it is accurate enough to think of consciousness as "whatever is on one's mind at the moment,"[2] including the thoughts and feelings that we are aware of and are more or less able to control. But a lot of ideas never seem to get into our conscious minds. If you drive to work along the same route every day, you are likely to stop for red lights, turn at the right places, and avoid other cars, all while "your mind is somewhere else." Clearly, experienced drivers can operate a car without thinking consciously about what they are doing.[3] Most of us walk around objects, avoid danger, use good grammar, perform skills, and do routine tasks, all without conscious thought. Our sense organs are bombarded with innumerable stimulations all the time, but as we saw earlier, the brain is able to sort through these, to ignore most of them, and to let only important ideas filter through to our conscious attention. All of this sorting is done automatically and without getting direction from the conscious mind.

Everyone knows about mothers who can sleep soundly through the night even when there is considerable noise, but who are quickly awakened by the slightest sound from the baby. More recently it has been found that anesthetized patients really do perceive what surgical teams are saying during operations. This has led some physicians to argue that there should be less banter in surgery and more care to avoid making statements about the patient's condition that could be depressing or frightening.[4]

The thinking, perceiving, feeling, and deciding that takes place apart from conscious awareness is what we mean by unconscious mental processes. Often these influence our lives without ever becoming conscious. As we will see later, some advertisers, political indoctrinators, and other mind changers attempt to reach people at the unconscious level and persuade them to make purchases or change their thinking. Even those who disagree with Freud tend to accept the fact that behavior isn't always under our conscious control. Some of our dreams, fantasies, creative productions, attitudes, and urges spring from the unconscious.

It appears, too, that the ideas and attitudes that we and others feed into our minds, can come back later to influence our thinking and behavior. Early computer programmers used to talk about GIGO: when *Garbage* goes *In*, *Garbage* comes *Out*. The same is true of the mind. This raises some sobering implications about how we think and what we put into our mental computers.

THE ALTERED MIND

I taught my first course in psychology back in the 1960s when campuses all over the world were exploding in violence and when students were blatantly attacking the values, morals, and economics of what they called "the military-industrial complex." Part of the rebellion included challenges to conventional lifestyles, dress, and behavior. Casual, even dirty and messy clothing became common, along with bare feet, long hair, beards, and experimentation with drugs, meditation, encounter groups, alternate lifestyles, uncontrolled sex, commune living, radical politics, and the "Jesus movement."

Students who enrolled in psychology courses might have expected to learn more about these relevant issues, but instead they heard about rats in mazes, debates over psychological methods, intelligence testing, and other issues that must have seemed trivial and unimportant.

Introductory college courses still tend to be dull, but at least there is more awareness of the importance of hypnosis, dreams, fantasies, religious experiences, extrasensory perception, the influence of drugs, and the effects of sensory deprivation. These topics are not part of the mainstream of psychology, but each is now being studied scientifically and each deals with *altered states of consciousness*, usually abbreviated ASC's.

Let us assume that all of our mental experiences could be put on some kind of a yardstick, which had "alert conscious thinking" at one end and "unconscious coma" at the other. In between, there would be a variety of experiences. Some, like deep sleep, would be close to the unconscious end of our scale. Others, like daydreaming, would be nearer the other end.

A whole host of mental experiences could be placed along the ruler. Dreams, drug-induced ecstasy, the experience of drunkenness, hypnotic trances, meditation, delirium, intense concentration, anesthetized states, deep depression, intense excitement over athletic successes, and even some religious "mountain-top" experiences, could all be placed on the scale. Each of these is partly conscious and partially unconscious. Perhaps all could be considered altered states of consciousness.

According to one writer, an ASC refers to any mental state in which either the person knows, subjectively, that "this isn't the way I usually think," or some other observer knows that "this isn't the way he or she normally thinks."[5] Usually, such altered states are characterized by many or all of the following:[6]

- *Changes in thinking.* Sometimes the thinking is irrational, memory or attention is bad, concentration is poor, and judgment is impaired.
- *Confusion about time.* There may be feelings of timelessness, a nonawareness of time, or a sense that time has speeded up or slowed down.
- *Loss of control.* The person may feel that he or she has lost self-control, or has no power to adapt to circumstances. Think, for example, of the person who is drunk, hypnotized, controlled by drugs, or experiencing a mystical state. Most sense a lack of control.
- *Change in emotional expression.* Often there is a marked change in feelings and in the way one expresses emotion.
- *Changed body image.* Sometimes people sense that their bodies are distorted, dizzy, excessively light or heavy, weak, numb, tingling, perhaps floating, or otherwise altered.
- *Distorted perceptions.* ASC's often are accompanied by hallucinations, visual images, the intense awareness of light, color, or sounds, and other unusual perceptions.
- *Change in meaning or significance.* People see the world in a different light and sometimes find great meaning in things that they otherwise would take for granted.
- *A sense of uniqueness.* This is the feeling that "this is too wonderful, too awful, or too intense for anyone else to ever be able to experience or understand, unless the other person has had a similar experience."
- *Feelings of rejuvenation.*
- *Hypersuggestibility.* The person is very much influenced by suggestions from others.

ASC changes such as these may come from a variety of circumstances, including the influence of alcohol or other drugs, the reduction of stimulation from the environment, fever, or other physiological influences, intense excitement or stimulation, intense mental absorption in some task or work, or the passive state of mind that comes with meditation or daydreaming.

In the Western world, we tend to value alert conscious thinking and want to shy away from any altered states that sound mystical, emotional, or out of our control. Some sincere Christians, as we will see in the next chapter, describe such altered states as always being wrong or satanic, but it is impossible to have a normally functioning mind that does not shift frequently to altered states. Sleep and dreaming are surely altered states, and so are mental fatigue, the confusion that may come with high fevers, or the enthusiasm of intense religious experiences. But perhaps one of the most controversial of the altered states is that which Benjamin Franklin's commission considered two centuries ago—the issue of hypnosis.

THE HYPNOTIZED MIND

When he was a young boy, Mark Twain volunteered to be the subject for a visiting stage hypnotist. To everyone's amazement, the boy went into a deep trance and even permitted people to stick needles through his flesh while he showed no evidence of pain or discomfort. In later years, the famous novelist tried to convince people that he had faked the whole thing and had never gone into a trance as everyone had assumed.[7] But even his own mother doubted the story of her grown son. She had seen the original performance and was convinced that the young Mark Twain had, indeed, been in a deep hypnotic state.

Stage hypnotists are performers. They are paid to put on a good show and nobody objects if they fool people, create illusions, wear fancy clothing, give esoteric explanations of their "strange powers," or perhaps even find some accomplices who can act in ways that add to the performance. All of this drama contributes to the notion that hypnosis is mystical, phony, eerie, or not to be taken seriously.

But many people now do take it seriously. Research into the nature of hypnosis has mushroomed since the days of King Louis' commission, hundreds of therapists have found value in the use of clinical hypnosis, and many of their patients have been helped through hypnotherapy. Professional athletic teams have been using hypnotists to help their athletes perform better, and police departments have turned to hypnosis to help them solve crimes. When a busload of school children was kidnapped in

California several years ago, the bus driver was hypnotized and enabled to recall most of the license plate numbers on the abductors' car. With that clue, the police were able to make the arrest that led to conviction of the kidnappers.[8]

In 1852, James Braid first introduced the term "hypnosis," which is based on the Greek word *hypnos,* to sleep. Today, however, almost no one believes that hypnosis is a form of sleep. The brain waves of a hypnotized person do not resemble the brain waves of sleep. Instead, hypnotic brain patterns are indistinguishable from those of people who are awake and relaxed.[9]

It is widely accepted, therefore, that hypnosis involves a state of deep relaxation, intense concentration, and high suggestibility. Some people are more easily hypnotized than others, but there is no evidence for the popular beliefs that hypnotizable people are especially gullible, hysterical, weak-willed, passive, or easily controlled by dominant people.[10] It does appear, however, that people whose thinking is predominantly right-brain are more easily hypnotized than those who are left-brain dominated.[11] And the easily hypnotized have more vivid imaginations.[12]

The power of hypnosis. There are a variety of ways by which people can be hypnotized,[13] but most techniques include restricting sensory input and motor activity, helping people to concentrate their attention, repeating words or actions in a monotonous way, defining the relationship between hypnotist and subject, and in some way communicating how the person is likely to act when hypnotized.[14] Usually the subject is encouraged to relax and the hypnotist uses some form of imagery (like, "Your arm is getting lighter and lighter," "Your eyelids are getting heavier and heavier," or "Your breathing is getting deeper and deeper"). With a little coaching, it is likely that most of us could learn how to hypnotize another person, but since the nature and power of hypnosis are still being studied, it would be unwise for untrained amateurs to play with something that *might* be a powerful force.

Some critics have argued that hypnosis is nothing more than a relaxed state in which people let themselves be highly influenced by the hypnotist's suggestions. Others have argued that hypnotic feats are overexaggerated and easily replicated by people who are not under hypnosis. Then there are those who believe that hypnosis is a powerful force for good or evil, and some who are convinced that all hypnosis is an occult phenomenon that is dangerous and even satanic.

Whatever your view, it seems clear that hypnosis does help people tolerate, and sometimes not even feel, pain. Hypnotized people have also been able to control their blood flow so their wounds stop bleeding, to stop stuttering or overeating, to remember past events, to mentally remove warts, to reduce anxiety, and to cope more effectively with stress. As we have seen, however, each of these can be done without hypnosis. Perhaps a similar realization led Freud to conclude that hypnosis might be useful, but it wasn't necessary. As in Freud's lifetime, however, not everyone today would agree with this conclusion.

Recently, I was speaking at a Bible College in western Canada. The students and visitors were clearly interested in the lectures on the mind and there was a lot of curiosity, especially over the subject of hypnosis. One pastor, for example, told about a neighbor who couldn't stop smoking. "I counseled with him," the minister stated. "I prayed with him, and prayed for him, but the compulsive smoking continued. Then he went to a hypnotist and after one session the smoking stopped and has never returned again. I have a one word question: 'Why?' "

There is no easy answer, but it may be that hypnotic suggestions help people find the satisfactions in nonsmoking that they originally found in smoking. In one study, subjects were taught to relax whenever they felt like smoking,[15] so there was no need to use a cigarette to unwind. Another gave this suggestion: "Each time you feel a desire to light a cigarette, the thought will come to mind that you can wait a while. Then, when you put the pack of cigarettes back in your pocket without taking one, you will experience a bright, rosy glow."[16] When people are both motivated to stop smoking, and convinced that hypnosis will give them the power to quit, then smoking often ceases.

What about age regression? When I was a teenager, magazines and newspapers reported great interest in the story of Bridey Murphy. As first reported in the *Denver Post,* a Colorado housewife named Virginia Tighe would speak in an Irish brogue when under hypnosis and told detailed stories of her past life as an Irish woman living in Cork in 1806. One of the newspaper editors decided to "check out" the story and wrote a book that was on the best-seller list for weeks.[17] There was a popular song written about Bridey Murphy, a new interest in hypnosis, and at least one suicide by an Oklahoma teenager who wanted to investigate the story in person.[18]

It soon became clear that Mrs. Tighe's stories about Ireland had no basis in fact. Instead of remembering a nineteenth century life in Ireland, Mrs. Tighe was remembering what she had learned as a child in Chicago. A lady whose maiden name was Bridey Murphy had impressed the young girl with stories about Ireland. She had taught Mrs. Tighe the Irish jig she danced during her hypnotic trances. In addition, it was found that an aunt who spoke with a brogue had taught the young girl about Irish ways and had given her a great love for the Emerald Isle. Under the influence of an impressive hypnotist whom she wanted to please, Mrs. Tighe had responded to subtle suggestion and had unconsciously composed a story that had no basis in reality.

But if hypnosis gives no support to the notion of previous lives, is it possible that hypnosis can take us back to relive some earlier period in this life? If a hypnotist tells a subject, "You are now five years old," the person will often speak, act, and draw like a young child. Experiments have tried to determine whether the person under "hypnotic age regression" really has returned to an earlier stage in life, but the results have been contradictory. Some critics believe that the subjects are trying to act according to how they think the hypnotist expects them to act. Others suggest that age-regressed subjects are role-playing and acting like they think a young child would act.[19]

In one fascinating report, a hypnotist took a subject back to the time when he was six years old and spoke only German. "Do you understand any English?" the hypnotist asked. "Nein," came the reply, followed by an explanation, in childlike German, that he did not comprehend English as a child. Additional English questions brought similar answers, each of which was stated in German but each of which came in response to a question asked in English—the language that the "child" claimed he did not understand.[20]

Does this mean that the age-regressed subjects are deliberately being deceptive? Not necessarily, but there is clear evidence that hypnotically regressed people do bring their present attitudes and knowledge back into their memories of the past. Pure hypnotic age regression, like hypnotic reincarnation, does not exist.

What does exist is something called trance logic. Deeply hypnotized people think differently than those who are pretending to be hypnotized. If you tell a subject that a chair in the room does not exist, the hypnotized person will nevertheless walk around the chair, but the pretender will walk into it. It has been suggested that this is because the pretender fails to realize that it is possible to register a fact at one level, even while we remain unaware of it at another. By ordinary logic, it makes no sense to see and to not see a chair at the same time; trance logic makes no such assumption. Some researchers have used the presence of trance logic as a test to determine whether or not a person is really hypnotized.[21]

Perhaps all of this has little impact on our day-to-day lives, but technical research into the nature of hypnosis continues, and there *is* evidence that hypnosis can be a useful aid to professional counselors. Evidence also exists suggesting that many of the exaggerated claims for hypnosis are overstatements. The hypnotized mind may not be as mysterious or as powerful as many of its supporters claim.

THE HALLUCINATING MIND

More powerful, perhaps, is the hallucinating mind which sees visions, hears sounds, or smells odors that do not really exist. It is well known that psychiatric patients sometimes experience hallucinations, but so do people who take psychedelic drugs, individuals who are deprived of normal sensations, those who are deprived of sleep, and some people who are deeply religious. In 1486, two Dominican monks published a book which proposed that anyone who hallucinated was possessed of the devil and, therefore, should be punished by torture or by being burned at the stake. A more recent writer has suggested that all religions begin with hallucinatory visions or trances. These are assumed to be divine revelations but express the needs and desires of one's culture or group.[22]

Cognitive scientists still do not know why people hallucinate. In an earlier chapter we saw that hallucinations can be produced when groups of neurons in the brain are stimulated by electrodes. Some specialists have suggested that we all need to experience a certain amount of fantasy or imagination if we are to maintain our mental balance. When this is blocked, hindered, or excessively stimulated, the brain in some way is triggered to fire the neurons that make us experience hallucinations. No one knows for certain why hallucinators have reduced periods of REM sleep, or why some people seem more prone to hallucinations than others.[23]

Hallucinations and out-of-body experiences. The word "hallucination" comes from a Latin term that means to "wander in the mind." Some have wondered if people who report out-of-body experiences are really "wandering in the mind." Do we assume, therefore, that out-of-body experiences are specialized forms of hallucinations?

Psychologists have tended to ignore these experiences, even though they are fascinating and probably much more common than we might assume. Out-of-body experiences are sometimes known as OBE's but more often are referred to as "autoscopic hallucinations." "Autoscopy" means to see oneself the way we are seen by another. The suggestion that this is an hallucination implies that people are not really leaving their bodies, except by their own mental visions.

OBE's are more common than we might expect, most often seen in young people (between the ages of fifteen and thirty-five), in those who have a creative imagination, in people who are under stress, and in those who are concerned about their identities or physical state.[24] In one interesting experiment, a lady who claimed to have OBE's was brought to sleep in a laboratory and instructed to read some numbers on the top of a cabinet whenever she floated out of her body and up to the ceiling of the room. For three nights the lady failed to read the numbers, and when she did so on the fourth night, the experimenter had some reason to believe that she had found another way to get the information.[25]

Most investigators, therefore, tend to assume that out-of-body experiences do not really exist, except as mental fantasies. Some Oriental philosophies do not agree, however, and there are Christians who believe that OBE's, hypnosis, psychic healings, fantasies, altered states of consciousness, and many of the other issues discussed in this and previous chapters, are really the result of satanic forces. This is an issue that must be considered if we want to understand the magnificent mind.

16
THE
DEMONIC
MIND

Edgar Cayce is dead!

His life ended following a stroke in early 1945, but for thousands of Cayce's followers, the influence of the man lives on. The Association for Research and Enlightenment, the Edgar Cayce organization in Virginia, publishes books, sponsors conferences and research studies, propagates Cayce's teachings, and maintains a clinic in Arizona where patients are treated in accordance with the advice that came from the several thousand psychic readings Edgar Cayce gave during his lifetime. A biography of Cayce attracted great popular interest when it was published a number of years ago,[1] and even though he never went beyond a grade school education, Cayce's diagnoses and treatment techniques have attracted the attention of many people in the medical professions.

Who was Edgar Cayce? Born on a Kentucky farm in 1877, he was raised as a fundamentalist Christian, attended church regularly, believed in the literal interpretation of the Bible, and taught a Sunday school class for many years.[2] As a child, Cayce had visions of "angels" and unexpected "supernatural" experiences. Later, he developed a physical problem that changed his life.

On a business trip in 1900, Cayce was found wandering in a daze in a railroad station. Rescued by a family friend, he regained conscious awareness only to realize that his voice was gone. Numerous physical examinations did nothing to correct the problem and the young man concluded that he would never again be able to speak above a whisper.

One day, however, he went into a hypnotic trance and with a strong, clear voice, diagnosed his own problem, commanded the blood in his body to circulate to the affected area, and awoke with his speech restored. A local osteopath suggested that Cayce's trance statements might be able to diagnose and suggest cures for others. Before long, the enthusiastic osteopath and a reluctant Edgar Cayce opened an office where the doctor would read names of patients to Cayce while he was in a trance, and he in turn would give diagnoses and recommend therapies, many of which seemed to work. Whenever Cayce's voice would disappear, he would go back into a trance and pronounce his own treatment. Throughout his lifetime, Cayce gave over 14,000 "readings." He was called "the sleeping prophet," and in time he became known as this century's greatest psychic.

But Edgar Cayce was a troubled man. He knew that his readings were helpful to many, and he sincerely wanted to do good. But he realized, too, that his teachings were moving farther and farther away from the biblical truths that he had learned in childhood. He began to believe in reincarnation, in salvation by works, in the reliability of clairvoyance, and in the view that Jesus was no more than a man who lived as an example and died as a human. There is evidence that he wanted to forsake his psychic powers, but he couldn't.[3] It was not Edgar Cayce who possessed powerful mind forces—the forces possessed him.

Two recent observers have pondered the developments in Cayce's life. His life, they suggest,

> . . . illustrates the classic pattern of those caught up in demonic fascination. He was first ensnared through the "good" being done through his gift, and his philosophy had a neutral character. Once he had done enough good to become emotionally committed to his powers, it became very difficult to abandon them. Cayce then came to the test phase, when antibiblical doctrines began to enter his teachings and practices. He began to be willing to abandon all claim to legitimate Bible doctrine and, instead, to "follow his star." Finally the ultimate phase—control by the negative spirits—was accomplished. Now Cayce was being used, in his view of things, as a puppet—a double-agent, as it were, since he was known originally as a biblical teacher. In the demonic realm, control eventually reaches a point at which the individual has no will left. Even if he chooses to

escape, he cannot, which is the ultimate end of anyone opening himself to such powers. Like so many others, Cayce was unable to outsmart or stop the forces working through him. . . .

Cayce's abilities were simply beyond solely human potential; hence they must have originated from a nonhuman source. The hostility to Christ and Scripture displayed so clearly in his readings is sufficient evidence of the ungodly source of Cayce's information—demons, who are the source of supernaturally received antibiblical teachings.

When we examine Cayce's heavily occult background, super-natural abilities, anti-Christ theology, and false prophecies, we are left with no other choice. The study of the man's life is a classic in the study of the subtlety of spiritual warfare.[4]

There were two forces at work in the thinking of Edgar Cayce. The first was the God-centered power Cayce had learned in church as a child; the second was the antibiblical teaching that dominated his later readings. As the first of these was distorted and faded, the second took over with increasing strength.

This battle between the forces of God and the powers of evil did not cease with the death of Edgar Cayce. According to the Bible, the battle still rages. Some have given in to the "spiritual forces of evil,"[5] and others seem to be unaware that a battle exists. But there *is* a struggle, and the chief battleground appears to be the human mind.

THE CONTEMPORARY MIND

"Did you know you have a second mind?"

That is the heading of an advertisement in a magazine that came to my house sometime ago. The reader is told that psychologists now know how "to harness the powers of the hidden mind." It is possible, says the advertisement, for us to stimulate the subconscious mind so we feel better, look younger, get more out of life, get rid of hangups and misconceptions about ourselves, find more fulfillment, and attain lasting happiness.

Ten or fifteen years ago it is unlikely that such a message would have appeared as a full-page ad in *Psychology Today*.[6] But times have changed, and there now is increasing and widespread interest in a variety of phenomena that deal with the mind but border on the occult. Mind control, imagery, meditation, faith healing, holistic medicine, dream interpretation, positive mental attitudes, the development of human potential and even acupuncture are not necessarily bad or wrong in themselves. But contemporary movements such as these tend to capture the popular imagination and they often pull people away from biblical teaching, toward ideas that the Bible would call dangerous and occult-like.

There are those within psychology who reject anything supernatural and give naturalistic scientific explanations for events that Christians might consider to be demonic.[7] Such writers can, at times, be persuasive, and their work shows that many "strange" events in this world can have logical, natural explanations. Sometimes, I suspect, the devil gets credit for doing things that can be explained in other more "down to earth" ways.

But even scientists, practicing physicians, college professors, and other intelligent people are turning to Eastern, esoteric, and occult explanations to account for the strange powers that appear to reside within human grasp. Numerous seminars, conferences, and college courses now exist to discuss and study reincarnation, psychic healing, parapsychology, extrasensory perception, out-of-body experiences, Chinese medicine, Oriental philosophy, transcendental meditation, and a variety of intriguing new psychotherapies.

Common to most of these is belief in the existence of some kind of universal energy or life force.[8] This goes under different names—including Ch'i, orgone energy, vital energy, prana, cosmic energy, mana, or even the animal magnetism that brought such criticism to Anton Mesmer—but it is assumed to be universal and the source of both healing and personal power. Those who attempt to harness "the force" appear to have little interest in God, almost no inclination to study the Bible, great belief in human potential, but no appreciation for such Christian doctrines as the Lordship of Christ or the sinful nature of individuals. Some have used the term "New Consciousness" to describe their thinking, and many would argue that the new movement is meant to bring a change in the way people view themselves, their potential, the universe, and the realm of the supernatural.[9] Few would be as honest or as perceptive as Edgar Cayce who wondered about the source of those psychic forces that came through his trances. He suspected that "the devil may be tempting me to do his work by operating through me when I was conceited enough to think God had given me special power."[10]

THE SATANIC MIND

Modern thinkers who show great interest in mysticism, spiritism, occultism, animism, psychic healing, universal energy, and other unusual phenomena, rarely seem to give much attention to the devil. Often Satan is seen as a little gremlin with horns, wearing a red suit, carrying a pitchfork, and doing little harm except to tempt people to do what they want to do anyway. Such an image is far removed from the teachings of the Bible.

The word "Satan" means adversary or enemy. According to the Bible, he is a being of intense power who is deceptive, filled with lies, and intent on seeking to trap and devour individuals, even as he walks about the earth posing as an angel of peace and light.[11] His major technique of deception and entrapment is to blind people's minds so they develop arguments against God, are led away from devotion to Christ, and cannot even understand the gospel or see the glory of Christ, God's Son.[12] By displaying "all kinds of counterfeit miracles, signs and wonders," the devil deceives people, so that they do not know the truth.[13] Like Adam and Eve, people today look for enlightenment, insight, and knowledge apart from God. The evil one is happy to comply with this search. But the more one submits to satanic sources of knowledge, the more one is trapped—like an Edgar Cayce.

The devil is not divine, all powerful, all knowing, or ever present. But he does rule over a vast and powerful force of spirit-beings who do his bidding and are obedient to his directions.[14] This demonic force is in control of the world,[15] and although it ultimately will be destroyed,[16] it presently works in our minds to deceive and cause faulty thinking.

Is it possible that Satan and his forces control people by working through many of the mind powers which have been described in this book? Could the evil one use positive mental attitudes, holistic healing, hypnosis, imagery, dream interpretation, creative thinking, and similar mental ideas to advance his cause and to turn people away from Jesus Christ? I believe the answer is yes, but this does not mean that we should try to turn off our minds and stop using them. That wouldn't be possible and neither would it be Christ-honoring. Instead, we must be alert to what enters our minds and be careful that we are not deceived in our thinking.

On 5 July 1941, C. S. Lewis sat at his desk in Magdalen College at Oxford, and wrote the foreword to his famous *Screwtape Let-*

ters. He could never have guessed how often his words would be quoted, but they are worth repeating again. He wrote: "There are two equal and opposite errors into which our race can fall about the devils. One is to disbelieve in their existence. The other is to believe, and to feel an excessive and unhealthy interest in them. They themselves are equally pleased by both errors."[17]

We begin to avoid such errors by recognizing that Christ has already established his control over the world and its forces. His Holy Spirit, who lives within each believer, is greater than the satanic force within the world.[18] This does not imply that we should ignore the devil. The Bible tells us to be mentally alert to his schemes and to resist his activity through our closeness to Christ, our reliance on the Holy Spirit, and our knowledge of the Scriptures.[19] All of this implies, however, that the battle against demonic forces is a battle that takes place in the mind.

THE ALERT MIND

Perhaps one of the keys to successful warfare is to be alert so that one is not taken by surprise. In summarizing their warnings about satanic influence, both Paul and Peter warned us to be alert, so that we are not fooled, caught off guard, or "taken in" by demonic deception.[20]

Johanna Michaelsen would agree, but she learned the hard way. A possessor of psychic powers almost from birth, this young lady encountered a variety of strange experiences and mental depressions as she grew up in Mexico and later attended college in Georgia and North Carolina.

In a captivating book describing her experiences,[21] Johanna described her involvement with "The Mind Control Method," a training program designed to teach relaxation and self-improvement through the use of visualization and image creation. The students in the course were taught that they could have full control over their minds. They were taught to create a mental "laboratory" where they could work at solving their problems. And they were told to imagine the existence of a spiritual counselor or guide who could give them direction.

Johanna Michaelsen began to have visions, insights into the past and future, and the ability to get information through vibrations that came from objects. Eventually she went to work with a psychic surgeon and stayed for fourteen months. She was sincere in her desire to please God, but there was no peace inside. She was distressed when her sister raised some disturbing questions—questions that echoed some of Johanna's own hidden doubts.

"You say you can tell the difference between good and evil spirits, but how do you know you haven't been deceived?" "You watch the psychic healer perform amazing operations but how do you know they are from the power of God?" "You say you believe in Jesus, but how do you know that the Jesus in your clinic is the Jesus of the Bible?" "You believe that demons are being cast out, but how do you know that they aren't play-acting?"

"I had to admit," Johanna wrote later, "I didn't really know. The only argument I could fall back on was my experience—my feelings and perceptions. Yes, I had read and studied the masters, Edgar Cayce, Allan Kardec. I could give eloquent explanations when asked about reincarnation, karma and cosmic consciousness, and astral planes and psychic manifestations. But when it came right down to it, I knew there was no solid, truly objective way of testing the source behind them, and that troubled me. How could I be sure the source was God? I had no absolutes against which to compare my experience."[22]

Eventually, Johanna Michaelsen went to L'Abri, the Christian community in Switzerland, where she began to understand the errors in her thinking. In time, she committed her life and mind to Christ.

Looking back on her life, Johanna began to recognize that the things which seemed to be so beautiful and good were really deceptive and evil. She saw, too, that occult mind activities and thinking are becoming more and more prevalent in our society, perhaps because they so often are seen as innocent, harmless pastimes or mental activities. People who claim to be Christians, Johanna concluded, let their minds dabble in dangerous occult activities, often without even knowing that their interests are satanic. The minds of these people are not alert to spiritual issues or to the subtleties of spiritual warfare.

Not long ago I gave a series of talks about the mind at a local church. Some members of the audience enthusiastically approached me after the lectures and urged me to read the writings of several contemporary authors who appear to be on crusades against atheistic humanism, holistic medicine, the "New Age" movement, secular psychotherapy, and several other modern and sometimes disturbing trends in our society. I had read some of the recommended books[23] and was impressed with the sincerity of the authors, with their lack of scholarship, and with the personal vindictiveness that seemed to characterize their writings. There *are* dangerous trends in contemporary thinking. There *is* a battle going on for the minds of people. We *do* need to be alert to the devil's schemes and subtle teachings that masquerade as truth in our society. But the way to resist such mental error is not with emotional diatribes. Instead, there needs to be a clear understanding of the Bible's teachings about demonic error, accompanied by a committed submission to the commands of Scripture.

THE SPIRITUALLY SENSITIVE MIND

Recently I read the story of a man who grew up in a family of committed Christians, attended a church where the Bible was taken seriously, but fell under the influence of a cult when he reached the late teenage years. He explained later that he had become a Christian at age ten, but the Bible teaching in his church was so dull and irrelevant that he never grew. When a cult group came along, expressing love and convincing answers, he was a ripe candidate for conversion.

The Scriptures warn of church people who have a form of godliness, but have no power. They claim to love God, but their lives demonstrate that their beliefs are more talk and show than evidence of true dedication.[24] Does this kind of weakened thinking characterize your mind—or mine?

To keep our minds free of satanic influence there are several guidelines that are crucial to remember.

First, we must maintain a skepticism toward reports of strange occurrences and promises of new power through mind control. The popular press, the followers of psychic leaders, and the devotees of new movements like to cite case histories to "prove" the unusual. We sometimes hear, for example, that Jeane Dixon, the well-known psychic, made a number of accurate predictions, including the assassination of President Kennedy, but few people are aware of her many false predictions.[25] We know of people who proclaim that their visions, tongues-speaking, prophecies, dream interpretations, and healings come from God, but each of these can have satanic counterfeits which are not from God. Superlearning, visualization, positive thinking, and stress management techniques may all bring benefits, but are they consistent with biblical teaching? Ideas, trends, and techniques that are beautiful and helpful are, sometimes, also demonic and satanic.

The Scriptures tell us to "examine everything carefully," holding on only to that which is good.[26] We are warned to not "always believe everything you hear just because somebody says it is a message from God: test it first to see if it really is."[27]

The second guideline is that we should avoid contact with any idea or practice that even hints of being occult. The Old Testament commanded the Israelites, "Do not turn to mediums or seek out spiritists, for you will be defiled by them."[28] "Let no one be found among you who sacrifices his son or daughter in the fire, who practices divination or sorcery, interprets omens, engages in witchcraft, or casts spells, or who is a medium or spiritist or who consults the dead. Anyone who does these things is detestable to the Lord."[29] Isaiah later wrote that it is foolish to consult mediums and spiritists when we can have contact with the living God.[30]

Some have argued that these verses were written for a different era and are no longer applicable. Is it logical to assume, however, that the God who so strongly forbid such occult practices in the past would change his mind about the harmfulness of their influence? Apparently the early disciples didn't think that God had changed his mind. Following Paul's preaching at Ephesus, the new believers were instructed to bring their occult objects to a fire where they were destroyed completely.[31] The history of occult involvement is a history of people who became trapped following their contacts with Ouija boards, horoscopes, séances, and other occult practices.

Third, we must "test the spirits" to make sure that our minds are not embracing a spiritual counterfeit. There are at least two ways in which this is done:

1. We can recognize that anything or anyone who denies that "Jesus Christ has come in the flesh and is from God" is a false prophet.[32] There can be no clearer test. Some people claim to be followers of Jesus, but they don't mean the Jesus who is Lord.[33] Anyone who makes someone else lord, or anyone who denies that Jesus Christ is the Son of God, is deceived, and a deceiver.[34] We must be careful of the teachings of such people.

Many of the modern mind philosophies encourage people to find an "inner guide" who can advise and give direction. Such guides can be harmful substitutes for Christ who alone is sufficient to give us direction. Such inner guides may not be much different from the false Christs and false prophets that sometimes appear to do miracles and are so convincing that they even fool believers.[35]

2. It is clear that the true follower of Christ will have a life that is characterized by the fruit of the Spirit: love, joy, peace, patience, kindness, goodness, faithfulness, gentleness, and self-control.[36] There are counterfeits here too, of course, but the true believer is growing in these characteristics, consistently seeking to avoid involvement in sinful practices, and active in attempting to understand and obey the Scriptures.[37]

Fourth, in order to stand solidly against demonic influences, it is important that we be firmly grounded in the teachings of the Bible. Sincerity or good intentions do not act as a magical protection to keep us from demonic intrusion and deception.[38] Johanna Michaelsen wrote about this following her conversion. "I did not understand the importance of carefully, systematically studying His Word," she wrote. "I had no real understanding of *what* I believed or *why* I believed it. And so, in time, I began to build my relationship with God based on my experience. . . . Because of my ignorance of the Word of God, I became deceived."[39]

The apostle Paul wrote about this in his second letter to Timothy. He warned that times would come when people would not want to hear sound doctrine but would, instead, prefer to listen to speakers who would say what the listeners wanted to hear. To prevent such watered-down teaching, believers are instructed to be thoroughly familiar with the teachings of the Bible.[40] Ignorance of God's Word and failure to obey his teachings are among the major reasons that people's minds fall into error.

Finally, there must be a willingness to confront and resist demonic opposition. This cannot be done in our own strength, since no human being is powerful enough to resist the devil or smart enough to avoid his deceptive tactics.

When I was a college student, I once visited a church in British Columbia and heard the preacher speak on spiritual warfare. I don't remember the message being particularly inspiring or profound, but I do remember the text. It was 1 John 1:7: "The blood of Jesus Christ, God's Son, purifies us from all sin." The preacher urged his congregation to remember this whenever temptation came along. Because of the death of Christ on the cross, and the shedding of his blood for the sins of mankind, we are freed from satanic control.

Stating 1 John 1:7 or any other Bible verse can become a meaningless gimmick—a magic charm that we hope will get us out of difficult situations. That is not how the Bible should be used. But reminding ourselves (and the devil) of Scripture, especially Scripture that deals with the blood of Christ and his victory over Satan, can be the most powerful weapon to use in times of temptation.

Do you remember how Jesus responded when he was tempted by the devil in the wilderness? Jesus quoted Scripture.[41] Several years later, Paul stated that the best way to resist the devil was to "put on the whole armor of God," and to take the Word of God as our sword.[42]

All of this must be done in an attitude of prayer. We who are believers must never underestimate the power of prayer to bring protection in the midst of spiritual battles.[43]

Cults, Psychic War, and the Mind

It has been said that cults are always extrabiblical. They survive by adding to the Bible, taking away from it, distorting it, ignoring it, or publishing "keys" to help people understand it. Most of these movements resist any suggestion that there should be serious Bible study, and many—often with the sincerest of intentions—are intent on attracting people into their ways of thinking. No Christian is likely to be led astray if he or she is grounded in biblical teachings and willing to be obedient to its commands. Edgar Cayce made the tragic mistake of forsaking his biblical roots.

Is it possible that nations and governments can do the same? A recent report estimates that the Soviet Union spends several million dollars annually on research to investigate how telepathy and psychic mind powers can be useful in conducting war. Faced with the possibility of Russian psychic superiority, the United States now is spending about $500,000.00 annually (most from private foundations) to study the possible use of psychic mind powers as an aid to military intelligence.[44]

We have come a long way from the declaration of King David who wrote that the nation is blessed when their God is the Lord.[45] In this age of fascination with psychic activity, we would be wise to remember the message that God gave to King Solomon: "If my people who are called by my name will humble themselves and pray and seek my face and turn from their wicked ways, then will I hear from heaven and will forgive their sin and heal their land."[46]

Religious cults, psychic readers, and new movements that promise mind changes rarely say much about God as the Lord, but they are powerful and persuasive. Often they use careful mind-control techniques. It is to these techniques that we turn in the next chapter.

17
THE
CONTROLLED
MIND

Have you ever heard of Stephan Jones? He's married, hand-some, tall, in his mid-twenties, and employed as an installer of office systems. He lives in California but has nothing to do with the entertainment industry. He's not a writer, professional ath-lete, or politician, but stories about him have appeared from time to time in newspapers throughout the country. Stephan Jones doesn't like to give interviews but reporters and their read-ers find him intriguing. Why?

Stephan Jones is the only son of a famous father.

His father was Jim Jones, powerful leader of the Peoples Tem-ple cult, and the man who so controlled the minds of his fol-lowers, that 913 were persuaded to drink cyanide and die in a South American jungle camp known as Jonestown. Stephan Jones was away at the time of the massacre, so he escaped the fate of his fellow Jonestown dwellers. But the local authorities didn't know that the son was vehemently opposed to his father's mad schemes. Stephan had helped to build Jonestown and he knew many of the victims. Perhaps it isn't surprising, therefore, that he was arrested and thrown in jail when news of the murders became known.

The prison conditions were deplorable. The food was awful, the cells were infested by rats and cockroaches, and the other inmates were constantly threatening him. But Jim Jones' son used the time to think about his life. "For me," he told a reporter, "my therapy was prison. I found I could be totally alone and at peace with myself."[1]

Other Jonestown survivors have not been able to cope so well, and the relatives of those who died doubtless will always struggle with the incomprehensible issue of "why?" How could one man exert so much control over the minds of so many others?

THE MANIPULATED MIND

Shortly after the second World War, a British psychiatrist named William Sargant published a disturbing and highly influential book, *Battle for the Mind*.[2] Sargant had observed British soldiers and civilians collapsing under the stress of war, he had read about the stressful conditioning experiments, he knew about the brainwashing activities of the Communist Chinese, and he had pondered the reports of revival published in John Wesley's journals. In every case, Sargant concluded, people were changed by being aroused emotionally and sometimes physiologically until they reached a point of collapse. At that point they were much more open to accepting new ideas, especially ideas that offered relief from the aroused tension. The essence of revival meetings, according to Sargant, was the creating of guilt and fear in the congregation, followed by the promise of salvation and abundant life. It isn't surprising that some Christians reacted with quick and concise challenges to the Sargant theory.[3]

It has been suggested that history is largely a record of people's attempts—sometimes very successful—to impose their wills on others. Often this has been done by tyranny and war, but increasingly it appears that the battleplace is within the human mind.[4]

Mind-manipulation research has been conducted for decades by hundreds of scientists in dozens of countries on thousands of people hundreds of thousands of times. Behavior modification, a major school of psychological thought, dominates many university psychology departments; psychosurgery has been endorsed by a national commission established to investigate its dangers; microminiature electronic circuits are making control of the mind through direct brain stimulation a real possibility; drugs to control moods and emotions have become the largest and most profitable part of the pharmaceutical industry; the techniques of brainwashing appear to have been revived with great success by numerous religious sects; computer technology now makes possible monitoring (and therefore control) of intimate aspects of behavior by health, welfare, police and other government agencies, as well as by private employers, insurance companies, and credit bureaus;

... and branches of government for twenty-five years have applied to unwitting American citizens, and others, the fruits of centuries of tinkering with alteration of the mind. ...

Mind manipulation is no longer the exclusive domain of imaginative science-fiction writers, no longer the exceptional weapon to be used only on the enemy. Mind manipulation is present fact, and it affects all our lives.[5]

Everyone recognizes that lobotomies, brainwashing, torture, and electrical stimulation of the brain are all dangerous and unethical ways to influence human minds. But could it be argued that education, psychotherapy, preaching, advertising, book publishing, and television documentaries can also use dangerous and unethical ways to persuade and manipulate minds, sometimes by subtle means?

Each of these more traditional persuasive techniques assumes that the person who gets the message has the freedom to either accept or reject what is presented. Researchers have shown, however, that people don't always have as much freedom as they assume. And apparently they are especially likely to change when they think they have free choice and when the pressure to change is subtle and not very intense.[6]

This was shown dramatically in a study of fifty very successful salespeople.[7] When compared to less successful people, the effective sellers tend—consciously or unconsciously—to make use of three powerful but almost unnoticed techniques.

First, there is *rapport building*. Usually this begins with casual talk about the weather, the customer's family, or something equally relaxed but designed to build a bond between the seller and potential buyer. If the customer raises an objection to the sale or the product, the seller agrees but then goes on to add some opposing arguments. "Insurance is surely a waste of money," one prospective buyer said, and the agent heartily agreed. "But then," he added, "it does have a few uses such as . . ."

Research found that the good salesperson matches voice tone, rhythm, volume, speech rate, and even slang to that of the customer. If the customer seems depressed, the seller mentions that "As a matter of fact, I've been feeling a little down lately, too." To use the researchers' slang term, the goal of this part of the selling process is to "get in sync" with the customer.

Only after a bond of trust has been built do top salespeople move into *the soft sell*. They do this by working suggestions into the conversation, and even by giving the customer commands:

"If you look at the advantages and see the benefits, Tom, I am sure you will want to buy this car." Notice the last three words. They are a command, set within a sentence, and positioned after mentioning the customer's name. If spoken by a successful seller, there would also be a change in tone or speech rate so that a subtle emphasis would be put on these last three words.

Third, there is *frequent use of stories and anecdotes*. Have you ever thought about how a movie or television play can teach values about sex and morals? The viewer is not expecting to be persuaded, so he or she hasn't put up any defenses, and as a result the message is more likely to "get through." Some of the most successful salespeople in the research study did almost nothing except tell stories. They used parables to get attention, to build trust, and even to deliver product information, all tucked within interesting tales.

I cringed a little when I read about this research. These were exactly the techniques used by the salesperson who sold me the word processor that I am using to type these words. I was naive enough to think that I had made the decision to buy—all by myself!

That is what makes mind control so powerful and so dangerous. The controllers' tactics are subtle, and so casual that the "victim" does not see the need to resist or to put up a defense.

THE MARKETING MIND

Sometimes, however, a skilled writer can stir up controversy by dealing with an issue "head on." Vance Packard, for example, once wrote a highly popular exposé of the advertising industry, maintaining that Madison Avenue had now begun to bypass the conscious mind in order to control customers. According to Packard, it was possible to reach the consumer's unconscious and to stimulate sales, all apart from the buyer's awareness.[8]

As a college student, I can still remember the debates we had in psychology class about the validity of Packard's claims. In the midst of all this, an advertising executive announced the discovery of "subliminal perception."[9] It was now possible, he said, to flash words on a television or movie screen with such speed that viewers would not even realize what they were seeing. Appeals to buyers could thus be made directly to the unconscious mind, bypassing the consumer's conscious defenses altogether. Later research showed that subliminal advertising wasn't as powerful or as possible as its advocates claimed. But concern and discussion over commercial control of the mind continued, as they have to this day.

Positioning and the mind. Mind control has become of increasing concern as our society has shifted from an industrial to an information society.[10] It is estimated that about 60 percent of the population works on information jobs, including education, banking, secretarial work, computer use and programming, media work, counseling, and business. The blue-collar industrial worker is in a minority, and the trend is continuing toward increasing emphasis on the production and exchange of information.

Every year thousands of pamphlets, scientific papers, and magazine articles are published and distributed. In the United States alone, 30,000 books are published every year—books that the publishers compete with each other in trying to sell. The phenomenal boom in the personal computer industry means that information on virtually any subject can be available to people in their own homes. Add to this the information that comes by way of the media, advertising, education, or church meetings—and the information flow is staggering. As we saw in chapter ten, each mind can contain only an infinitesimal fraction of the information that is available.

All of this has been of concern to advertisers who want to market their products. How does one compete for attention and get one's advertising message into the minds of potential buyers who already are overwhelmed by too much information?

The answer, say two advertising executives, comes with "positioning."[11] People are not likely to respond solely to factual information and advertiser's claims about a product. In this information-saturated society, people don't need, and neither do they notice, more facts and information. So the advertiser (and presumably the educator and theologian) must look for holes in the receiver's thinking, and position one's messages so they enter the mind at these open points.

The best way to do this is to be first on the scene with a new idea. Kodak was first in photography, IBM in computers, Hertz in rent-a-cars, and Xerox in copiers. Those who come later can't dethrone the leaders by giving reports of a better product. More successful would be an emphasis on what the new product does that the leader does not. The name of one's product is important (for some reason "Cadillac" was better than "Edsel"), and so is the length of the message.

People are so overloaded with information that they aren't

impressed with long, complicated details of a product—even when the product is religion. Information-saturated advertisements, like long, flowery sermons, rarely get into people's minds. Instead, the good advertiser and communicator must "jettison the ambiguities, simplify the message," and sharpen the content so the idea can cut into the mind.[12] Professors, like me, might not like this conclusion, but it is surely true. To cope with complexity, people have learned to simplify everything. To reach contemporary minds, messages must be concise, carefully positioned, and unique enough to be noticed. Perhaps it isn't surprising that the advertising executives who plan these messages are well paid, and often are not very secure in their jobs. A good advertising campaign can earn millions; a bad advertising decision can lead to a company's bankruptcy.

The Perceiving Mind

If people's minds were passive, waiting patiently to receive incoming information, it might be easier to be an educator or advertiser. But, as we are well aware, minds aren't passive or like empty buckets waiting to be filled. Instead, our minds have been shaped by education and past experiences. Each of us has learned a variety of attitudes, expectations, opinions, biases, and viewpoints that cause our minds to exclude some messages, distort some, and misinterpret others.

This is what makes the psychology of perception so interesting. Introductory books in psychology often include visual illusions, like those in Figure 17-1, to show how our perceptions can be influenced by the environment. Business lunches are built on the premise that prospective deals look different over a casual lunch than they do in a cold office. Brainwashers realize that resistance is best broken down when the environment is controlled, so the persuader's message is more palatable. Films, even films of people preaching sermons, are assumed to carry more impact than live speeches or sermons, because the film is shown in the dark where many distractions are removed from view. Good perception depends on the environment as much as on the message.

It also is true that we see what we want to see, and what we expect to see. Everyone has heard that love is blind; we see good points in the one we love and often fail to notice the weak points. Psychologists call this "selective perception."

A.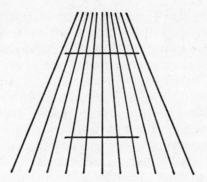

B.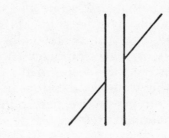

C.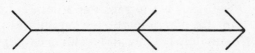

D.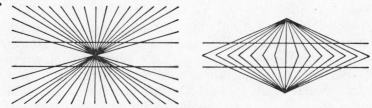

FIGURE 17-1

Optical illusions showing how the "setting" is important in perception. In A, the two horizontal lines are of equal length. In B, the lower half of the diagonal is an extension of the upper half. In C, both parts of the line are of equal length. In D, the pairs of horizontal lines are parallel.

But there is also something called "selective exposure." We let ourselves experience things that we enjoy or agree with, but we don't even seem to notice ideas that oppose our beliefs and attitudes. Several years ago the meter reader at a municipal waterworks noticed sharp rises in water consumption, exactly on the hour, every hour between 7:00 and 11:00 P.M. This is prime-time for television and apparently many people watch the programs, but then go to the bathroom and flush toilets all over the community whenever the commercials appear. Someone quickly named this the "flush factor." It is further proof of the selective exposure idea. People stay in their chairs during the programs but leave for the commercials.

You might want to think about this the next time you are subjected to a political campaign. Most people probably assume that their votes are influenced by the issues, but is it possible that we more often respond to the candidate's looks or personality? Most of us pay more attention to candidates who belong to "our party" and don't even read the views of the opposition. We would like to believe that we make decisions based on rational evaluation, but more often selective perception, selective exposure, bias, and emotional preferences determine how we vote.[13]

Do such perceptions also influence the votes of jurors in murder trials? Apparently, the answer is yes, and attorneys know this so well that many hire experts in communications, marketing, and the psychology of perception, to help in jury selection. "We can help predict and influence what takes place in a juror's mind during a trial," one California firm recently advertised.[14] They can do this by taking community surveys, finding the characteristics of jurors who are most likely to vote for conviction, and informing the defense attorneys so these pro-conviction people are rejected from the jury.

It should be emphasized that some lawyers question the effectiveness of such procedures, and so many challenged the ethics and fairness of such techniques that several states have passed laws to change jury selection procedures. But jury members still are influenced by the way a defendant is dressed, the way he or she sits, the looks and personalities of the lawyers, and the persuasive abilities of the courtroom participants. Add to this the jurists' personalities and perceptual biases and it is easy to wonder whether anyone can have a completely unbiased, fair trial.

THE PERSUADED MIND

None of us likes to think that our minds are being manipulated, and neither do we want to believe that our minds are closed. It is much more comforting, and self-flattering, to think that we are open to persuasion. This implies that we can accept or reject a message, based on careful, rational evaluation.

But effective persuasion is not as neutral or as free from pressure as we might like to believe. At the time of Socrates and Aristotle, there were men known as sophists who were paid to deliver speeches. Plato ridiculed such people because they were more interested in swaying minds than in presenting truth.[15] But even people who want to present truth use persuasive techniques. Some of these techniques have been known for centuries and within recent years social scientists have been able to determine the methods that really work.

Consider the following, for example.[16]

- People are more likely to change their opinions if you state your beliefs than if you let the audience draw their own conclusions.
- Pleasant forms of distraction can increase the effectiveness of a persuasive appeal.
- Information, by itself, almost never produces permanent changes. In time, the effects of oratory and persuasive communication wear off.
- People are more likely to change when the message is repeated more than once, and when the desired conclusion is presented at the beginning or at the end of the presentation, instead of in the middle.
- A persuasive appeal is more effective when people are required to be active (for example, by discussing an issue or by having to exert oneself to get information) than when they are merely passive listeners.
- Attempts to change people by arousing guilt and fear rarely bring lasting, internal change.
- People are most likely to be persuaded when they perceive that the communicator is in some way similar to themselves. A communicator's effectiveness is increased if he or she expresses some views that are also held by the audience.
- An audience is more likely to be persuaded if they perceive that the communicator has high credibility.
- If you assume that the audience might be hostile, it is most

effective to present facts first (building a case), give more than one side of the argument, and present your position at the end.

• Communication is most effective when information comes through different channels (for example, through pictures, brochures, media "spots," and rational arguments), from different people who present the same message, and repeatedly over a period of time.

THE PROCLAIMING MIND

This information about persuasion can be interesting, but it doesn't affect us much until we begin to consider two personal and practical questions: How can we persuade others? and How can we resist the attempts of other people to persuade us?

One way to consider these questions is to look at the issue of religious persuasion. In his letter to the Colossian church, Paul summarized his life purpose. All of his energies, he said, were directed toward proclaiming Christ, warning and teaching anyone who would listen.[17] Generations of Christians have had similar goals, as they have attempted to follow Christ's "Great Commission" to make disciples of all nations.[18]

How can we persuade others? Em Griffin is a professor at Wheaton College whose book, *The Mind Changers,*[19] has summarized many of the proven principles of good communication. It is important, he suggests, to decide first who we are trying to reach, then work on altering that person's beliefs, feelings, and plans.

All of this is done in the same way that people make candles. The wax must first be melted, then molded, and finally made hard. The same three steps must be part of any proclamation of the Christian message.

Melting, the first stage, takes time and is best done not by a bombastic "hard sell" but by the demonstration of consistent love, openness, gentle humor, dialogues (monologues don't do much to change people), and presentation of parables and images that help people think in terms of pictures.

The second stage, *molding,* comes by giving people incentives and reasons to change, by showing that change is credible, and by building one's case slowly. The good communicator, says Griffin, is honest, informed, enthusiastic, willing to disclose something about himself or herself, kind, pleasant, cheerful, sensitive, and responsive to others. Although people may be changed by powerful orators, dogmatic monologues, or speakers who vehemently attack the opposition, such changes are temporary and soon wear off. In contrast, the apostle Paul, whose life and communication were guided by the Holy Spirit, took a more sensitive approach.

> I have freely and happily become a servant of any and all so that I can win them to Christ. When I am with the Jews I seem as one of them so that they will listen to the Gospel and I can win them to Christ. . . . When with the heathen I agree with them as much as I can, except of course that I must always do what is right as a Christian. And so, by agreeing, I can win their confidence and help them too.
>
> When I am with those whose consciences bother them easily, I don't act as though I know it all and don't say that they are foolish; the result is that they are willing to let me help them. Yes, whatever a person is like, I try to find common ground with him so that he will let me tell him about Christ and let Christ save him.[20]

The third stage of Em Griffin's approach, *making hard,* comes through such techniques as modeling the way you want believers to act, putting them in contact with other believers, encouraging people to talk about their new beliefs, and guiding people as they live out their new beliefs in practice. Perhaps this was Paul's goal in proclaiming the gospel first, then "admonishing and teaching" individuals so they would move toward Christian maturity.[21]

How can we resist persuasion? The first "book" I ever wrote was really a thirty-two-page pamphlet dealing with the subject of how Christian students could be helped in their resistance of the anti-Christian arguments of professors and students on the secular campus. All of my formal education took place in secular universities and I had watched with real concern as some of my fellow Christians appeared to forsake their faith in response to the persuasive arguments of our teachers.

At the time that I wrote my booklet, I was impressed with the work of a communication researcher named William McGuire. My recent reading indicates that McGuire's conclusions of twenty years ago still command respect among his professional colleagues.[22]

Just as we vaccinate people against disease, McGuire proposed, so we can use persuasive inoculation as a "vaccine for brainwash." To do this, we should warn people that an attack is coming, expose them to a small dose of the arguments they will hear later, and give them experience in answering these arguments. Don't spoon-feed with answers, McGuire warned, because that robs people of the opportunity to do the mental calisthenics that will strengthen them and help them resist the attack. It helps, too, if people can keep in contact with others who share their beliefs. For the Christian there is the crucial importance of regular and consistent prayer and study of the Bible.

I once read of a camp where Christian high school seniors spent a week preparing to attend college. There were lectures on Bible study, discussions with Christian college students, and talks about the arguments that might be encountered in the future. Most helpful, however, were the attempts to put the vaccination theory into practice. One camp staff member wore a sign that said "Atheist" and tried to present the atheistic position all week, wherever he went. Other staff members took the roles of "Playboy," "Communist," "Humanist," "Skeptic," and several other philosophies. The students were thus made aware of perspectives that opposed their Christianity, and were given practice in dealing with these viewpoints.[23]

WHAT ABOUT MIND-CONTROL ETHICS?

Not long ago, a Stanford professor raised some thoughtful questions about "would-be mind controllers" who are springing up everywhere and whose tactics are subtle, whose strategies are insidious and whose influence is pervasive. "They sell us, educate us, treat us, service us and minister to us—after first persuading us of the need to pay willingly and dearly for their product."[24]

The professor was especially concerned about religious persuaders whose power seems to be increasing, and whose methods often are manipulative and insensitive to human needs. Is it right, some have asked, to pressure people into making decisions, to manipulate individuals by offering special gifts in return for an offering, to pair Christianity with patriotism or political movements in order to attract followers, or to use guilt arousal and emotionally charged pressure tactics in evangelistic services?

The Bible never gives examples or instructions to suggest that we should manipulate people against their wills, restrict their freedom to choose, or try to force them into making a decision to follow Christ. Such tactics are both wrong and certain to fail because they treat people like things to be manipulated, instead of like humans to be respected. Jesus never forced anyone to follow him, and he doesn't expect his followers to use high-pressure tactics to attract disciples.

It has been argued that people are much harder to change than most of us tend to believe, that stories of brainwashing and mind control are based more on fantasy than on reality, and that resistance to change is more effective than most of us think.[25] This may be true, but it is difficult to discount the power of a man like Jim Jones or to ignore the harmful influence of professional mind-controllers in our society. As individuals we must be careful not to fall into their selfish and dehumanizing tactics, especially when we want to persuade people of the truths of the gospel.

While the young Stephan Jones lives at peace in California, a survivor of another massacre has been living alone since 1948 at Spandau Prison in West Berlin. Rudolf Hess was Hitler's deputy and has been called "the last Nazi." Now in his nineties, Hess remains a mystery, and it appears that no one will ever understand his real motives for serving Hitler and participating in one of the most powerful and destructive mind-control movements of this or perhaps any century. Rudolph Hess is an old but living reminder of the awesome power of individuals who attempt to manipulate the minds of others.

But what can we say about people who are intent on controlling their own minds? That is the issue to which we now turn.

18
THE
DETERMINED
MIND

They've been doing it in India for centuries. It's been seen in Japan, incorporated into elaborate religious ceremonies in the Pacific Islands, and even demonstrated occasionally on American TV talk-shows. The initial rituals differ from place to place, but the end results are the same: human beings walk barefooted and without apparent pain across a bed of white-hot glowing coals.

The religious reasons for fire-walking are varied. Some do it to please their gods in hopes of getting better crops. Others do it as a purification rite. And some apparently do it to demonstrate their holiness. Critics call it occult, amazed onlookers may call it mystical, but a number of scientists have argued that it can be explained rationally.

"This fire-walking stuff is an old vaudeville trick," says UCLA professor Bernard Leiking. According to one popular explanation, little beads of sweat or droplets of dew from the grass form a protective vapor layer that insulates and protects the feet from burns. Some have suggested that calloused feet protect many fire-walkers, and others point out that most fire-walks are so rapid that the feet contact the coals for only a fraction of a second each time. It's like passing your finger through the flame of a candle. If you do it fast enough, you don't get burned, even if you do it repeatedly.

Perhaps it was inevitable that an enterprising young man would incorporate fire-walking into a self-help seminar and propose that it has something to do with the mind. Tony Robbins lives in Beverly Hills and conducts weekend "Fear into Success" workshops that are designed to help participants face their insecurities. The culmination comes when class members, some in three-piece suits or stylish dresses, walk barefoot across a ten-foot long bed of red-hot wood coals.

"It's fantastic," reported one fire-walker, a Pasadena therapist. "If all my clients did this, they wouldn't need me anymore." Others have concluded that this is positive proof the mind is powerful enough to block pain and even prevent flesh from burning.[1]

Most of the fire-walkers are determined people. They are facing their fears. They want to prove to themselves and to others that they can march across the hot coals and feel no pain. These are walking illustrations of the power of mental determination.

The history books are filled with other examples of determined minds. Everyone knows about people like Lincoln and Churchill who rose to prominence and a secure place in history after repeated failures early in life. We admire people who suffer strokes or heart attacks and yet are able to fight back and regain their health. We applaud those who succeed in casting off addictions so they can live productive lives. And we look with favor on the crusaders, explorers, missionary pioneers, and biblical heroes who persisted in their goals despite great resistance. Do you remember the workers in Nehemiah's lifetime who succeeded in rebuilding the walls around Jerusalem? They faced incredible opposition, but the job was completed, according to the Bible, because "the people had a mind to work."[2]

THE ATHLETIC MIND

Today we are best able to see determination and the "mind to work" when we watch athletic events. It isn't easy to train long hours and to face the tension of competitive sports. It takes time and patience to develop athletic skills. Nobody becomes a proficient competitor without discipline, discomfort, and determination.

But sometimes the most determined and highly trained athletes fail to win because they are too tense, too easily distracted, and too self-critical. Consider Paul Annacone, for example. At seventeen he was widely regarded as a young tennis prodigy, but he was also temperamental and easily distracted. When he lost an important championship match, he stomped off the court, slammed his fist into one of the lockers downstairs, and broke his hand. Paul Annacone demonstrated what coaches, players, and sports psychologists are beginning to see with increasing frequency. In sports, the greatest opponent you have is yourself and what goes through your mind, especially when you are not winning.

As a group, athletes are not psychologically maladjusted or more hostile than nonathletic people.[3] But athletes are often under great pressure. Think about how you would feel as a skier, standing at the top of a 90-meter ski jump, about to fly 400 feet into the air and land on ice—all while television cameras and thousands of countrymen back home are watching to see if you will win a medal—or maybe break your neck.

Even athletes who never compete in the Olympics often have a great need to succeed. Many struggle with envy or fear of failure. Professional team members sometimes don't know how to communicate or handle the intimacy of living, traveling, and working together for long periods of time. When such competitors become tense, their muscles don't relax, injuries become more likely, concentration is hindered, and performance slips.[4] Is it surprising that many of these people are turning for help to a new group of professionals known as sports psychologists?

While he was nursing his broken hand, for example, Paul Annacone received professional help in learning how to relax, how to maintain his concentration, and how to keep from condemning himself (and getting tense and inefficient) whenever he made a mistake. Before long, the young tennis player's game improved considerably.[5]

Almost forty years ago, the owner of the Chicago Cubs wanted to hire a psychologist to help his team members train their minds. The idea was ridiculed and the proposal was dropped, but in other parts of the world the training of athletic minds was being pursued with enthusiasm. There is now some evidence that the superiority of Soviet and Eastern bloc athletes is at least partly due to their mind-training. Dr. Raymond Abrezol believes this, and several years ago he had an unusual opportunity to test his beliefs.

The leader of the national Swiss ski team asked Dr. Abrezol if he would help the athletes prepare for the Olympics. A program was designed to help the skiers combat nervousness, lack of concentration, fatigue, fear of errors, lack of confidence, and anxiety about defeat. Four skiers were coached by Dr. Abrezol;

three won medals in the 1968 Olympics. Four years later, three different Swiss skiers won medals. According to Abrezol, his mental programs had liberated the competitors from unconscious fears that could cost them several hundredths of a second and cause them to lose the medal.[6]

Athletic mind-training programs are not all the same, but at least three characteristics are common: relaxation training, teaching people to concentrate, and showing athletes how to develop imagination skills.

Relaxation and the athletic mind. The Boston Marathon is a grueling, twenty-six-mile race that for many runners really begins at mile twenty. We who are nonjoggers might drop out at the end of the first half block, but the trained runners in the Marathon often run for eighteen to twenty miles before they begin to recognize their fatigue and sense that their bodies are dehydrated and beginning to hurt. To make matters worse, it is at this point that the runners face "Heartbreak Hill," a long, gradual climb, several miles from the finish line. Some call this "the wall," and it is at this point that many become dizzy and light-headed, and are forced to drop out of the race.

But for some runners, the wall doesn't exist. They keep on going to the finish line, without the mental struggle of having to fight the fear of dropping out. When those who saw the wall were compared with those who did not, some interesting differences appeared. The more successful runners tended to be less tense, less depressed, and more extroverted than the wall-facing group. And the two groups of runners used their minds differently during the race. Those who thought about other things as they ran—music, building a house, or going on a vacation—encountered the wall, and sometimes were so caught up in their fantasies that they failed to notice even if their bodies were injured. The other, more successful group thought more about the race—the pace they were keeping, the state of the body, and the need to relax. "I constantly remind myself to relax, hang loose, not tie up," one runner reported.[7] These successful runners had learned to apply some common relaxation techniques: concentrate on what you are doing at the moment, break your tasks into smaller blocks of time and more narrow goals, learn to breathe carefully, and don't dwell on your mistakes.[8]

Concentration and the athletic mind. There is a story about a professional football player who always left for a game at precisely the same time, always dressed from left to right, always kicked a specific locker room door twice before going on to the field, always stood on the forty-nine-yard line while the national anthem was played, and sometimes would run back to repeat the ritual if he missed a part of it before the game began. Not all athletes are this ritualistic, but many have little activities that they do regularly hoping these will help reduce anxiety, bring them luck, or help them concentrate.

Mental concentration is a major characteristic of successful athletes. Sports hypnotist Harvey Misel has stated this emphatically. "When athletes reach a professional level, they all have talent, ability, and brawn," Misel said in a recent interview. "How many times have you wondered why an athlete never reached his potential? His potential was in his mind. . . . It's not the mind alone. It's mind and body together. But nobody pays attention to the mind."[9]

That is changing. Psychiatrist William Glasser suggests that mind concentration is at the core of effective play,[10] and Timothy Gallwey's best-selling book, *The Inner Game of Tennis,* has an entire chapter on quieting the mind and another on the skill of concentration.[11] Many experts recognize that concentration is most successful when the individual is relaxed, and many programs suggest that one of the best ways to improve one's concentration and overall game is through the use of imagery.

Imagination and the athletic mind. In the 1984 Winter Olympics, two American brothers, Phil and Steve Mahre, won the gold and silver medals in skiing. On the night before the race they were pictured on television, standing at the top of the ski run, mentally rehearsing the coming competition. Clearly, the brothers had learned what other athletes are discovering: There can be great value in mentally visualizing a coming sports event, running through the entire sequence in vivid and finite detail. The skier, for example, starts at the top of the run, performs every maneuver mentally, and goes back to start over if there is a mistake. Jack Nicklaus and Gary Player reportedly have used this technique repeatedly with golf. Arnold Schwarzenegger, the body builder, maintains that a large part of weight lifting begins in the mind. "As long as the mind can envision the fact that you can do something, you can," he has stated. "I visualized myself being there . . . having achieved the goal already."[12]

It even seems that mental practice can be helpful. In one study, high-school basketball players of equal ability were divided into three groups. One group practiced twenty-five basketball free throws daily. Another group came to the gym and imagined themselves shooting twenty-five free throws. A third group did nothing. Fourteen days later everyone was tested. There was no improvement in the third group. The first group showed a twenty-five percent improvement, but the second group improved almost as much, simply by imagining the free throws.[13] Nobody proposes that an athlete should simply sit on the sidelines and practice mentally, but when visual imagination and practice are combined, concentration and athletic performance both improve.

THE BECOMING MIND

Jesse Owens was one of the most famous athletes that America ever produced. In 1936 he won four gold medals at the Olympics in Germany and embarrassed Hitler in his own home town. How did Owens do it? How did he change from a "little skinny, scrawny black boy" to gain international fame as the world's fastest human being?

It began when a coach visited Jesse Owens' junior high school and gave a talk about mental determination. "You can pretty well become what you make up your mind to be," the speaker exclaimed. "God will help you."

After the speech, young Jesse went over to the coach and told him "I've decided what I want to be—the fastest man in the world!"

"That's a great dream," the coach replied, "but there is one problem. Dreams have a way of floating high in the sky and drifting around like clouds. A dream never becomes a reality unless you have the courage to build a ladder to your dream."

Then the coach told Jesse how the ladder could be built. "You build one step at a time. The first rung is determination—a refusal to give up. The second is dedication. Then comes discipline and the fourth rung is your attitude."[14] Jesse Owens learned his lesson well and stuck with his dream until it became a reality.

Some people don't have any dreams and others have visions that are as intangible as clouds. But according to Gordon Allport, a famous Harvard psychologist, we are all in the process of becoming what we will someday be. Allport even gave one of his books the simple title *Becoming*.

Athletic trainers, like Jesse Owens' coach, train young competitors to use their minds so they determine to win and imagine that they are successful. Many find that they are able to become what they imagine. Similar approaches are used with people who want to become successful salespeople, better public speakers, or effective performing artists. Think about what you can become, the trainers suggest, and in time you will find yourself moving in that direction.

This kind of visualizing undoubtedly is helpful for improving one's self-confidence or skills, but mental pretending and self-centered determination can also be dangerous. When students in a speech class pretend to defend a position in which they don't really believe, there often is a move in the direction of the position they are defending. If, for the sake of discussion, you pretend to be an atheist, in time you might find yourself becoming more sympathetic to the atheistic position. Convince yourself that you are "oversexed" and in time you will find yourself acting on your convictions. *It doubtless is true that people become what they think about.*[15] C. S. Lewis once warned that "all mortals tend to turn into the thing they are pretending to be."[16]

It is important, therefore, that each of us determines to become the kind of person we really want to be and whom God wants us to be. "We are the children of God," John wrote in his first epistle. "What we will be has not yet been made known. But we know that when he appears, we shall be like him."[17]

There probably is nothing wrong with determining to be competent or successful, but the Christian should also be determined to be Christlike. That isn't easy, and it brings us to an issue of self-control that may be more difficult than winning a tennis game, breaking through an invisible wall in the Boston Marathon, or "climbing a ladder to the clouds."

In one of his epistles, John wrote that everyone who hopes to see Christ again should seek to be pure, just as Christ is pure.[18] The Christian, therefore, should be determined to develop and keep a mind that is pure.

THE PURE MIND

The apostle Peter must have been an impulsive fellow. He once got out of a boat in the middle of a lake and started walking across the water to meet Jesus. In the Garden of Gethsemane, he swung his sword at a well-armed soldier, and later he denied Jesus with cursing and swear words. Following the resurrection, Peter jumped out of a boat again and swam to greet Jesus on the shore, this time leaving his fellow fishermen to pull in the catch without his help.

But it appears that Peter changed, and when he wrote his two biblical epistles, he was deeply concerned about a different and devastating kind of impulsiveness that was creeping like a cancer into the early church. People who were claiming to be Christians had given in to their lusts and were seducing others away from wholesome thinking.

These people, Peter wrote,

carouse in broad daylight. They are blots and blemishes, reveling in their pleasures while they feast with you. With eyes full of adultery, they never stop sinning; they seduce the unstable; they are experts in greed—an accursed brood! They . . . mouth empty, boastful words and, by appealing to the lustful desires of sinful human nature, they entice people who are just escaping from those who live in error. They promise them freedom, while they themselves are slaves of depravity—for a man is a slave to whatever has mastered him.[19]

These people had minds that thought about adultery and this led them into sin. They were intent on leading unstable people astray and were motivated by personal greed. Their thinking was so distorted that, like many people in our day, they boasted about their sexual freedom and liberation but failed to realize that they really were enslaved by their own passions. Their minds were filthy, distorted, and determined to ignore God's standards of purity.

They probably didn't reach this kind of thinking overnight. Minds are changed in small steps. A casual idea, a fleeting glance, a savored fantasy, a pondered seduction—each of these can add up to the kind of overt immorality that ruined the life and reputation of King David.

Recently, I heard about a pastor who had run off with a female member of his congregation. I was distressed at this news but not as shocked or surprised as I might have been a few years ago. Most of us have heard similar stories too frequently. How often we need to remember Paul's warning that "if you think you are standing firm, be careful that you don't fall."[20] No thinking human mind is immune from temptation.

How, then, does one keep a pure mind? To keep the mind pure, we must avoid contact with pornography, immorality on the television screen, and other sexually arousing materials, insofar as this is possible in our sex-saturated society. We must openly resist evil[21] and make a habit of letting our minds dwell not on immoral fantasies but on whatever is true, noble, right, pure, lovely, admirable, excellent, and praiseworthy.[22] It is helpful to pray about one's sexuality, asking for divine help with self-control and fulfillment. There also can be value in finding an understanding Christian friend of the same sex with whom one can pray and give account of one's struggles with sexual lusts.

Some people have also been helped by a psychological gimmick known as "thought stopping." Whenever one has an immoral thought say "Stop!"—out loud if no one else is around. Sometimes the technique is more effective if a rubber band is worn loosely around the wrist. When the undesirable thought occurs, say "Stop!" and flick the rubber band to give a slight punishment.

Ultimately, however, thought stopping may be a temporary measure that must be set within the context of more powerful mind-purification procedures. These have been summarized in the last few verses of Peter's second letter.

- Make it a habit to read and understand the Scriptures, including the teachings of Old Testament prophets, New Testament apostles, and Jesus himself.[23] The Bible is not a magic defense against temptation, but the Bible *is* "God-breathed and useful" for teaching us, rebuking, correcting, and training us to be righteous.[24]
- Be alert to temptation and on guard against the arguments of the people who tempt.[25] It is easiest to resist an attack when we know it is coming.
- Be aware of God's nature.[26] Sometimes we forget that God is patient, forgiving, willing to help, aware of our thoughts or struggles, and able to protect us from overwhelming temptation.[27] When our view of God is too small, we feel powerless and are more inclined to fall into impure thought and actions.
- Make a consistent and determined effort to live holy, spotless, blameless lives.[28] Sometimes, of course, we will fail at this, but with God's help we can resist temptation and live in purity.
- Recognize that we cannot keep pure minds in our own strength. Instead, we need to rely on God's wisdom, trusting him to help us grow in the knowledge of God.[29]

Some well-meaning Christians have suggested that with special prayer services, the committed believer can be delivered from temptation and freed immediately from immoral thinking. But that rarely happens—if ever. The purification of one's mind is an ongoing process. It may involve confessing sinful thoughts or actions and receiving forgiveness several times every day. When we expect to pray and get pure minds immediately, and then find that this does not happen, we can be discouraged because we fail to recognize that pure minds come slowly.[30]

THE PERSISTENT MIND

Rick Little is a young man with a purpose. As a teenager, he was injured so seriously in a car accident that the doctors wondered if he would ever walk again. But he persisted in his therapy and recovered completely. After being released from the hospital, he started interviewing other young people about their emotions and struggles in coping with life. It came as no surprise when he found that many were unprepared for facing stress and unable to find the needed help.

Recently, the superintendent of California's Orange County Department of Education described Rick Little as "a modern day Paul Revere intent on awakening America to the need for . . . character education for youth."[31] But nobody paid much attention to this young Paul Revere at first. He approached 155 foundations, asking for funds to support his goal of helping young people to develop life skills and sound moral values. All 155 turned him down.

But on the next try, he acquired some funds. He started an organization called Quest[32] and has seen a massive character-building program develop that will soon be operating in thousands of schools in countries around the world. The work is now supported by over thirty foundations, by well-known people such as comedian Bill Cosby, and by the International Lions Clubs. Rick Little is a living example of a Christian who had a dream and was determined to see something good accomplished.

Determination and persistence are good qualities, but they can be dangerous if they are used selfishly to build personal empires or to put down other people. But persistence, purity, and self-control can be awesome, powerful forces for good when the determined mind is also a mind that is committed to Christ and willing to contemplate his nature and goodness.

19
THE
CONTEMPLATIVE
MIND

Henri Nouwen had always wanted to live in Rome. Born and raised in Holland and ordained there as a Catholic priest, Nouwen had spent a number of years in the United States. He had taught at Notre Dame and Yale, written several highly acclaimed books, and seriously considered the possibility of pastoral work in South America. Still, he wanted to spend some time in Rome, so when the opportunity arose, he accepted eagerly.

Those of use who are not Roman Catholics probably cannot appreciate the euphoria that a dedicated priest might feel, given the opportunity to live within sight of the Vatican. Henri Nouwen was moved by the red-robed cardinals and the impressive ceremonies in Piazza San Pietro. He was jolted by the Red-Brigade activists and the distressing political violence in Piazza Venezia. But he was most impressed by the unsung acts of service performed every day by little-known people whom he affectionately called "the clowns of Rome."

"I started to realize," Nouwen wrote in describing his experiences, "that in the great circus of Rome, full of lion tamers and trapeze artists whose dazzling feats claim our attention, the real and true story was told by the clowns."

Clowns are not in the center of the events. They appear between the great acts, fumble and fall, and make us smile again after the tensions created by the heroes we came to admire. The clowns don't have it together, they do not succeed in what they try, they are awkward, out of balance, and left-handed, but . . . they are on our side. We respond to them not with admiration but with sympathy, not with amazement but with understanding, not with tension but with a smile. Of the virtuosi we say, "How can they do it?" Of the clowns we say, "They are like us." The clowns remind us with a tear and a smile that we share the same human weaknesses.[1]

The longer he stayed in Rome, the more Nouwen enjoyed and appreciated the clowns. He called them "peripheral people who by their humble, saintly lives evoke a smile and awaken hope."[2] They are at work, even in places terrorized by violence, immobilized by apathy, or enslaved by self-centered materialism. Such "clowns" are not inclined to be pompous or demanding. They don't boast about their accomplishments or say much about their dedication. They don't spend time criticizing, accumulating wealth and honors, or trying to undercut the work of others.

Instead, these people tend to be humble servants, committed to Christ, and dedicated to serving others. When we are tempted to join the "lion tamers and trapeze artists who get most of the attention," these people remind us that "what really counts is something other than the spectacular and the sensational."[3] Clowns like this offer consolation, comfort, hope, encouragement, realistic values, and a little humor when we are inclined to take life too seriously. And often the minds of these rare people seem to be molded by consistent times of meditation and prayer.

THE MEDITATING MIND

In the mid-1960s, when college campuses around the world were in turmoil and revolution, an insightful little man from India, with a strange sounding name, was quietly launching a missionary movement that was to have great impact, especially in America. Mararishi Mahesh Yogi wanted to spread the doctrine of Transcendental Meditation (TM) around the world. To potential converts, he said little about the Hindu basis of TM, but instead emphasized its ability to calm troubled minds, remove anxiety, and bring inner peace.

Thousands of people embraced the TM message. Therapists began to recommend its use to their clients. The United States government allocated money to study its effectiveness, and education departments around the country began to introduce it into high school curricula until court challenges proved that TM was not a science, as it claimed, but was really a subtle religion.

Undaunted, many Christians began to learn TM techniques, and some might have agreed with the man who wrote to a magazine proclaiming that TM could be "a valuable aid to Christian living and Christian counseling."

"I tried the easy practice" of TM, the man wrote in his letter, "and it worked. No memorizing, analyzing, concentrating or exercising. The anxieties, stresses, aches, frustrations, and pressures gradually slip off and serenity slips in. And at the end of fifteen or twenty minutes I arise energized and glad."

The writer wondered if TM could free Christians from their need to use tranquilizers and could give them more energy and harmony to serve the church. He stated that TM exercises left him refreshed, unlike his times in prayer and Bible study when he had to use his mind rationally. Bible study is work, he complained, but TM is simple and relaxing.[4]

How do we evaluate Transcendental Meditation? Since its introduction and initial popularity several years ago, TM has been evaluated both scientifically and theologically.

Initially, the scientists were like the TM believers—enthusiastic, impressed, and convinced that they had found a new way to calm the mind. But the scientific research didn't back up these enthusiastic hopes. Early research found that TM did not alter the personality, change one's self-image, or reduce anxiety. It is a waste of time, one Stanford researcher concluded. When meditators are compared with nonmeditators who take time to sit still periodically, there are no differences.[5]

A more recent report showed similar findings. After evaluating the meditation research done over a fifteen-year period, the report reached this concise conclusion: There is no evidence that meditation is more effective for "reducing somatic arousal" than is simple resting.[6] Meditation in itself does not have the power to calm people down and reduce anxieties.

Christian theologians are not surprised by such research. It is now well known that TM is a form of Hindu religion that believes in the innate goodness of human beings, the ability of individuals to save themselves by works and without Christ, the worship of a swami named Guru Dev, and the conviction that TM is a path to God.[7] All of this contradicts the Bible's teachings that salvation is by faith in Christ, not by works (and certainly not by the reciting of Hindu words);[8] that only through Jesus Christ can humans come to God;[9] and that it is useless to pray in "meaningless repetition," saying the same words over and over again.[10]

This does not mean that all meditation is useless. Many of the greatest saints throughout history have been meditators, and the Bible mentions meditation in several places. But biblical meditation is different from TM and other Eastern meditations. Eastern meditation attempts to empty the mind and to focus on meaningless words known as mantras. Christian meditation seeks instead to fill the mind with biblical truths and thoughts about God.[11] Psalm 1, for example, calls the person "blessed" who meditates on God's law both in the morning and evening. Psalm 119 mentions meditation five times, and each time the meditation contemplates God or his precepts. Joshua learned that the secret of his success as a national leader could only come if he would meditate on God's law and be careful to practice what he read there.[12]

J. I. Packer once defined meditation using words that are both thought-provoking and difficult to understand. Meditation, he suggests, is "the activity of calling to mind, and thinking over, and dwelling on, and applying to oneself, the various things that one knows about the works and ways and purposes and promises of God. It is an activity of holy thought, consciously performed in the presence of God, under the eye of God, by the help of God, as a means of communication with God."[13] Unlike the intellectual study of Scripture, meditation is a process of pondering the Scriptures and applying them to our own lives. "The act of meditation is calling to mind those thoughts which are already in your memory, bringing them up and thinking about them, weighing them, evaluating them, discussing them with yourself, trying to explore the depth of a certain memorized passage. It is a kind of mental massaging" that involves a quiet contemplation of divine truths.[14]

There is no scientific data to suggest that such meditation will remove anxieties or solve all of one's problems. To live is to have problems and tensions, but Christian meditation can calm the mind. This is the kind of meditation that gives one a greater awareness of God's nature, a greater purity, less selfishness, more hope, a desire to reach out to others, and the assurance that comes when we know that God is in control.

THE PRAYING MIND

Is God in control when you experience a tragedy? My mind says yes to that question, but I confess that I wondered about it on the morning that our church burned. It had been a beautiful building, filled so often with fine people, a dynamic program, helpful preaching, and outstanding music. But some disgruntled person slipped into the building late one night, poured gasoline throughout the sanctuary, struck a match, and left. By the time a passing policeman noticed the fire, flames were already licking skyward through the roof.

The high school kids were among the first to appear with buckets and mops to start the cleanup of what was left of our building. The church members talked bravely of reconstruction, the local newspaper commented on our determination and unquenchable spirit, the community rallied around with offers of help or support, and many agreed that this must have been in accordance with God's perfect will.

But a lot of my enthusiasm had gone up in the flames. I didn't make much effort to attend the congregational meetings that were called to talk about rebuilding, and I tended to be somewhat critical of the fund-raising campaign that followed. Imagine my dilemma, therefore, when the church leadership asked if I would give a series of lectures on prayer, to help us keep our priorities straight during the crucial days following the fire.

I was aware that talking about prayer, reading about prayer, and even thinking about prayer can often distract one from praying. I was convinced that no one person could be an expert on prayer—certainly not me—and I feared that my talks might be politely received but ignored in practice. Nevertheless, I agreed to give the series and launched into a study that had a great influence on my own mind and prayer life.

The purpose of prayer. To begin, I had to ask honestly why any of us should take valuable time to pray, especially when we are busy with work, planning, and things that *need* to be done. I was jolted when I read the conclusion of Jacques Ellul, the French theologian and social critic. Most of us get along very well without prayer, he wrote. Even in our churches we spend more time planning than praying. We tend to dismiss prayer as a ritual at the beginning or end of a meeting, but rarely do we think of prayer as a sincere indication of our dependence on God.

In spite of this, there is one main reason why we must pray: God has commanded it.[15]

Andrew Murray was a missionary and writer who once wrote about "the sin of prayerlessness."[16] When we don't use our minds to pray, we are being disobedient, self-centered, spiritually weakened, and hindered by Satan. The disciples asked Jesus to teach them to pray; many of us need help in even wanting to pray.

Perhaps it would be helpful for us to ponder what prayer does.

Prayer lets us draw closer to God. William Carey once wrote that "secret, fervent, believing prayer—lies at the root of all personal godliness."[17] Without prayer we cannot hope to grow spiritually, please God, or experience the inner joy and peace that comes from closeness with the heavenly Father.

Prayer lets us serve God more effectively. We are great believers in self-help books and programs, careful planning, money-raising appeals, and management by objectives. In themselves, none of these is wrong. Too often, however, we plan ahead, using our own creative minds, but without much inclination to pause for a consideration of what might be the mind and will of God.

Patti Roberts is a Christian singer who once was involved in a popular and influential religious television program. The performers were sincere people who really wanted to serve God and help others. But the scheduling and pressure of rehearsals kept the television personalities separated from the very people they sought to serve. Audience acclaim had let them become Christian superstars, addicted to the intoxicating power and prestige that comes with fame. The busy schedules and concerns about finances had so distorted their values that many of their efforts were directed toward little else than keeping the program alive.

> We lived luxurious, storybook lives, but all of our acquisitions and acclaim still left us very lonely and tired and spiritually hungry. We had built a wonderful machine in the name of God, and now all of our efforts were focused on keeping it running. At all costs it must never be allowed to stop. So, the masters eventually became the slaves and the machine that we had created now controlled us.[18]

People who write about positive thinking rarely mention conclusions such as this. These television people were dedicated individuals with all kinds of creativity and drive. Their planning and positive mindset had created a machine, designed to serve God. Apparently, however, the creators had forgotten to seek God's direction. They had given little prayerful thought to what *he* wanted. Any one of us could fall into the same error.

Prayer lets us get closer to others. When we are praying for or with another person, it is difficult to hold grudges, criticize, undercut, refuse to forgive, or not get along. Is this one of the reasons why group prayer is so often mentioned in the Bible? It isn't easy to stay mad at a prayer partner. Before Christ, the walls of criticism and partition tend to come down.

The psychology of prayer. Psychiatrist Eric Berne, the founder of a popular form of therapy known as transactional analysis (TA), wrote a best-selling book, *Games People Play.*[19] The author believed that most of us go through life playing mental "games" that keep us from facing reality, hide ulterior motives, and sometimes keep us from honestly dealing with our doubts and insecurities.

Is it possible that we use similar mind games when we face the subject of prayer? Consider, for example, the game that we might call *genie*. This sees prayer as a magic gimmick for bargaining with God and manipulating him into giving us what we want. God is pleased when people pray fervently and persistently. He expects us to make our wants and requests known to him, and he has promised to supply our needs.[20] But prayer should be entered into with an attitude of submission, not with demands and attempts to manipulate. By treating God as a genie we are trying to control the divine will and in so doing we make prayer powerless.

When we play the game of *conscience-soothing*, we often feel better. Sometimes we pray before meals, before a meeting, or before a trip, because it gives a nod to God, eases the conscience, and reduces guilt. Often these prayers also become meaningless rituals that aren't very sincere and don't mean much to anyone.

Somewhat different is the game of *protest*. Here we try to undercut someone else by telling God what is wrong with another person and piously reminding the Almighty that our side is the right side. Verbal broadsides in public prayer may help us feel superior, but they rarely change anyone and they disobey the scriptural injunction that we are not to be judgmental.[21]

The games of *heavy* and *quickie* are more easily challenged. The first of these assumes that true prayer is always long and boring. It fails to realize that when prayer is too ponderous and difficult, it is also dull and not very effective. Prayer can be brief and concise. It can involve communication with God wherever we are and whenever our minds think about praying. But prayer that is always quick and "on the run" never leads to much spiritual depth. To learn to pray, we need to set aside time to pray.

On close examination, the *yes-but* game can be seen as a type of doubting. We think, "Yes, God provided in the past—but I don't think he is likely to do that again." "Yes, he is powerful—but surely he couldn't do what I want." "Yes he has helped others—but I doubt that he will help me." These thoughts show a wavering faith and a questioning of God's promises and faithfulness.

When we think like this, it is helpful to ask God to strengthen our faith. It is good, too, to look again at the promises of God recorded in the Bible.

Perhaps one of the most common psychological prayer games is something we might call *self-talk*. This is where we wonder if prayer is really a form of mind deception by which we talk to ourselves and then pretend or persuade ourselves that we are communicating with God. This type of thinking implies that prayer is a mental escape from reality. It is thinking that sees prayer as an activity which calms minds and stimulates hope, even though it might not have anything to do with the supernatural.

This is a difficult view to challenge. The skeptic who believes that "answers to prayer" are only coincidences or examples of selective perception is unlikely to be changed by hearing personal testimonies. Most of us who believe in prayer would have to agree that for some people, prayer *is* little more than a calming form of mental self-talk.

But biblical prayer involves faith in God, a belief in his power, and an awareness of someone greater than ourselves. Biblical prayer involves much more than the sharing of requests and the listing of personal needs. It is an act of worship and dedication, involving commitment and a willingness to be a servant. We see this when we look at the practice of prayer.

The practice of prayer. On the outskirts of Rockford, Illinois, a nine-acre plot of land sits encircled by a low wall and surrounded by a neighboring community of low-income homes. The walls enclose "The Corpus Christi Monastery of the Poor Clare Sisters," a community of twenty-one women who range in age from twenty-six to ninety-two and who live twenty-four hours a day within the religious complex. They almost never leave except for medical emergencies. Instead, they have taken a vow of "enclosure" and have committed themselves to poverty, chastity, obedience, and a lifestyle of continued prayer and penance. The sisters believe that the best ways to help people and change the world are to devote one's life and nonworking hours to prayer.[22]

It would be easy to admire and to criticize these religious women at the same time. Their devotion and dedication is admirable, but is withdrawal into a monastery the best way to change the world? Whatever your opinion might be, it seems that the Poor Clares have accepted some principles that often are ignored or overlooked by many of us whose lives are more hectic and busy. The sisters believe that the praying mind can make a difference in this world and they are determined to take prayer seriously.

According to the Bible, it doesn't much matter where, when, or how long we pray. There is no one best position for prayer and neither are we expected to pray using specific words. The "Lord's prayer" that Jesus gave his disciples focuses both on praise to God and on the needs of humans, but apparently it was intended to be more a model for prayer than a form to be recited.

Lloyd John Ogilvie, senior pastor of Hollywood's First Presbyterian Church, has written that we often come to God with our requests and petitions, but we fail to realize that the most effective prayer begins by asking God to show us what he wants us to pray for, and how *he* wants us to pray. We must come to him with open minds that are attentive to what God wants.[23] And we need to recognize that effective, powerful prayer includes several parts.[24]

- *Adoration* involves pondering God's nature and praising him for his characteristics. "Praising Him reestablishes the fact in our minds that He knows what He is doing and makes us receptive to His guidance."[25] It is tempting to rush past this part of prayer but to do so is to make prayer times less meaningful or effective.
- *Confession* is the act of admitting our sins and failures, and then asking for his forgiveness. It also means that we ask God to point out the things that he wants us to confess, change, and correct in our lives.
- *Thanksgiving* is not something we reserve only for a special time each year. The mind of the believer should be filled with gratitude, and spilling into expressions of thanks to God.[26]
- *Commitment* has been called the missing ingredient of contemporary Christianity, and the reason why many people find prayer to be boring. Many people believe in Christ but have never really committed their lives, families, careers, and plans to his leadership and control. This needs to be a regular part of prayer.
- *Meditation* comes next. The psalm writer knew that meditation leads to understanding.[27] Meditation is a pondering of God's will and a restatement of our openness to his leading. It is also a time of asking God to show us what and who we should pray for.
- *Supplication*, the next step, involves making requests for ourselves and for others—and asking God to show us what we should request.

• *Dedication* involves taking action following prayer. This does not mean that we end the time of prayer by taking matters back into our own hands. Instead, it is a determination to do what we can to "back up our prayers" with whatever practical action we can take.

Too often, I suspect, we find prayer to be dull, boring, and irrelevant for contemporary minds. We don't like to admit that prayer is sometimes a struggle,[28] but prefer instead to think of it as a therapeutic technique or a friendly "little talk with Jesus." True prayer involves a willingness to "break out of our monologue with ourselves and to follow Jesus by turning our lives into an unceasing conversation with our heavenly Father."[29]

The Open and Closed Mind

It would be simplistic to think that meditation and prayer are the only marks of true spirituality. Various writers have talked about the spiritual growth that comes from study, service for others, worship, giving, fasting, submission, and other spiritual disciplines. Each of these can characterize the contemplative mind.

Recently, my wife and I traveled to the campus of a nearby university where I had been invited to give a lecture on the mind. As we were leaving the lecture hall, an effervescent lady approached us and began to talk about her view of personality. She radiated enthusiasm but demonstrated that she had made up her mind and was not open to any ideas that might challenge or conflict with her theory. It was hard for us to get away. The lady was convinced that my wife and I needed to be converted to the system that she embraced so completely—a system of thought that we had rejected on the basis of published psychological research.

As we drove home, I was reminded of a friend who believes that we are moving into an era of "new legalism." We have become so flexible and open to new ideas in our society, that many people don't know what they believe. When people are floundering, they quickly latch on to any speaker or other leader who offers a concise, logical system that gives easy answers and claims to have the truth.

This has happened in the secular society, but it is also seen in church people like the lady who followed us out of the lecture. Christian groups are often influenced by writers, pastors, and seminar leaders who have attracted great followings. "Forget everything you have ever heard about the issue I am discussing," a famous preacher said in a sermon recently. "I want to tell you what the Bible says, so you will know what is true." Members in the audience nodded their heads in agreement, apparently not realizing that other Bible scholars had reached contrasting conclusions about the same issue.

Several years ago, a psychological researcher named Milton Rokeach produced a massive study on open and closed minds. Closed minds, he concluded, are dogmatic, prejudiced, rigid, too threatened to consider new ideas, and hard to change. People with closed minds sometimes have a clear idea of what they believe, but they are unwilling to hear other perspectives and refuse to change. Sometimes these people even boast about their open minds, but their thinking is really closed.

Can contemplation help us know what we believe but, at the same time, keep us from being rigid and insensitive to those who think differently? In the chapters of this book we have considered a variety of issues. Some statements have been controversial and undoubtedly have stimulated disagreement. I hope they have also stimulated our minds to clearer thinking.

It may be, however, that the most important issue of all is the one that we consider now as we move to the last chapter. What does it mean to have a Christian mind?

20
THE
CHRISTIAN
MIND

Who could have predicted that Miss Santmyer would become famous—at age eighty-eight? She was born in the little town of Xenia, Ohio, lived there for most of her life, taught English at a local college, and later worked as a reference librarian. When she retired, Helen Santmyer started work on a huge novel about a local women's club.

The book took years to complete, and when it was finished, no one wanted to publish it. The story described the events of a small Ohio town—a town very much like Xenia—as seen through the eyes of a group of matrons, spinsters, and clergymen's wives who were members of a literary club between 1868 and 1932. Critics called the book irrelevant, boring, uninspiring, tedious, repetitious, and small-minded. Readers complained that it was too long, too ponderous, and not very fashionable because it had no violence, no dirty language, and no sex scenes.

But the manuscript was "discovered" by a housewife whose son was in the publishing business, accepted as a main selection by the Book-of-the-Month Club, propelled into best-seller status, and touted by the publisher as a literary phenomenon. Bedridden, frail, and almost blind, Miss Santmyer mustered all the strength available in her eighty-four-pound frame and rose to accept the acclaim and attention when her book was produced. She was the subject of a three-page spread in *Life* magazine, described in newspapers around the country, and interviewed by representatives from the major television networks. From all over the world, letters came to the author's nursing home address, expressing excitement over her achievement, and thanking her for proving that it is never too late to be successful. People who didn't like the novel[1] nevertheless found hope and encouragement in the story of an obscure little old lady who had found fame and fortune in the last days of her life.

One report called Miss Santmyer "the darling of the news media." Hardened reporters were captured by her charm and modesty, and several noted that her weakened body supported a sharp, alert mind.

THE SECULAR MIND

Have you ever wondered what your mind might be like if you survive long enough to be as old as Helen Santmyer? Will you be modest, compassionate, and joyful, or will your thinking be cynical, self-centered, and bitter? Will your mind, or mine, be so sensitive to the needs of others and so characterized by humility that our thinking will be like that of Christ?[2] Or will our attitudes be so molded by our contemporaries that there will be almost nothing Christian about the way we think?

According to Harry Blamires, a respected British thinker and former student of C. S. Lewis, most of us don't think much like Christians. Our minds, instead, have become "secularized." We look at almost everything from a human point of view and fail to recognize that God is still in control of the universe. We are reluctant to take unpopular stands on moral issues and sometimes convince ourselves that "fence-sitting is pre-eminently the posture of the charitable Christian leader."

Even we Christians are so influenced by the values of our secular society that there is nothing unique about our lifestyles, literary efforts, business practices, political positions or approaches to education. Instead of "thinking Christianly," we have assumed that non-Christian perspectives are the most tolerant, the most scholarly, and the most accurate ways of looking at the world. The Bible may influence our thinking in church and Christianity may effect our personal ethics, but apart from these areas, we think like everyone else. The minds of modern people have surrendered to secularism, says Blamires. "There is no longer a Christian mind."[3]

Over twenty years have passed since these ideas were first published, but it would be difficult to argue that things have changed for the better during the past two decades. Situational ethics, insensitivity to the needs of others, and disregard for authority have become widely accepted. Although there are still many compassionate people in this world, the majority appear to be self-centered and concerned primarily with satisfying their own needs. Few people take much time to worship God, and, according to psychologist Paul Vitz,[4] many have embraced a "cult of self-worship" that is concerned primarily with self-fulfillment and self-satisfaction.

A few weeks before his death, theologian-philosopher Francis Schaeffer wrote a moving appeal to Christians. He argued that we have so compromised our stand on truth and morality that there appears to be almost nothing unique about the Christian message or lifestyle. He ended with a challenge for believers to care enough to challenge secular thinking with firm but loving confrontation.[5] Without using these words, was Schaeffer calling for us to develop Christian minds?

What is a Christian mind? According to Blamires, secular thinking sees everything from the perspective of life on earth. There is no awareness of God's perspective and no thought of our eternal destiny as God's children.

In contrast, Christian thinking has an eternal point of view. It recognizes that we are servants of Christ, pilgrims on earth, and aliens whose home is in heaven. While we are on this planet, the Christian recognizes that his or her mind and behavior should be characterized by love, compassion, sensitivity, and a willingness to forgive. The Christian mind avoids gossip, greed, and overinvolvement with thoughts of self. Instead, there is a recognition that one of our purposes for living is to bring salt and light[6] to a sin-saturated secular world.

The Christian mind recognizes that human life and history, including the future, are held in the hands of God. Such thinking can be so provocative, revolutionary, and threatening that it is likely to bring opposition and perhaps even persecution from those whose minds are more secular. This opposition has come to committed Christians throughout history and is much in evidence today in some parts of the world.

The Christian mind, by cultivating the eternal perspective, will bring a totally different frame of reference to bear on all that touches human success or human failure, human joy or human misery, human health or human pain. In short *there is nothing in our experience which will not look different to the Christian mind than to the secular mind.*

And many of the issues and activities which will be most vitally transformed by being regarded Christianly are precisely those which are with us now as constant topics of public controversy—war, crime, delinquency, disease, divorce, insanity, vice. The question what is to be done about these problems is a very different question faced christianly and faced secularly, in that the pursuit of temporal well-being gives a twist to human thinking which the pursuit of eternal well-being will not always condone or permit.[7]

According to Blamires, the Christian mind is aware of evil, committed to discovering God's truth, willing to submit to biblical authority, concerned about people, and able to appreciate the richness and diversity of God's creation.

But these are not the only characteristics of Christian thinking. In earlier chapters we have mentioned that the Christian has a renewed mind,[8] a prepared mind,[9] a self-controlled mind,[10] and a pure mind.[11] Perhaps all of this is summarized in Paul's first letter to the Christians at Corinth. "Who has known the mind of the Lord?" he asked. "We have the mind of Christ."[12]

The Mind of Christ

The Christian is expected to think like Christ thinks. His mind was knowledgeable about the Scriptures, constantly aware of the heavenly Father, and sensitive to the guidance of the Holy Spirit. Jesus "did nothing out of selfish ambition or vain conceit."[13] He was compassionate, forgiving, and deeply concerned about others. Even though he was God, he "made himself nothing," and developed a humble, obedient, servant attitude and mentality.

Jesus had a caring mind. In teaching the disciples, Jesus stated that the greatest characteristic of a Christian must be love.[14] His whole life reflected a caring concern for people and he commanded his followers to be servants, as he was a servant.

Caring and servanthood are not popular or comfortable ideas in any era, including ours. To be a caring servant is to be inconvenienced, misused, and sometimes hurt. To be compassionate means that we may feel distressed, guilty, and sometimes convicted about our own selfish motives or struggles to accumulate material goods. One of my friends expressed this concisely when he described a recent Caribbean cruise. "I thoroughly enjoyed it," he said, "but I would have enjoyed it more if they hadn't sailed so close to poverty-stricken Haiti."

Jesus had a heavenly mind. The Christian mind is "set on things above, not on earthly things."[15] This does not mean that we are to be oblivious to current events and human problems. Jesus was well aware of the thinking, personal struggles, and politics of the people with whom he lived. But he also was aware of eternity and saw things from God's perspective.

The Christian mind is clear and informed. It is alert to dangers, able to make plans, and capable of coping with the stresses of life. It also realizes that we are only on this planet for a short time and that our goal during this earthly journey is to serve and please God until we reach our heavenly home.

Jesus had an obedient mind. Frequently, he mentioned his desire to submit to the Father's will. "When Christ came into the world he said: . . . I have come to do your will, O God."[16] He became obedient, even to the point of dying on a cross.[17]

In writing about the Christian mind, Blamires comments that we move in a world which has a distaste for authority unparalleled in history. "Our age is in revolt against the very notions of authority that are crucial to Christian thinking and acting. . . . The Christian mind has an attitude to authority which modern secularism cannot even understand."[18]

Many people in our society are willing to admit that God exists but they don't feel the slightest impulse to bow before him. There is no sense of gratitude, dependence, or submission. There is little awareness of sin, and no knowledge that one needs to be forgiven. God is seen as an elder brother (or sister), an equal among equals, and one whose "views" can be accepted or rejected at will. Such a viewpoint fails to realize that there can be only two reactions to a holy God and his standards. There is either a bowed head or a turned back.[19]

THE ENDURING MIND

If we were to take a survey of neurophysiologists, psychiatrists, psychologists, and other cognitive scientists, most would agree, I suspect, that the mind cannot exist apart from the brain. Many neuroscientists believe that in time we will be able to understand how the mind works, based on our understanding of the brain's activity.[20] At last, say these specialists, we will have biological answers to many of those questions about the mind that have concerned philosophers, theologians, and scientists for centuries.

One of these ancient questions concerns the state of the mind after death. When I die, and my brain deteriorates, will my mind continue to exist? If the mind depends on the brain, then the mind will die when the brain dies. But if the mind somehow exists apart from the brain, then the brain can die but the mind can go on living.

As we saw in chapter two, Wilder Penfield, the famous neurosurgeon, tended to believe that the mind was greater than the brain and he speculated that the mind might go on living even after death.[21] Two eminent thinkers, philosopher Sir Karl Popper and physiologist Sir John Eccles, tended to agree, and they wrote a massive book to support their ideas.[22] More recently, researcher Alan Gevins of EEG Systems Laboratory in San Francisco has admitted that it is difficult to believe that creativity, inspiration, and the more mysterious aspects of the mind will someday all be reduced only to the flow of electrons.[23] All of this leaves us with an important philosophical and practical question: Does the mind endure beyond the grave?

The psychology of life after death. Several years ago, a Gallup poll reported that about 70 percent of the people in the United States believe that life exists after death. An earlier survey found that 44 percent of the people polled in Los Angeles claimed to have been in contact with others who were known to be dead.[24] These people are unlikely to be impressed with arguments that the mind disappears when the brain dies. The recent upsurge of interest in ghosts, mediums, reincarnation, parapsychology, and similar topics indicates that there is a lot of popular interest in the issue of life after death. There is professional interest in the topic as well.[25]

For example, Raymond Moody is a physician whose book *Life after Life* has sold over three million copies.[26] Moody interviewed more than a hundred people who had been pronounced dead, then revived. Their experiences were remarkably similar. Usually there are feelings of peace and quiet, the awareness of a dark tunnel through which one passes, the meeting of guides and spirits including one's dead relatives or friends, the awareness of a great light, and then the return back to life.

Moody describes the experience as something like the following: A man is dying and hears the doctor state that he is dead. Almost immediately he hears a loud buzzing or ringing noise and soon he feels himself moving rapidly through the dark tunnel. As he moves along, he looks back and sees the medical personnel working to revive his lifeless body, but soon he is distracted by other things. He sees an instantaneous playback of the major events of his life, and soon he meets the spirits of previously departed acquaintances who come to greet him, accompanied by a warm spirit aglow with light. Eventually the man reaches a barrier which represents the line between life and death. He wants to step over, but he learns that he must go back to earth and take up residence in his body for a while longer. He doesn't want to leave the feelings of joy, love, and peace, but eventually he goes back. After he recovers, he tells people about his experiences, but people scoff so he says nothing. But the man has been changed, especially in his views about life after death.[27]

Does all of this prove that there is life after death and that the mind endures forever? Many of Moody's readers believe that the book gives scientific proof of a pleasant life after death. Moody himself doesn't go that far, and some of his professional colleagues are much more critical.

A UCLA psychologist carefully evaluated all of the "afterlife" reports that he could find. He read the scientific literature, studied religious writings, reviewed the testimonies of people who had once been declared clinically dead, and even attended a show at the California Museum of Science and Industry which attempted to demonstrate that energy—including life energy—is indestructible.

The psychologist, Dr. Ronald Siegel, tried to be objective and honest in his evaluation. He attempted to treat the reports fairly and showed no inclination to attack or discredit those who had experienced or written about the afterlife experiences. Nevertheless, he found several flaws in the work of Dr. Moody and others.[28]

Sometimes, for example, the researchers had asked biased and leading questions. This was not always done deliberately, but often such questioning led to distortions and inaccuracies. Thus, biased data was then used to support the idea that people had indeed been in contact with some other world.

It was noticed, too, that the afterlife experiences are almost identical to the hallucinations people experience when they are under the influence of drugs, afraid, or cut off from sensory stimulation. When organs degenerate, apparently there is a reduction in the brain's ability to perceive sensations. As a result, the individual's attention turns inward. There are fantasies, reflections, a sense of detachment, feelings of unreality, and often thoughts of death and memories of people who lived in the past. All of this suggests, therefore, that the afterlife experiences can have psychological explanations. Visions like this are nothing new; they have been observed by physicians and psychiatric researchers for many years.

The ultimate deception. Based on the afterlife experiences, one popular writer has concluded that death is really a pleasant experience, as thrilling and harmless as an amusement park ride.[29] The afterlife reports imply that everyone will experience intense feelings of joy, love, and peace after death. It is implied that each of us will be surrounded by a warm, loving spirit of light when we arrive in another place after we die.

The Bible has a different story. Although we read that God is light,[30] we are also warned that Satan masquerades as an angel of light in order to be deceptive.[31] Death, according to the Bible, is an enemy[32]—not a joy-ride, and death is followed by judgment, not by warmth and joy.[33] It is the devil's ultimate deception to imply that there is nothing worse than a journey through a dark tunnel after death.

Jesus once told a story about an afterlife experience. It wasn't a report of someone who had been at death's door and had then recovered. Instead, it was a parable about two men, one of whom had been rich in this life and the other poor. After death, the poor man found himself in a place of peace and security reserved for believers, but the rich man was in hell. In the midst of his torment, he asked that a messenger be sent to warn his living brothers so they could avoid such misery after death.

"But there is no need to send a messenger," the rich man was told. The living have the Bible to instruct them.

The rich man protested that his brothers could only be convinced if they had contact with someone who had returned from the dead.

"If they do not listen to Moses and the Prophets," the reply came back, "they will not be convinced even if someone rises from the dead."[34]

Since that story was told, someone has risen from the dead—Jesus Christ—but many people refuse to listen to his message. They prefer, instead, to put their confidence in afterdeath reports that are of highly debatable validity.

The reincarnated mind. Within recent years there has been an upsurge of interest in reincarnation and an increased willingness to believe that when we die, the mind leaves the body and returns in some other body. Hinduism, Buddhism, and other Eastern religions have taught this doctrine of reincarnation for centuries, but it was never very popular in the West. Now, however, it is estimated that one-third of all Westerners agree that some form of reincarnation is at least a good possibility.[35]

Many of these people have read the writings of Helen Wambach, a San Francisco hypnotist who claims to have hypnotized more than two thousand people and explored their past lives.[36] Her reports are interesting but inconsistent, and some have concluded that she is a practicing medium who clearly is in sympathy with occultists, spiritists, and psychics.[37]

More credible, and more careful as a researcher, is Ian Stevenson of the University of Virginia. He has tried to be objective in his studies of reincarnation, but critics have also challenged his conclusions. He, himself, seriously entertains the idea of demon possession and accepts the fact that his observations may be the result of satanic deception.[38]

Professor Ernest Hilgard, one of this country's best known psychologists and an expert on hypnosis, has made a strong statement about reincarnation reports, especially those discovered under hypnosis. "New identities claimed during trance are not uncommon and easy to produce. Invariably, they're related to long buried memories, and anybody who makes claims to the contrary has not based them on scholarly judgments."[39] Mark Albrecht would agree. His intensive studies of reincarnation[40] have led to the conclusion that most of the experiences can be explained naturally. On occasion, it appears that the reports seem to have been frauds, but there is also reason to suspect that some reincarnation stories show evidence of demonic influence.

Is this what happened to King Saul? He wanted to talk to a dead man, so Saul disguised himself and consulted a medium who in turn brought up the image of Samuel.[41] More recent are the reports of an American bishop who consulted a medium and claimed later that he had been able to communicate with the ghost of his dead son. While some would dismiss this as "magic performed under the special conditions of the séance room,"[42] others, including some Bible scholars, are more inclined to see supernatural influences at work.

The Bible is clear about such practices, however. The use of mediums or spiritists is forbidden because such practices are defiling and dangerous.[43] The prohibition is strong: "Let no one be found among you who . . . practices divination or sorcery, interprets omens, engages in witchcraft, or cast spells, or who is a medium or spiritist or who consults the dead. Anyone who does these things is detestable to the Lord."[44]

It could be argued that these instructions were part of the law and thus not applicable to modern Christians. But if God spoke so powerfully about such issues in the past, are we justified in ignoring the warnings today? Surely not, especially in the light of

New Testament examples where sorcerers and fortunetellers are seen as people who are "captives to sin" and in opposition to the ways of God.[45] Sorcery is satanic[46] and clearly not needed by anyone.

The resurrected mind. Science, of course, cannot tell us what happens to the mind when the body dies, and some would argue that the Bible doesn't speak with great clarity about this issue either. Apparently something persists immediately after death because the believer is "present with the Lord" as soon as he or she dies and is "absent from the body."[47] That which goes to be with the Lord following death is conscious and surely this would imply the mind.

At some time in the future, we will all be resurrected, not in a reincarnated state, but in new bodies. At that time there will be judgment,[48] followed by eternal life with God or eternal punishment.[49] Believers will get new, disease-free bodies,[50] and it seems logical to assume that our minds will be changed as well, because we will not think impure thoughts or be inclined to sin.[51]

THE MELLOWING MIND

It may be interesting for our minds to think about the past and the future, but for now we live in the present and our minds must deal with current realities.

I began writing this book in the winter, when snow whirled about my window and there was ice outside my door. But then came spring, and now I look out on green grass and flowers that are approaching the full bloom of summer. Some day soon, I will take my camera outside and photograph the flowers in all their beauty. In time, the colors will fade, the petals will fall, the leaves will turn brown, and winter will return. But I will have my photographs and my memories of the beauty of summer.

In many respects, this cycle is similar to the growth of a mind—your mind or mine. As children, our minds are easily influenced, not very strong, and sometimes twisted by the winds of change and the destructive forces from our sin-saturated culture. Sometimes we let our minds get distorted. We dwell on ideas that are wrong, self-defeating, and destructive. We fail to develop our minds and wonder why we don't think clearly or productively. We notice that our minds don't have much beauty.

But minds, unlike plants, can always be changed. We can fertilize our minds with enriching ideas, positive attitudes, and biblical concepts. We can determine to let our minds dwell on things that are pure, positive, and praiseworthy. We can resist the tendency to let our minds grow wild and to be filled with the weeds of bitterness, cynicism, immoral thoughts, impure fantasies, self-centered ambition, revenge, and anger.

It isn't easy, and perhaps it isn't even possible, to change our minds by mere determination. But God can help us renew our minds and think thoughts that are pleasing to him[52] and beneficial to us. He can help us develop minds that are mellowing— getting richer, more mature, sensitive, wise, and Christlike.

At the beginning of chapter one, we considered the sad story of Phineas Gage whose mind became distorted when a steel rod destroyed part of his brain in an accident. At the beginning of this chapter we pondered the heart-warming story of Helen Hooven Santmyer, a sharp-minded lady who attained fame and success as an author at eighty-eight.

But we end the book with the story of other minds—yours and mine. Some day we too might have damaged minds, like that of Phineas Gage. Some day we might reach old age and have minds that are sharp, like that of Miss Santmyer. But some of our minds will deteriorate with age. Others of us may die prematurely and never have the opportunity to attain our mind's goals or to reach our mental potential.

But for now we are alive and able to think. We have minds that are alert enough to be developed and molded. From this point on we need to ponder a significant question:

What are you doing with your magnificent mind?

NOTES

Chapter 1

1. J. M. Harlow, "Recovery from the Passage of an Iron Bar through the Head," *Publ. Mass. Med. Soc.*, 1868. The vivid report of Dr. Harlow appears in a number of more recent books. See, for example, James C. Coleman, James N. Butcher, and Robert C. Carson, *Abnormal Psychology and Modern Life*, 6th ed. (Glenview, Ill.: Scott, Foresman & Co., 1980), 452.
2. Photographs of the rod and the skull, and information about their present location, are reported by D. Gareth Jones in his book, *Our Fragile Brains* (Downers Grove, Ill.: InterVarsity Press, 1981), 87–90.
3. Cited by Daniel Goleman, "New View of Mind Gives Unconscious an Expanded Role," *New York Times*, 7 February 1984.
4. 1 Corinthians 2:16.
5. Acts 14:2.
6. For a fascinating, but perhaps overly dramatic account of this, see Alan W. Scheflin and Edward M. Opton, *The Mind Manipulators* (New York: Paddington Press, 1978).
7. This example is taken from Paul Watzlawick, *The Language of Change: Elements of Therapeutic Communication* (New York: Basic Books, 1978), 3.
8. Ibid.
9. Psalm 139:14.
10. The idea of self-fulfilling prophecies is widely accepted in psychology. The conclusion that self-talk is at the basis of much thinking and behavior has been stated most clearly in the early writings of psychologist Albert Ellis. See, for example, Ellis' book *Humanistic Psychotherapy: The Rational-Emotive Approach* (New York: The Julian Press, 1973).
11. See, for example, Norman Vincent Peale, *The Power of Positive Thinking* (New York: Prentice-Hall, 1952); or *You Can If You Think You Can* (Englewood Cliffs, N.J.: Prentice-Hall, 1974).
12. Robert H. Schuller, *Self-Esteem: The New Reformation* (Waco, Tex.: Word Books, 1982).
13. See, for example, Napoleon Hill and W. Clement Stone, *Success Through a Positive Mental Attitude* (Englewood Cliffs, N.J.: Prentice-Hall, 1960). The positive thinking mentality will be discussed later in this book. (See chapter 4.)
14. See, for example, the chapter by Ellis in Leonard Hersher's *Four Psychotherapies* (New York: Appleton-Century-Crofts, 1970). Note, especially, pages 50 and 61. For a concise summary of RET, see the chapter by Ellis in

Current Psychotherapies, ed. Raymond J. Corsini, 2nd ed. (Itasca, Ill.: F. E. Peacock, Pubs., 1979).
15. John 14:2, 25, 26.
16. John 14:27, TLB.

Chapter 2

1. Other "groups" were G.I. Joe in 1950 and Middle Americans in 1969.
2. John Naisbitt, *Megatrends* (New York: Warner Books, 1982).
3. The computer as machine of the year is described in *Time,* 3 January 1983.
4. Alvin Toffler, *The Third Wave* (New York: Wm. Morrow & Co., 1980), 187, 188.
5. Ibid., 189. (Italics added.)
6. Charles Furst, *Origins of the Mind: Mind-Brain Connections* (Englewood Cliffs, N.J.: Prentice-Hall, 1979), 4.
7. David G. Myers, *The Human Puzzle: Psychological Research and Christian Belief* (New York: Harper & Row, 1978), 45.
8. This is the opinion of William Shoemaker of the Salk Institute in La Jolla, California. He is quoted in an article entitled "How the Brain Works," *Newsweek,* 7 February 1983, 41.
9. Ibid.
10. D. Gareth Jones, *Our Fragile Brains: A Christian Perspective on Brain Research* (Downers Grove, Ill.: InterVarsity Press, 1981), 39.
11. Morton Hunt, *The Universe Within: A New Science Explores the Human Mind* (New York: Simon & Schuster, 1982), 41.
12. Some scientists are predicting that the near future will see the transplanting of brain tissue into damaged brains. See Don Marshall Gash, "Brain Transplants Are Next," *Psychology Today,* vol. 15, December 1981, 116; and "A Conversation with Richard Jed Wyatt," *Psychology Today,* Vol. 17, August 1983, 30–41.
13. Since the development of the CAT scan, neuroscientists have been able to get accurate "cross-sectial" pictures of brains without the need for surgery or autopsies. See Monte S. Buchsbaum, "The Mind Readers," *Psychology Today,* vol. 17, July 1983, 58–62.
14. Hans J. and Michael Eysenck, *Mindwatching* (Garden City, N.Y.: Anchor Press, 1983), 177.
15. The procedure described here is technically known as a frontal leucotomy: a type of lobotomy done without making surgical incisions into the skull.
16. Maya Pines, "The Human Difference," *Psychology Today,* vol. 17, September 1983, 62–68.
17. For a more detailed report of split brain research see R. W. Sperry, "The Great Cerebral Commissure," *Scientific American,* January 1964; R. W. Sperry, "Cerebral Organization and Behavior," *Science,* vol. 133, June 1961, 1749–57; and Robert Ornstein, *The Psychology of Consciousness,* 2nd ed. (New York: Harcourt Brace Jovanovich, 1977).
18. There is some evidence that the brain may be organized a little differently in left-handed people who come from families where left-handedness is common. These left-handed people appear to have verbal and language abilities spread more evenly throughout the two hemispheres. See R. Hardyck and L. Petrinovich, "Left-Handedness," *Psychological Bulletin,* vol. 84, 1977, 385–404.

19. Marcel Kinsbourne, "Sad Hemisphere, Happy Hemisphere," *Psychology Today*, vol. 15, May 1981, 92.
20. This experiment is suggested by Robert E. Ornstein, *The Psychology of Consciousness*, 32.
21. Some writers have attempted to help people capitalize on right-brain functioning. See, for example, Betty Edwards, *Drawing on the Right Side of the Brain* (Los Angeles: J. P. Tarcher, 1979); and Gabriele Lusser Rico, *Writing the Natural Way: Using Right-Brain Techniques to Release Your Expressive Powers* (Los Angeles: J. P. Tarcher, 1983).
22. Kinsbourne, "Sad Hemisphere, Happy Hemisphere."
23. Ibid.
24. Ibid.
25. Howard Gardner, "How the Split Brain Gets a Joke," *Psychology Today*, vol. 16, June 1982, 91–93.
26. William James, *The Principles of Psychology*, vol. 1 (1890; reprint, New York: Holt, Rinehart, & Winston, 1950), 177.
27. The phrase is Penfield's. For a nontechnical report of his work and conclusions about the mind-brain problem, see Wilder Penfield, *The Mystery of the Mind* (Princeton, N.J.: University Press, 1975).
28. Ibid., xiii.
29. Ibid., 79–80.
30. Ibid., 86–87.
31. Ibid., 114.
32. Howard Gardner, *The Shattered Mind* (New York: Vintage Books, 1974).
33. Ibid., 442.
34. Hunt, *The Universe Within*, 81.
35. See, for example, Arthur C. Custance, *The Mysterious Matter of Mind* (Grand Rapids: Zondervan, 1980).
36. Ibid., 65.
37. Penfield, *The Mystery of the Mind*, 115.

Chapter 3

1. D. M. Lake, "Mind," in *The Zondervan Pictoral Encyclopedia of the Bible*, vol. 4, ed. Merrill C. Tenney (Grand Rapids: Zondervan, 1975), 228–9.
2. This quotation from Nehemiah is taken from the King James Version of the Bible (KJV) which uses the words "mind to work." The NIV says "the people worked with all their hearts."
3. James 1:8.
4. Luke 1:29, KJV.
5. Acts 17:11, TLB. The KJV describes how the Bereans received Paul's message "with readiness of mind."
6. Matthew 22:37.
7. These words are used in Acts 14:2; 2 Corinthians 3:14; 2 Corinthians 11:3; 1 Timothy 6:5; Proverbs 21:27; Daniel 5:20; Luke 12:29; Romans 1:28; Ephesians 4:17; and Colossians 3:18, KJV.
8. See 2 Corinthians 8:12; Philippians 2:3; Colossians 3:12; 2 Timothy 1:17; 2 Peter 3:1, and Romans 12:2.
9. Isaiah 26:3,4.
10. Romans 14:5.

11. 1 Corinthians 1:10; 2 Corinthians 13:11; Philippians 2:2; 1 Peter 3:8; 4:1, KJV.
12. 1 Corinthians 2:16, TLB.
13. Lake, "Mind," 229.
14. Deuteronomy 28:65, 66; 2 Corinthians 2:13.
15. Isaiah 32:6.
16. Romans 8:7.
17. 1 Timothy 6:5.
18. Luke 21:14.
19. 1 Peter 1:13.
20. Proverbs 23:7. The KJV is most familiar: as a man "thinketh in his heart, so he is." The New American Standard Bible (NASB) renders this: "as he thinks within himself, so he is."
21. This tripartite view is expressed clearly by a Christian psychiatrist who sincerely seeks to build his conclusions on biblical teachings. See Frank B. Minirth, *Christian Psychiatry* (Old Tappan, N.J.: Fleming H. Revell, 1977), 57–70. It should be noted that other Christian writers present a dualistic or two-part view of human nature.
22. See G. C. Berkouwer, *Man: The Image of God* (Grand Rapids: Wm. B. Eerdmans, 1962), 208.
23. The well-known theologian Emil Brunner once wrote that the Scriptures never attempt to give a "scientific description of man." See E. Brunner, "Biblische Psychologie," in *Gott und Mensch*, 1930; cited in Berkouer, *Man: The Image of God*, 195.
24. Lake, "Mind," 228–9.
25. Berkouwer, *Man: The Image of God*, 198, 200.
26. Romans 7:25.
27. Mark 7:20–23.
28. Cited in John R. W. Stott, *Your Mind Matters* (Downers Grove, Ill.: Inter-Varsity Press, 1973), 30.
29. Dorothy L. Sayers, *Creeds or Chaos*, 23; quoted in George Buttrick, ed., *The Interpreter's Bible*, vol. 11 (New York: Abingdon Cokesbury, 1951), 145.
30. 1 Peter 1:13.
31. 1 Peter 1:10–12.
32. William Barclay, *The Letters of James and Peter* (Philadelphia: Westminster Press, 1958), 216.
33. Francis Darwin, ed., *The Life and Letters of Charles Darwin*, vol. 1 (reprint, Saint Clair Shores, Mich.: Scholarly Press, 1977), 81–82.
34. Romans 12:1.
35. John the Baptist described Jesus as "The Lamb of God who takes away the sin of the world" (John 1:29, 36). The same idea is expressed in 1 Corinthians 5:7 and 1 Peter 1:19.
36. See Karl Menninger, *Whatever Became of Sin?* (New York: Hawthorn Books, 1973); M. Scott Peck, *People of the Lie* (New York: Simon and Schuster, 1983). See also the book written by psychologist O. Hobart Mowrer, *The Crisis in Psychiatry and Religion* (Princeton, N.J.: Van Nostrand Reinhold Co., 1961).
37. In his translation of this verse, J. B. Phillips writes, "Don't let the world around you squeeze you into its own mould, but let God re-mould your minds from within."
38. Ephesians 4:23.

39. Proverbs 3:5, 6; Philippians 4:13 characterized by "righteousness and holiness."
40. You can read this list in detail in Romans 12:3–21. Try to read in a modern translation such as *The Living Bible.*

Chapter 4

1. Dr. Peale's life story has been told by Arthur Gordon in *One Man's Way* (Pawling, N.Y.: Foundation for Christian Living, 1972).
2. Norman Vincent Peale, *The Power of Positive Thinking* (New York: Prentice-Hall, 1952), ix.
3. Ibid., 1.
4. Ibid., ix.
5. For a broader survey of possibility thinkers, see Donald Meyer, *The Positive Thinkers* (New York: Pantheon Books, 1965).
6. These quotations are from Peale, *Positive Thinking*, 12, 15, 65, 83, 227.
7. The previous five quotations are taken from Norman Vincent Peale's book *You Can If You Think You Can* (Englewood Cliffs, N.J.: Prentice-Hall, 1974), xi, 1, 82, 199, 308.
8. Robert H. Schuller, *Self-Esteem: The New Reformation* (Waco, Tex.: Word Books, 1982).
9. See, for example, Norman Vincent Peale, *Favorite Stories of Positive Faith* (Pawling, N.Y.: Foundation for Christian Living, 1974); and Robert H. Schuller, *Tough Times Never Last But Tough People Do* (Nashville: Thomas Nelson, 1983).
10. See, for example, W. Clement Stone, *The Success System That Never Fails* (Englewood Cliffs, N.J.: Prentice-Hall, 1962); and Napoleon Hill and W. Clement Stone, *Success Through a Positive Mental Attitude* (Englewood Cliffs, N.J.: Prentice-Hall, 1960).
11. Stone, *Success That Never Fails*, 30.
12. Hill and Stone, *Positive Mental Attitude*, 46–47.
13. Ibid., p. 15.
14. The message is contained in books such as Zig Ziglar, *See You at the Top* (Gretna, La.: Pelican Publishing Co., 1974); and Zig Ziglar, *Zig Ziglar's Secrets of Closing the Sale* (Old Tappan, N.J.: Fleming H. Revell Co., 1984).
15. Schuller, *Self-Esteem.*
16. John MacArthur, Jr., "Questions for Robert Schuller," *Moody Monthly*, vol. 83, May 1983, 6–10.
17. These theological statements are found in Schuller's *Self-Esteem*, 67, 68, 15, 99.
18. MacArthur, "Questions for Robert Schuller," 6.
19. John R. W. Stott, *Your Mind Matters* (Downers Grove, Ill.: InterVarsity Press, 1973), 34–36.
20. Paul C. Vitz, *Psychology As Religion: The Cult of Self-Worship* (Grand Rapids: Wm. B. Eerdmans, 1977), 72.
21. Viktor E. Frankl, *Man's Search for Meaning* (New York: Washington Square Press, 1959).
22. Ibid., 117.
23. Some of the material in the remainder of this chapter is adapted from Gary R. Collins, "Handling Our Mental Attitudes," *Christian Herald*, vol. 103,

May 1980, 30–33. This was reprinted in the author's book *Calm Down* (Ventura, Calif.: Vision House Pubs., 1981).
24. Philippians 4:8.
25. Peale, *Positive Thinking.*
26. Colossians 1:17; Hebrews 1:13.
27. John 15:5.
28. Matthew 20:25–28.
29. Matthew 19:26.

Chapter 5

1. A fascinating report of Nolen's journey to the Philippines is found in his book. William A. Nolen, *Healing: A Doctor in Search of a Miracle* (New York: Random House, 1974). Most of the following material on psychic surgeons is adapted from this book.
2. Recently I discovered a difficult-to-find but dramatic book on the Philippine faith healers. The author concludes that the "healers" are really engaged in sleight-of-hand activities, but the book's greatest value is its many impressive color photographs of the "surgeries." See Gert Chesi, *Faith Healers in the Philippines* (Austria: Perlinger VerlagGesmbH, Brixentaler Strasse 61, 6300 Worgl, Austria, 1981).
3. Quoted by Myra Pines, "Psychological Hardiness: The Role Challenges in Health," *Psychology Today,* vol. 14, December 1980, 34–44, 98. For other observations on voodoo spells, see Ari Kiev, ed., *Magic, Faith, and Healing Psychiatry* (New York: Free Press, 1972); and E. Fuller Torrey, *The Mind Game: Witchdoctors and Psychiatrists* (New York: Emerson Hall Pubs., 1972).
4. W. B. Cannon, "Voodoo Death," *Psychosomatic Medicine,* vol. 19, 1957, 182–90. Cannon's physiological conclusions are not necessarily at odds with those who see demonic involvement in voodoo death. Surely the devil can work through the means that Cannon describes.
5. Daniel Hack Tuke, *Illustrations of the Influence of the Mind upon the Body in Health and Disease Designed to Elucidate the Action of the Imagination* (London: J. and A. Churchill, 1884).
6. Walter McQuade and Ann Aikman, *Stress* (New York: E. P. Dutton, 1974).
7. For a fascinating discussion of this, see Kenneth R. Pelletier, *Mind as Healer, Mind as Slayer* (New York: Delta Books, 1977). Notice the descriptive title of Pelletier's book.
8. James C. Coleman, James N. Butcher, and Robert C. Carson, *Abnormal Psychology and Modern Life,* 7th ed. (Glenview, Ill.: Scott, Foresman & Co., 1984), 282–4.
9. Pelletier, *Mind as Healer,* 169–73.
10. E. B. Blanchard and F. Andrasik, "Psychological Assessment and Treatment of Headache: Recent Developments and Emerging Issues," *Journal of Consulting and Clinical Psychology,* vol. 50, 1982, 859–79.
11. Robert Ader, "The Little Black Box for the Body's Defenses," *Psychology Today,* vol. 15, August 1981, 92; and Alan Anderson, "How the Mind Heals," *Psychology Today,* vol. 16, December 1982, 51–56.
12. Signe Hammer, "The Mind as Healer," *Science Digest,* April 1984, 47–49, 100.
13. See Pines, "Psychological Hardiness."
14. Ibid., 39.

15. This term was used by the author in an earlier book. See Gary R. Collins, *Beyond Easy Believism* (Waco, Tex.: Word Books, 1982).

16. Martin E. P. Seligman, *Helplessness: On Depression, Development, and Death* (San Francisco: W. H. Freeman, 1975). One study showed that people *can* function well under stress if they sense that life is meaningful, that they are in control of their lives, and that they have strong personal goals. See S. C. Kobasa, "Stressful Life Events, Personality and Health: An Inquiry into Hardiness," *Journal of Personality and Social Psychology*, vol 37, 1979, 1–11.

17. This is documented in a humorous article written by Cousins' wife. See Eleanor Cousins, "The Irrepressible Spoofer Strikes Again," *The Saturday Evening Post*, vol. 254, April 1982, 26–29, 105.

18. Norman Cousins, *Anatomy of an Illness* (New York: W. W. Norton & Co., 1979), 31.

19. Proverbs 17:22.

20. Cousins, *Anatomy of an Illness*, 39.

21. Norman Cousins, *The Healing Heart* (New York: W. W. Norton & Co., 1983), 158.

22. Norman Cousins, *Human Options* (New York: W. W. Norton & Co., 1981), 205, 209, 207.

23. See Pelletier, *Mind as Healer*, and Hammer, "The Mind as Healer."

24. For a description of ways in which the mind can bring physical relaxation, see Herbert Benson, *The Relaxation Response* (New York: Wm. Morrow & Co., 1975).

25. Richard Cheng and Bruce Pomeranz, "Electroacupuncture Analgesia Could Be Mediated by at Least Two Pain-Relieving Mechanisms: Endorphin and Non-Endorphin Systems," *Life Sciences*, vol. 25, 1979, 1957–62. See also James Hassett, "Acupuncture Is Proving Its Points," *Psychology Today*, vol. 14, December 1980, 81–89. For a Christian critique of acupuncture, see Paul C. Reisser, Teri K. Reisser, and John Weldon, *The Holistic Healers* (Downers Grove, Ill.: InterVarsity Press, 1983).

26. This theory is described in a cover story in *Time* magazine. See "Unlocking Pain's Secrets" *Time*, 11 June 1984, 58–66.

27. Nolen, *Healing: A Doctor in Search*, 254. The following conclusions are based largely on Nolen's conclusions about the psychic surgeons.

28. Agu Pert, "The Body's Own Tranquilizers," *Psychology Today*, vol. 15, September 1981, 100.

29. Bertrand Russell, *Why I Am Not a Christian* (New York: Simon & Schuster, 1957), 22.

30. Dr. Nolen did an intensive study of the Katherine Kuhlman healing meetings, with the full cooperation of the healer. He concluded that there was no healing among the people who claimed to have been healed at a Minneapolis crusade, and who later submitted to medical examination. See Nolen, *Healing: A Doctor in Search*, 90.

31. Chapter 16.

32. The statement is taken from the wellness inventory designed by Dr. John Travis, a physician (with training at Tufts and Johns Hopkins) who operates a wellness clinic in California. This is reported in a book by John D. Adams, *Understanding and Managing Stress* (San Diego: University Associates, 1980), 30. See also Carin Rubenstein, "Wellness Is All," *Psychology Today*, vol. 16, October 1982, 28–37.

33. See, for example, Michael Halberstam, "Holistic Healing: Limits of 'The

New Medicine,'" *Psychology Today*, vol. 12, August 1978, 26–27. The new
medicine is also discussed in *The Holistic Healers* by Reisser, et. al.

Chapter 6

1. William E. Burrows, "Cockpit Encounters," *Psychology Today*, Vol. 16, November 1982, 42–47.
2. Hans Selye, *The Stress of Life* (New York: McGraw-Hill Book Co., 1956).
3. Selye dedicated *The Stress of Life* to "those who are not afraid to enjoy the stress of a full life, nor too naive to think that they can do so without intellectual effort" (ibid., v).
4. Hans Selye, *Stress Without Distress* (Philadelphia: J. B. Lippincott Co., 1974). One section in this book is titled "Stress is the spice of life."
5. A. Kent MacDougall, "Stress," *Success*, vol. 30, November 1983, 37–40.
6. See, for example, Robert D. Rutherford, *Just in Time: Immediate Help for the Time-Pressured* (New York: John Wiley & Sons, 1980).
7. Ibid., 38.
8. Ibid.
9. Susan Witty, "The Laugh-Makers," *Psychology Today*, vol. 17, August 1983, 22–29.
10. Jacob Levine, "Humor and Mental Health," *Encyclopedia of Mental Health*, vol. 3 (New York: Franklin Watts, 1963), 786–799.
11. George Gmelch and Richard Felson, "Can a Lucky Charm Get You Through Organic Chemistry?" *Psychology Today*, vol. 14, December 1980, 75–78.
12. B. F. Skinner, "Superstition in the Pigeon," *Journal of Experimental Psychology*, vol. 38, 1948, 168–72.
13. Gustav Jahoda, *The Psychology of Superstition* (Baltimore: Penguin Books, 1970).
14. Within the past decade, literally hundreds of stress-management books have been published. These include one by the author: Gary R. Collins, *Spotlight on Stress* (Ventura, Calif.: Vision House Pubs., 1982).
15. James Hassett, "Teaching Yourself to Relax," *Psychology Today*, vol. 12, August 1978, 28–40.
16. Herbert Benson, *The Relaxation Response* (New York: Wm. Morrow & Co., 1975).
17. For a "how-to-do-it" book on relaxation, see John D. Curtis and Richard A. Detert, *How to Relax: A Holistic Approach to Stress Management* (Palo Alto, Calif.: Mayfield Publishing Co., 1981).
18. Within recent years, a number of relaxation tapes have appeared. One company, for example, offers tapes with titles such as "Relaxation Training," "Pain Control," "Stress Management," "Personal Enrichment through Imagery," and "Quieting Reflex Training." The author has not heard these tapes and for this reason cannot recommend them. There is no evidence in the brochure that the tapes work. Nevertheless, the speakers on the tapes are among the best researchers in the field, and it is likely that their methods are based on scientific data that proves their effectiveness.
19. For a popular introduction to biofeedback, see Barbara B. Brown, *New Mind, New Body* (New York: Harper & Row, 1974).
20. See, for example, Gerald Caplan and Marie Killilea, eds., *Support Systems*

and Mutual Help (New York: Grune & Stratton, 1976); and Benjamin H. Gottlieb, ed., *Social Networks and Social Support* (Beverly Hills: Sage Publications, 1981).

21. Acts 2:42–47; 4:32–35.
22. Cited in David D. Burns, *Feeling Good: The New Mood Therapy* (New York: Wm. Morrow & Co., 1980).
23. These suggestions, and the guidelines of the following paragraphs are adapted from John D. Adams, "Guidelines for Stress Management and Life Style Changes," *The Personal Administrator,* June 1979, 35–38, 44.
24. Galatians 6:22, 23.
25. Isaiah 26:3, kjv; Philippians 4:6,7.

Chapter 7

1. Hebrews 1:1–3.
2. Carol Tavris, *Anger: The Misunderstood Emotion* (New York: Simon & Schuster, 1983).
3. Reported in Tavris, ibid.
4. The Bible notes the futility of anger ventilation in passages such as Proverbs 14:29; 15:18; 19:11; 22:24, 25; 29:11, 20, 22.
5. Reported in Tavris, ibid.
6. Some of this research work is summarized in D. Gareth Jones, *Our Fragile Brains* (Downers Grove, Ill.: InterVarsity Press, 1981), 121–33.
7. K. E. Moyer, "The Physiology of Violence," *Psychology Today,* vol. 7, July 1973, 35–38.
8. See Hebrews 12:15; Matthew 7:14, 15. For a good discussion of anger and the Bible, see Jay E. Adams, *The Christian Counselor's Manual* (Grand Rapids: Baker Book House, 1973), chapter 31.
9. Carol Tavris, "Anger Defused," *Psychology Today,* vol. 16, November 1982, 29.
10. Revenge is a natural response to anger, but the Bible teaches nonviolence instead. See Matthew 5:38–48 and Romans 12:17.
11. This is the suggestion of Archibald D. Hart in his excellent book, *Feeling Free* (Old Tappan, N.J.: Fleming H. Revell, Co., 1979).
12. Ephesians 4:26, 31.
13. Galatians 5:23.
14. Marcia Yudkin, "Young Activists," *Psychology Today,* vol. 18, April 1984, 24.
15. Jack Mack and William Beardslee. Cited in Marcia Yudkin, "When Kids Think the Unthinkable," *Psychology Today,* vol. 18, April 1984, 18–25.
16. Arthur Levine, *When Dreams and Heroes Died* (San Francisco: Jossey-Bass Pubs., 1980).
17. See Luke 12:19–21.
18. Don Baker and Emery Nester, *Depression: Finding Hope and Meaning in Life's Darkest Shadow,* (Portland, Oreg.: Multnomah Press, 1983), 11.
19. A discussion of the biological basis of depression, including some of the research on which these conclusions are based, can be found in John White's book, *The Masks of Melancholy* (Downers Grove, Ill.: InterVarsity Press, 1982). There are a variety of books on depression. In addition to White's book, see Roger Barrett, *Depression* (Elgin, Ill.: David C. Cook,

1977); Nathan Kline, *From Sad to Glad* (New York: Ballantine Books, 1974); and Baker and Nester, *Depression*.

20. The theory of learned helplessness is proposed by psychologist Martin E. P. Seligman, *Helplessness: On Depression, Development, and Death* (San Francisco: W. H. Freeman & Co., 1975).

21. See, for example, H. S. Akiskal and W. T. McKinney, "Overview of Recent Research in Depression: Integration of Ten Conceptual Models into a Comprehensive Clinical Frame," *Archives*, vol. 32, 1975, 285–305.

22. 1 John 1:9; James 5:16.

23. For a concise overview, see "New Hope for the Depressed," *U.S. News & World Report*, 24 January 1983, 39–42.

24. This is the view of David A. Taylor, *Mind* (New York: Simon & Schuster, 1982), 113.

25. Philippians 4:4–8.

26. Psalm 73 is labeled in the Bible as "a psalm of Asaph." If 1 Chronicles 16:5 refers to the same man, then we know Asaph played the cymbals.

27. Psalm 73: 3–12, TLB.

28. Psalm 73: 13, 14.

29. Psalm 73: 21–27.

30. It should be recognized that all anger is not bad. Some is healthy and motivating. Even Jesus became angry, and good came as a result of this. See Mark 3:5; 11:15, 16.

31. Psalm 37:23–27.

Chapter 8

1. Judith Allen Shelly, "Mental Health: A Personal Struggle," in Judith Allen Shelly, Sandra D. John, et al., *Spiritual Dimensions of Mental Health* (Downers Grove, Ill.: InterVarsity Press, 1983), 15, 16. A similar personal struggle was described by psychiatrist Solomon H. Snyder in *The Troubled Mind* (New York: McGraw-Hill, 1976).

2. Firsthand observations of this were reported several years ago when eight normal people—including one psychiatrist and three psychologists—checked themselves into different mental hospitals, acted normally, took notes about their experiences, and waited to see how long it would take for them to be released. The average length of stay was almost three weeks; one person stayed for fifty-two days. The subsequent report brought howls of criticism and protest. See D. L. Rosenhan, "On Being Sane in Insane Places," *Science*, vol. 179, 1973, 250–8.

3. For an analysis of anxiety in surgical patients see I. Janis, *Psychological Stress* (New York: John Wiley & Sons, 1958).

4. S. Epstein and W. D. Fenz, "Steepness of Approach and Avoidance Gradients in Humans as a Function of Experience: Theory and Experiment," *Journal of Experimental Psychology*, vol. 70, 1965, 1–12.

5. S. Freud, *The Problem of Anxiety* (New York: W. W. Norton & Co., 1936). Freud wrote that there were two kinds of anxiety: normal and neurotic. The second type, neurotic anxiety, could be divided further into two types: the first dealing with shame, the second with guilt.

6. Hans Selye, *Stress Without Distress* (Philadelphia: J. B. Lippincott Co., 1974).

7. See, for example, Seymour S. Kety, "The Biochemical Roots of Mental Illness," in Albert Rosenfeld, ed., *Mind and Supermind* (New York: Holt,

Rinehart & Winston, 1977); and Earl Ubell, "You're Not Crazy . . . You're Sick," *Reader's Digest*, April 1984, 145–8.

8. Cited in Shelly and John, *Spiritual Dimensions*, 25.

9. O. Hobart Mowrer, *The Crisis in Psychiatry and Religion* (Princeton, N.J.: Van Nostrand Reinhold Co., 1961); and Karl Menninger, *Whatever Became of Sin?* (New York: Hawthorn Books, 1973).

10. Ibid., 18–19.

11. Romans 3:23; 1 John 1:9; John 3:16; Romans 10:9; James 5:16.

12. An in-depth summary of secular approaches to therapy can be found in R. Corsini, ed. *Current Psychotherapies* (Itasca, Ill.: F. E. Peacock Pubs., 1979). For an overview of Christian theories see Gary R. Collins, *Helping People Grow: Practical Approaches to Christian Counseling* (Ventura, Calif.: Vision House Pubs., 1980).

13. The classification of therapies in the next paragraph is adapted from an article by Philip Brickman, et al., "Models of Helping and Coping," *American Psychologist*, vol. 37, April 1982, 368–84.

14. For a massive review of the literature on the effectiveness of psychotherapy, see Sol L. Garfield and Allen E. Bergin, eds., *Handbook of Psychotherapy and Behavior Change*, 2nd ed. (New York: John Wiley & Sons, 1978). See also S. L. Garfield, "Effectiveness of Psychotherapy: The Perennial Controversy," *Professional Psychology: Research and Practice*, vol. 14, 1983, 35–42.

15. Emory L. Cowen, "Help Is Where You Find It: Four Informal Helping Groups," *American Psychologist*, vol. 37, April 1982, 385–95.

16. O. Quentin Hyder, "On the Mental Health of Jesus Christ," *Journal of Psychology and Theology*, vol. 5, Winter 1977, 3–12.

17. This description is in Daniel 1:4, TLB. The story of Daniel is told in the Old Testament book that bears his name.

18. Daniel 1:8–15.

19. Daniel 1:17

20. Daniel 6:10.

21. Daniel 2:27–28.

22. Daniel 6:5–12.

23. Daniel 2:24.

24. Daniel 6:3–4.

25. This is the view of psychologist Albert Ellis who once wrote a highly vindictive paper in which he argued that religion undercuts emotional health and creates enormous amounts of mental disturbance. While accusing believers of bias and intolerance, Ellis' paper is a model of biased, intolerant rhetoric. See Albert Ellis, "The Case Against Religion," *Mensa Journal*, vol. 138, September 1970.

26. Hebrews 11:1

27. 2 Timothy 1:7.

Chapter 9

1. Israel Shenker, "Whistler's Art Came First; Enemies Were Next in Line," *Smithsonian*, vol. 15, April 1984.

2. H. A. Overstreet, *The Mature Mind* (New York: W. W. Norton Co., 1949).

3. H. A. Overstreet, *The Great Enterprise: Relating Ourselves to Our World* (New York: W. W. Norton Co., 1952).

4. The following analysis is adapted from a paper by John D. Carter, "Maturity: Psychological and Biblical," *Journal of Psychology and Theology*, vol. 2, Spring 1974, 89–96; from the work of Gordon W. Allport, *The Individual and His Religion* (New York: Macmillan Publishing Co., 1950); *The Pattern and Growth of Personality* (New York: Holt, Rinehart & Winston, 1961).
5. Carter, ibid., 92.
6. A. H. Maslow and B. Mittelman, *Principles of Abnormal Psychology*, (New York: Harper & Row, 1951).
7. This summary of Maslow is taken from Frank Goble, *The Third Force: The Psychology of Abraham Maslow* (New York: Grossman Pubs., 1970).
8. A. H. Maslow, *Toward a Psychology of Being* (New York: Van Nostrand Reinhold Co., 1962).
9. David D. Burns, *Feeling Good: The New Mood Therapy* (New York: Wm. Morrow & Co., 1980).
10. Thomas J. Peters and Robert H. Waterman, Jr., *In Search of Excellence: Lessons from America's Best-Run Companies* (New York: Harper & Row, 1982).
11. John W. Gardner, *Excellence* (New York: Harper & Row, 1961), 92.
12. Ibid., 86.
13. Ted Engstrom, *The Pursuit of Excellence* (Grand Rapids: Zondervan, 1982), 17.
14. Ibid., 26.
15. Ibid., 28–29.
16. This is the suggestion of William Barclay, in *The Letters of James and Peter* (Philadelphia: Westminster Press, 1958), 39.
17. See James 3:2–12.
18. James 3:13.
19. James 3:14–16.
20. Matthew 20:20–27.
21. James 3:17.
22. In Galatians 5:22–3, Paul lists the "fruit of the Spirit": love, joy, peace, patience, kindness, goodness, faithfulness, gentleness, and self-control. In 2 Peter 1:5–9 Peter writes about faith, goodness, knowledge, self-control, perseverance, kindness, and love.
23. James 3:18–4:4.
24. Quoted in "Lord of the Ring: A Conversation with Gunther Gebel-Williams," *Psychology Today*, vol. 17, October 1983, 27–32.
25. Adapted from chapter seven, "Healthy and Unhealthy Religious Beliefs," of Judith Shelly and Sandra John's book, *Spiritual Dimensions of Mental Health* (Downers Grove, Ill.: InterVarsity Press, 1983).
26. 1 John 1:9.
27. In his study of perfectionism, Burns (*Feeling Good: The New Mood Therapy*) takes this approach. He does not write from a Christian perspective, but he argues that perfectionists must be helped to change their thinking through cognitive methods. Then they can accept the fact that some things will not and need not be perfect.
28. David J. A. Clines, "Sin and Maturity," *Journal of Psychology and Theology*, vol. 5, Summer 1977, 183–96.
29. Ibid., 195.

Chapter 10

1. Bernard Rimland, "Inside the Mind of the Autistic Savant," *Psychology Today*, vol. 12, August 1978, 69–80.

2. Ibid., 79.
3. The study, by John J. Simmatore and Warren Blumefeld, was reported under the title "Mindless Redeeming," *Psychology Today*, vol. 17, November 1983, 81.
4. Ellen J. Langer, "Automated Lives," *Psychology Today*, vol. 16, 60–71.
5. This work was done by Ivor Brown at the Applied Psychology Research Unit in Cambridge, England. Reported in Hans J. Eysenck and Michael Eysenck, *Mindwatching* (Garden City, N.Y.: Anchor Books, 1983), 218–29.
6. Ibid.
7. Like language, gestures have a strong cultural meaning. See Paul Ekman, Wallace V. Friesen, and John Bear, "The International Language of Gestures," *Psychology Today*, vol. 18, May 1984, 64–69.
8. Stephen B. Douglass and Lee Roddy. *Making the Most of Your Mind* (San Bernardino, Calif.: Here's Life Publishers, 1983), 175–189.
9. Morton Hunt, *The Universe Within* (New York: Simon & Schuster, 1982), 264–5.
10. G. Alan Marlatt and Damaris J. Rohsenow, "The Think-Drink Effect," *Psychology Today*, vol. 15, December 1981, 60–69, 93.
11. Some researchers maintain that there is only one stage of memory; others propose that there are more than two stages. See Mark R. Rosenzweig, "Experience, Memory, and the Brain," *American Psychologist*, vol. 39, April 1984, 365–76.
12. This analogy is taken from Charles Furst, *Origins of the Mind* (Englewood Cliffs, N.J.: Prentice-Hall, 1979), 165.
13. Elizabeth F. Loftus, "Alcohol, Marijuana, and Memory," *Psychology Today*, vol. 13, March 1980, 42–56, 92.
14. Rosenzweig, "Experience, Memory, and the Brain."
15. "How the Brain Works," *Newsweek*, vol. 101, 7 February 1983, 43.
16. Furst, *Origins of the Mind*, 178.
17. Harry Lorayne and Jerry Lucas, *The Memory Book* (New York: Ballantine Books, 1974).
18. Eysenck and Eysenck, *Mindwatching*, 239.
19. K. R. Popper, *Objective Knowledge* (Oxford: Oxford University Press, 1972). More recently, another writer has proposed that we should add a fourth world, one consisting of the beliefs that people take for granted and use in their exploration of World 3. See J. W. Berry, *Human Ecology and Cognitive Styles* (New York: John Wiley & Sons, 1976).
20. The theme of choices is central to Leona E. Tyler's book, *Thinking Creatively* (San Francisco: Jossey-Bass Pubs., 1983).

Chapter 11

1. See, for example, Martin L. Gross, *The Brain Watchers* (New York: Random House, 1963).
2. Some of this debate is summarized in chapter 6 of a book by Morton Hunt, *The Universe Within* (New York: Simon & Schuster, 1982).
3. This is the title of a book commissioned by the international "think-tank" Club of Rome. See J. W. Botkin, M. Elmandjra, and M. Malitza, *No Limits to Learning: Bridging the Human Gap: A Report to the Club of Rome* (Oxford and New York: Pergamon Press, 1979).
4. Roderick MacLeish, "Gifted by Nature, Prodigies Are Still Mysteries to Man," *Smithsonian*, vol. 14, March 1984, 70–79.
5. Ibid., 78.

6. Ibid.
7. Robert J. Sternberg, "Who's Intelligent?" *Psychology Today*, vol. 16, April 1982, 30–39.
8. Questions 1 and 2 were designed by James Fixx and reported in Robert J. Sternberg and Janet E. Davidson "The Mind of the Puzzler," *Psychology Today*, vol. 16, June 1982, 37–44. Questions 3 and 4 were taken from Morton Hunt, *The Universe Within*, 241, 252.

    The answers are as follows:

    1. Remember that the trees do not need to be in parallel rows.

    2. If the lilies double in number every twenty-four hours, and if the lake will be completely covered on day 60, then the lake is half covered on day 59.

    3. Nobody said the triangles had to be two dimensional.

    4. In one hour each train will go 25 miles. That means they will meet in one hour. The bird flies 100 miles per hour. So in one hour the bird will have flown 100 miles.

    5. Moses didn't take any animals into the ark. Noah did.
9. Howard Gardner, *Frames of Mind: The Theory of Multiple Intelligences* (New York: Basic Books, 1983).
10. "Human Intelligence Isn't What We Think It Is," an Interview with Howard Gardner, *U.S. News & World Report*, 19 March 1984, 75–76. See also, "The Seven Frames of Mind: A PT Conversation with Howard Gardner," *Psychology Today*, vol. 18, June 1984, 20–26.
11. This term is described by John Naisbitt, *Megatrends* (New York: Warner Books, 1982).
12. The ideas in these and the following paragraphs are adapted from Sheila Ostrander and Lynn Schroeder, *Superlearning* (New York: Dell Publishing Co., 1979).
13. Ibid., 72.
14. Dorothy Retallack, *The Sound of Music and Plants* (Marina del Rey: DeVorss & Co., 1973).
15. Dennis M. Davis and Steve Clapp, *The Third Wave and the Local Church* (Champaign, Ill.: C-4 Computer Company, 1983).
16. Marc D. Schwartz, ed., *Using Computers in Clinical Practice* (New York: Haworth, 1984).
17. Alvin Toffler, *Future Shock* (New York: Wm. Morrow & Co., 1980), 191.
18. Ibid., 187.
19. Quoted in Hunt, *The Universe Within*, 318. See also, Patrick Huyghe, "Of Two Minds," *Psychology Today*, vol. 17, December 1983, 26–35.
20. The remainder of this section draws heavily on the work of Morton Hunt,

The Universe Within. His chapter on "Mind and Supermind" deals largely with artificial intelligence.

21. A computer could be programmed, for example, to distinguish between presidents who are living and those who are dead. For a popular consideration of artificial intelligence see Lester Brooks, "Towards the Supercomputer," *Sky* (Delta Airlines Inflight Magazine), March 1984, 26–35.
22. Morton Hunt, *The Universe Within*, 340, 345.
23. A. W. Tozer, *The Knowledge of the Holy* (New York: Harper & Row, 1961), 62.
24. Proverbs 9:1, TLB.
25. Romans 11:33, 34, 36.

Chapter 12

1. One such visitor was Howard Gardner whose critique of the Suzuki method appears in his book, *Frames of Mind* (New York: Basic Books, 1983).
2. Ibid., 378.
3. Robert S. Wieder, "How to Get Great Ideas," *Success,* vol. 30, November 1983, 29–31, 59.
4. Some of von Oech's seminar ideas have been published in a book. Roger von Oech, *A Whack in the Side of the Head* (New York: Warner Books, 1984).
5. Berkeley Rice, "Imagination to Go," *Psychology Today,* vol. 18, May 1984, 48–56.
6. Graham Wallas, *The Art of Thought* (New York: Harcourt Brace Jovanovich, 1926).
7. This concept of ideas suddenly coming together was at the core of a classic book by Arthur Koestler, *The Act of Creation* (New York: Dell Publishing Co., 1964). For a different thought-provoking approach, see Rollo May, *The Courage to Create* (New York: W. W. Norton & Co., 1975).
8. Donald R. Gentner and Donald A. Norman, "The Typist's Touch," *Psychology Today,* vol. 18, March 1984, 66–72.
9. Howard Gruber, *Darwin on Man: A Psychological Study of Scientific Creativity,* 2nd ed. (Chicago: University of Chicago Press, 1981).
10. Morton Hunt, *The Universe Within* (New York: Simon & Schuster, 1982), 284.
11. For a discussion of creative traits, see "Breakaway Minds," an interview with Howard Grober, *Psychology Today,* vol. 15, July 1981, 64–73; D. N. Perkins, *The Mind's Best Work* (Cambridge, Mass.: Harvard University Press, 1981); and Howard Gardner, *Art, Mind, and Brain: A Cognitive Approach to Creativity* (New York: Basic Books, 1982).
12. Perkins, *The Mind's Best Work,* 101.
13. John Naisbitt, *Megatrends* (New York: Warner Books, 1982).
14. Perkins, *The Mind's Best Work,* 137.
15. Reported in Sheila Ostrander and Lynn Schroeder, *Superlearning* (New York: Dell Publishing Co., 1979), 160.
16. John Gardner, *On Becoming a Novelist* (New York: Harper & Row, 1983).
17. Quoted by Madeleine L'Engle, *Walking on Water: Reflections on Faith and Art* (Wheaton, Ill.: Harold Shaw Pubs., 1979), 33.
18. Ibid., 18.
19. Gardner, *On Becoming a Novelist,* 60.
20. "Allegorical Fantasy: Mortal Dealings with Cosmic Questions: An Inter-

view with Madeleine L'Engle," *Christianity Today,* vol. 23, 8 June 1979, 14–19.

21. J. R. Hayes, *Cognitive Psychology: Thinking and Creating* (Homewood, Ill.: Dorsey Press, 1978). The Hayes-Flower research is reported by Morton Hunt, *The Universe Within,* 303–7.

22. The following paragraphs are adapted from Morton Hunt, *The Universe Within,* 296–303.

23. Quoted by Howard Gardner, "Children's Art: The Age of Creativity," *Psychology Today,* vol. 13, May 1980, 84–96.

24. Matthew 18:3–5.

25. Philip Yancey, *Open Windows* (Westchester, Ill.: Crossway Books, 1982), 212–3.

26. Luke 12:48.

Chapter 13

1. O. Carl Simonton, Stephanie Matthews-Simonton, and James Creighton, *Getting Well Again* (Los Angeles: J. P. Tarcher, 1978).

2. Some of these criticisms are included in an article by Maggie Scarf, "Images that Heal: A Doubtful Idea Whose Time Has Come," *Psychology Today,* vol. 14, September 1980, 32–46.

3. Some of the popularity can be traced to a significant article published in 1964. Notice the significance of the title: R. Holt, "Imagery: The Return of the Ostracized," *American Psychologist,* vol. 19, 1964, 254–64. A significant review of the literature appeared almost ten years later: Z. Pylyshyn, "What the Mind's Eye Tells the Mind's Brain: A Critique of Mental Imagery," *Psychological Bulletin,* vol. 86, 1973, 1–24.

4. For example, *Journal of Mental Imagery, Imagery Today,* and *International Imagery Bulletin.*

5. The definition is taken from Arnold Lazarus, *In the Mind's Eye* (New York: Rawson, Wade Pubs., 1977), 4.

6. This brief historical overview is adapted from Steven Starker, *Fantastic Thought* (Englewood Cliffs, N.J.: Prentice-Hall, 1982), 144.

7. M. Chappell and T. Stevenson, "Group Psychological Training in Some Organic Conditions," *Mental Hygiene,* vol. 20, 1936, 588–97.

8. Andrew Weil, *The Natural Mind* (Boston: Houghton Mifflin Co., 1972).

9. Quoted in an excerpt of Weil's book, published in *Psychology Today,* vol. 6, October 1972, 58.

10. Job 42:5.

11. This research, by Meichenbaum and Turk, is reported in Jerome L. Singer and Ellen Switzer, *Mind-Play: The Creative Uses of Fantasy* (Englewood Cliffs, N.J.: Prentice-Hall, 1980), 94.

12. Some of the research that addresses this question is summarized by D. C. Turk, D. H. Meichenbaum, and W. H. Berman, "Application of Biofeedback for the Regulation of Pain: A Critical Review," *Psychological Bulletin,* vol. 86, 1979, 1322–38; and by M. Weisenberg, "Pain and Pain Control," *Psychological Bulletin,* vol. 84, 1977, 1004–88.

13. J. J. Horan, F. C. Layng, and C. H. Pursell, "Preliminary Study of Effects of 'In Vivo' Emotive Imagery on Dental Discomfort," *Perceptual and Motor Skills,* vol. 42, 1976, 105–6.

14. For an overview of health psychology, see Robert J. Gatchel and Andrew

Baum, *An Introduction to Health Psychology* (Reading, Mass.: Addison-Wesley Publishing Co., 1983).

15. These and similar claims, in every case backed up with at least some evidence, are presented in *In the Mind's Eye*, by Lazarus and *Mind-Play: The Creative Uses of Fantasy* by Singer and Switzer.

16. See, for example, Beverly-Colleene Gaylean, "Guided Imagery in Education," *Journal of Humanistic Psychology*, vol. 21, Fall 1981, 57–68.

17. Ibid., 61.

18. Henri J. M. Nouwen, *¡Gracias! A Latin American Journal* (New York: Harper & Row, 1983), 32.

19. Quoted in Richard Foster, *Celebration of Discipline* (New York: Harper & Row, 1978), 22.

20. Ibid., 26.

21. Ibid., 27–28.

22. Ruth Carter Stapleton, *The Gift of Inner Healing*, 1976, and *The Experience of Inner Healing*, 1977. Both are published by Word Books, Waco, Texas.

23. For a critique of Stapleton's work see Jim M. Alsdurf and H. Newton Malony, "A Critique of Ruth Carter Stapleton's Ministry of 'Inner Healing,'" *Journal of Psychology and Theology*, vol. 8, Fall 1980, 173–84. The same journal includes several reactions to the Alsdurf-Malony critique.

24. Lazarus, *In the Mind's Eye*, 192.

25. The following suggestions are adapted from Singer and Switzer, *Mind-Play*, 161.

26. P. Bakan, "The Eyes Have It," *Psychology Today*, vol. 4, 1971, 64–7, 96.

27. M. S. Van Leeuwen, "Cognitive Style: North American Values and the Body of Christ," *Journal of the American Scientific Affiliation*, vol. 27, 1975, 119–25; and L. Rebecca Propst, "A Comparison of the Cognitive Restructuring Psychotherapy Paradigm and Several Spiritual Approaches to Mental Health," *Journal of Psychology and Theology*, vol. 2, 1980, 107–14.

28. There is initial research evidence that such imagery does have therapeutic effects. See Propst, "A Comparison."

29. Psalm 34:8.

30. Proverbs 18:24.

Chapter 14

1. Quoted by Montague Ullman, Stanley Krippner, and Alan Vaughan, *Dream Telepathy: Scientific Experiments in the Supernatural* (New York: Macmillan Publishing Co., 1973), 9.

2. Some of the conclusions from the preceding paragraphs are taken from summaries of sleep research. See, for example, A. Arkin, J. Autrobus, and S. Ellman, eds., *The Mind in Sleep: Psychology and Psychopathology* (Hillsdale, N.J.: Lawrence Erlbaum, 1978); W. C. Dement, *Some Must Watch While Some Must Sleep* (San Francisco: Freeman, 1972); C. Furst, *Origins of the Mind* (Englewood Cliffs, N.J.: Prentice-Hall, 1979); "What Dreams, Nightmares Tell You About Yourself: An Interview with Ernest Hartmann," *U.S. News & World Report*, 16 January 1984; and Wilse B. Webb, ed., *Sleep: An Experimental Approach* (New York: Macmillan Publishing Co., 1968).

3. Kilton Stewart, "Dream Theory in Malaysia," in Charles T. Tart, ed., *Altered States of Consciousness* (Garden City, N.Y.: Anchor Press, 1969), 160–170.

4. Patricia Garfield, *Creative Dreaming* (New York: Ballantine Books, 1975).
5. Rosalind Dymond Cartwright, "Happy Endings to our Dreams," *Psychology Today*, vol. 12, December 1978, 66–76.
6. For a summary and personal investigation of the Senoi phenomenon, see Kathryn Lindskoog, *The Gift of Dreams: A Christian View* (New York: Harper & Row, 1979). Lindskoog does not accuse Stewart of deliberate deception, but she does suggest that he reached his conclusions based on secondhand sources and without careful observation of the Senoi people.
7. Furst, *Origins of the Mind*, 100–103.
8. Theodore Melnechuk, "The Dream Machine," *Psychology Today*, vol. 17, November 1983, 22–34. The British researchers are Francis Crick (who won the Nobel prize as a co-discoverer of DNA's structure) and Graeme Mitchison.
9. I am grateful to Laura Meyer who shared this story in more detail than I could record and who gave me permission to include as much or as little as I wanted to use.
10. Abraham Schmitt, *Before I Wake . . . Listening to God in Your Dreams* (Nashville: Abingdon Press, 1984).
11. Herman H. Riffel, *Voice of God: The Significance of Dreams, Visions, Revelations* (Wheaton, Ill.: Tyndale House, 1978), 75.
12. Acts 2:17 is a quotation from Joel 2:28.
13. J. M. Lower, "Dreams," in Merrill C. Tenney, ed., *The Zondervan Pictoral Encyclopedia of the Bible*, vol. 2, 1975, 164.
14. Hebrews 11:1, 2, TLB.
15. Erich Fromm, *The Forgotten Language* (New York: Rinehart, 1951).
16. David Foulkes, *A Grammar of Dreams* (New York: Basic Books, 1978).
17. Schmitt, *Before I Wake*, 61.
18. Quoted in Lindskoog, *The Gift of Dreams*, 138. Apparently, the poem has been attributed to several authors, including William James.
19. Ibid., 142.
20. Stanley Krippner and William Hughes, "Genius at Work," *Psychology Today*, vol. 4, July 1970, 40–43.
21. Steven Starker, *Fantastic Thought* (Englewood Cliffs, N.J.: Prentice-Hall, 1982).
22. Scot Morris and Nicolas Charney, *Stop It!* (Garden City, N.Y.: Doubleday & Co., 1983).

Chapter 15

1. David A. Taylor, *Mind* (New York: Simon & Schuster, 1982), 168.
2. Charles T. Tart, *States of Consciousness*, (New York: E. P. Dutton, 1975), 5.
3. Ellen J. Langer, "Automated Lives," *Psychology Today*, vol. 16, April 1982, 60–71.
4. "Less Banter in Surgery?" *New York Times*, 7 February 1984, 20.
5. This is adapted from the definition of Arnold M. Ludwig who defined ASC(s) "as any mental state(s), induced by various physiological, psychological, or pharmacological maneuvers or agents, which can be recognized subjectively by the individual himself (or by an objective observer of the individual) as representing a sufficient deviation in subjective experience

or psychological functioning from certain general norms for that individual during alert, waking consciousness." The definition is taken from
page 11 of Arnold M. Ludwig, "Altered States of Consciousness," in
Charles T. Tart ed., *Altered States of Consciousness* (Garden City, N.Y.: Anchor Press, 1969), 11–24.

6. Adapted from Ludwig.
7. C. Neider, ed., *The Autobiography of Mark Twain* (New York: Harper & Row, 1959).
8. Elizabeth Stark, "Hypnotist on Trial," *Psychology Today*, vol. 18, February 1984, 34–36.
9. Charles Furst, *Origins of the Mind: Mind-Brain Connections* (Englewood Cliffs, N.J.: Prentice-Hall, 1979).
10. F. J. Evans. "Hypnosis." In Raymond J. Corsini (Editor) *Encyclopedia of Psychology*, vol. 2 (New York: John Wiley & Sons, 1984), 172–4.
11. Kenneth S. Bowers, *Hypnosis for the Seriously Curious* (New York: W. W. Norton & Co., 1976).
12. Steven Starker, *Fantastic Thought* (Englewood Cliffs, N.J.: Prentice-Hall, 1982).
13. See, for example, Milton H. Erickson, Ernest L. Rossi, and Sheila I. Rossi, *Hypnotic Realities* (New York: Irvington Pubs., 1976).
14. Starker, *Fantastic Thought*, 51.
15. M. V. Kline, "The Use of Extended Group Hypnotherapy Sessions in Controlling Cigarette Habituation," *International Journal of Clinical and Experimental Hypnosis*, vol. 18, 1970, 270–82.
16. J. G. Watkins, "Hypnotherapy," in Raymond J. Corsini, *Encyclopedia of Psychology*, vol. 2 (New York: John Wiley & Sons, 1984), 175–7.
17. M. Bernstein, *The Search for Bridey Murphy* (New York: Doubleday, 1956). See also, Harold Rosen, *A Scientific Report on "The Search for Bridey Murphy"* (New York: The Julian, 1956).
18. Leonard Zusne and Warren H. Jones, *Anomalistic Psychology: A Study of Extraordinary Phenomena of Behavior and Experience* (Hillsdale, N.J.: Law-rence Erlbaum, 1982).
19. W. E. Edmonston, Jr., "Hypnotic Age Regression," in Raymond J. Corsini ed., *Encyclopedia of Psychology*, vol. 2 (New York: John Wiley & Sons, 1984), 177–8. See also, T. X. Barber, "Hypnotic Age Regression: A Critical Re-view," *Psychosomatic Medicine*, vol. 24, 1962, 286–99.
20. M. T. Orne, "On the Simulating Subject as a Quasi-Control Group in Hypnosis Research: What, Why, and How?" in E. Fromm and R. E. Shor eds., *Hypnosis: Research Developments and Perspectives* (Chicago: Aldine-Atherton, 1972), 103–5.
21. See Bowers, *Hypnosis for the Seriously Curious*, 103–5.
22. Weston LaBarre, "Hallucinogens and the Shamanic Origins of Religion," in P. T. Furst ed., *Flesh of the Gods: The Ritual Use of Hallucinogens* (New York: Praeger Pubs., 1972).
23. Starker, *Fantastic Thought*.
24. Zusne and Jones, *Anomalistic Psychology*, 138. See also, D. Scott Rogo, "Strange Journeys of the Mind," *Human Behavior*, April 1976, 56–61.
25. C. T. Tart, "A Psychophysiological Study of Out-of-the-Body Experi-ences," *Journal of the American Society for Psychological Research*, vol. 62, 1968, 3–27.

Chapter 16

1. Jess Stearn, *Edgar Cayce: The Sleeping Prophet* (New York: Doubleday, 1967).
2. Many of the conclusions about Edgar Cayce in this section are adapted from a book by John Weldon and Zola Levitt, *Psychic Healing* (Chicago: Moody Press, 1982).
3. "He wanted to quit, yet he couldn't," writes Thomas Sugrue, an associate of Cayce. See Thomas Sugrue, *There Is a River* (New York: Holt, Rinehart & Winston, 1942), 112.
4. Weldon and Levitt, *Psychic Healing*, 71, 79.
5. The quotation is taken from Ephesians 6:12, which warns that every believer is in a struggle against "the rulers, against the authorities, against the powers of this dark world and against the spiritual forces of evil in heavenly realms."
6. The advertisement described in the text appears on page 37 of the February 1984 issue of *Psychology Today*.
7. See, for example, Leonard Zusne and Warren H. Jones, *Anomalistic Psychology: A Study of Extraordinary Phenomena of Behavior and Experience* (Hillsdale, N.J.: Lawrence Erlbaum, 1982); and James E. Alcock, *Parapsychology: Science or Magic?* (New York: Pergamon Press, 1981).
8. For an excellent discussion of universal energy and of the holistic healers, see Paul C. Reisser, Teri K. Reisser, and John Weldon, *The Holistic Healers: A Christian Perspective on New-Age Health Care* (Downers Grove, Ill.: InterVarsity Press, 1983).
9. Ibid., 13.
10. Sugrue, *There Is a River*, 210.
11. Ephesians 2:2; Revelation 12:9; John 8:44; 1 Timothy 3:7; 2 Timothy 2:26; 1 Peter 5:8; 2 Corinthians 11:13–15.
12. 2 Corinthians 4:4; 10:3–5; 11:3.
13. 2 Thessalonians 2:9, 10.
14. Matthew 12:28, 29; 25:41; Ephesians 6:12; Revelation 12:7.
15. John 12:31; 14:30; 16:11; 2 Corinthians 4:4.
16. Matthew 25:41; Revelation 20:1–3, 7–10, 12–14.
17. C. S. Lewis, *The Screwtape Letters* (Glasgow: Collins Fontana Books, 1942), 9.
18. John 16:33; 1 John 4:4.
19. 1 Peter 5:8, 9; James 4:7, 8; Ephesians 6:10–18.
20. Ephesians 6:18; 1 Peter 5:8.
21. Johanna Michaelsen, *The Beautiful Side of Evil* (Eugene, Oreg.: Harvest House, 1982).
22. Ibid., 137–8.
23. Since I am critical of these books I have chosen not to identify their titles or their authors here.
24. 2 Timothy 3:2–5.
25. Some of these are documented by James Bjornstad, *Twentieth Century Prophecy: Jeane Dixon, Edgar Cayce* (Minneapolis: Bethany Fellowship, 1969).
26. 1 Thessalonians 5:19–21.
27. 1 John 4:1, TLB.
28. Leviticus 19:31.

29. Deuteronomy 18:10–12.
30. Isaiah 8:19.
31. Acts 19:19.
32. 1 John 4:2, 3.
33. 2 Corinthians 11:4.
34. 1 John 2:22, 23.
35. Matthew 24:24.
36. Galatians 5:22, 23.
37. 1 John 2:3–6.
38. Michaelsen, *The Beautiful Side of Evil*, 182.
39. Ibid., 181.
40. 2 Timothy 3:16; 4:2–5.
41. Matthew 4:1–16.
42. Ephesians 6:10–17; Hebrews 4:12.
43. Ephesians 6:18.
44. "Psychic War and the Pentagon," *Science Digest*, May 1984, 38.
45. Psalm 33:12.
46. 2 Chronicles 8:14.

Chapter 17

1. Paul Galloway, "Remember Jim Jones? I'm His Son," *Chicago Tribune*, 15 April 1984.
2. William Sargant, *Battle for the Mind* (London: Heinemann, 1957).
3. The best example of this is D. Martyn Lloyd-Jones, *Conversations: Psychological and Spiritual* (Downers Grove, Ill.: InterVarsity Press, 1959).
4. Tim LaHaye makes this point in his analysis of humanism and its impact on the mind. See *The Battle for the Mind* (Old Tappan, N.J.: Fleming H. Revell, 1980).
5. Alan W. Scheflin and Edward M. Opton, Jr., *The Mind Manipulators* (New York: Paddington Press, 1978), 9–10.
6. This was the finding of Leon Festinger, as reported by Philip Zimbardo, "Mind Control in 1984," *Psychology Today*, vol. 18, January 1984, 71.
7. Donald J. Moine, "To Trust, Perchance to Buy," *Psychology Today*, vol. 16, August 1982, 50–54.
8. Vance Packard, *The Hidden Persuaders*, rev. ed. (New York: Pocket Books, 1981).
9. *New York Times*, 13 September 1957.
10. This is the observation of John Naisbitt, *Megatrends* (New York: Warner Books, 1982).
11. Al Ries and Jack Trout, *Positioning: The Battle for Your Mind* (New York: Warner Books, 1981).
12. Ibid., 8.
13. See Gene Wyckoff, *The Image Candidates: American Politics in the Age of Television* (New York: Macmillan Publishing Co., 1968).
14. Reported in Lori B. Andrews, "Mind Control in the Courtroom," *Psychology Today*, vol. 16, March 1982, 66–73.
15. Em Griffin, *The Mind Changers: The Art of Christian Persuasion* (Wheaton, Ill.: Tyndale House Pubs., 1976), 45.
16. Adapted from Griffin, ibid.; and from Marvin Karlins and Herbert I. Abelson, *Persuasion: How Opinions and Attitudes Are Changed* (New York:

Springer Publishing Co., 1970). Each of the conclusions in the text is built on convincing research evidence.

17. Colossians 1:28.
18. Matthew 28:18–20.
19. Ibid.
20. 1 Corinthians 9:19–22.
21. Colossians 1:28.
22. William J. McGuire, "Inducing Resistance to Persuasion," in Leonard Berkowitz, ed., *Advances in Experimental Social Psychology*, vol. 1 (New York: Academic Press, 1964), 192–231.
23. Reported in Griffin, *The Mind Changers*, 177.
24. Zimbardo, "Mind Control in 1984," 72.
25. These views are presented by Bernie Zilbergeld, *The Shrinking of America: Myths of Psychological Change* (Boston: Little, Brown & Co., 1983), chapter 12.

Chapter 18

1. Rogers Worthington, "Fire-Walkers Take a Stroll for the Soul," *Chicago Tribune*, 22 April 1984. For a more detailed discussion of fire-walking, see Leonard Zusne and Warren H. Jones, *Anomalistic Psychology: A Study of Extraordinary Phenomena of Behavior and Experience* (Hillsdale, N.J.: Lawrence Erlbaum, 1982), 61–65.
2. Nehemiah 4:6, NASB.
3. Jack R. Nation and Arnold D. Leunes. "Semi-tough and Supernormal," *Psychology Today*, vol. 15, September 1982, 66–67.
4. Sidney Lecker, *The Natural Way to Stress Control* (New York: Grosset & Dunlap, 1978). See the chapter entitled "The Stresses of Competitive Sports."
5. Emily Greenspan, "Mind over Muscle: Sports Psychology Teaches Athletes to Train the Brain," *Chicago Tribune*, 8 September 1983.
6. Reported by Sheila Ostrander and Lynn Schroeder, *Superlearning* (New York: Dell Publishing Co., 1979).
7. William P. Morgan, "The Mind of the Marathoner," *Psychology Today*, vol. 11, April 1978, 38–49.
8. Lecker, *The Natural Way to Stress Control*.
9. Skip Myslenski, "Sports and the Mind," *Chicago Tribune*, 14 November 1982.
10. William Glasser, *Stations of the Mind* (New York: Harper & Row, 1981).
11. W. Timothy Gallwey, *The Inner Game of Tennis* (New York: Random House, 1974). See also, W. Timothy Gallwey, *Inner Tennis: Playing the Game* (New York: Random House, 1976).
12. Ostrander and Schroeder, *Superlearning*, 159.
13. Cited in Claude Albee Frazier, ed., *Mastering the Art of Winning Tennis* (Toronto: Pagurian Press, 1974).
14. This story is often cited in books and lectures by possibility speakers. See, for example, Bill Glass, *Expect to Win* (Waco, Tex.: Word Books, 1981); and Skip Ross with Carole C. Carlson, *Say Yes to Your Potential* (Waco, Tex.: Word Books, 1983).
15. Em Griffin, *The Mind Changers* (Wheaton, Ill.: Tyndale House Pubs., 1982), 80. Griffin calls role play "the most effective way I know of to melt others toward a different position."

16. C. S. Lewis, *The Screwtape Letters* (London: Collins Fontana, 1942), 54.
17. 1 John 3:2.
18. 1 John 3:3.
19. 2 Peter 2:13, 14, 18, 19, NIV.
20. 1 Corinthians 10:12.
21. James 4:7.
22. Philippians 4:8.
23. 1 Peter 3:2.
24. 2 Timothy 3:16.
25. 2 Peter 3:3–7, 17.
26. 2 Peter 3:9.
27. 1 Corinthians 10:13.
28. 2 Peter 3:11, 14.
29. 2 Peter 3:15, 18.
30. For excellent discussions of sex and the mind, see John White, *Eros Defiled: The Christian and Sexual Sin* (Downers Grove, Ill.: InterVarsity Press, 1977); and Earl D. Wilson, *Sexual Sanity: Breaking Free from Uncontrolled Habits* (Downers Grove, Ill.: InterVarsity Press, 1984).
31. Quoted in an article by Pat. E. Crisci, "Quest: Helping Students Learn Caring and Responsibility," *Phi Delta Kappan*, October 1981, 131–3.
32. For more information, write to Quest, Inc., 4360 Maize Road, Columbus, Ohio 43224.

Chapter 19

1. Henri J. M. Nouwen, *Clowning in Rome* (Garden City, N.J.: Image Publishing, 1979), 2.
2. Ibid., 3.
3. Ibid., 110.
4. "Can TM Hurt Me?" *Eternity,* November 1974, 24.
5. John W. White, "Second Thoughts: What's Behind TM?" *Human Behavior,* October 1976, 70–71.
6. David S. Holmes, "Meditation and Somatic Arousal Reduction: A Review of the Experimental Evidence," *American Psychologist*, vol. 39, January 1984, 1–10.
7. Such conclusions are now documented in several places. For a brief and concise example, see Myra Dye, "The Transcendental Flimflam," *Moody Monthly,* January 1976, 33–35. A more detailed critique is found in chapter 6 of Os Guinness, *The Dust of Death* (Downers Grove, Ill.: InterVarsity Press, 1973).
8. Ephesians 2:8.
9. 1 Timothy 2:5.
10. Matthew 6:7.
11. This difference is pointed out by Richard J. Foster, *Celebration of Discipline* (New York: Harper & Row, 1978). See chapter 2 "The Discipline of Meditation." For a more controversial look at meditation, see Morton T. Kelsey, *The Other Side of Silence: A Guide to Christian Meditation* (New York: Paulist Press, 1976).
12. Joshua 1:8.
13. J. I. Packer, *Knowing God* (Downers Grove, Ill.: InterVarsity Press, 1973), 18–19.

14. John E. Bishop, "Meditation and Change," *Command,* vol. 16, Winter 1974, 12.
15. Psalm 50:15; Matthew 26:41; Luke 21:36; 1 Thessalonians 5:14–19. For a discussion of Ellul's "only reason for praying," see Jacques Ellul, *Prayer and Modern Man* (New York: Seabury Press, 1970).
16. Andrew Murray, *The Prayer Life* (Chicago: Moody, n.d.).
17. Quoted in Foster, *Celebration of Discipline,* 30.
18. Patti Roberts with Sherry Andrews, *Ashes to Gold* (Waco, Tex.: Word Books, 1983).
19. Eric Berne, *Games People Play: The Psychology of Human Relationships* (New York: Grove Press, 1964).
20. Philippians 4:6, 19.
21. Matthew 7:1–5.
22. Robert McClory, "Hidden Goodness: Rockford's Poor Clares: The World Is Their Cloister," *Chicago Tribune Magazine,* 6 November 1983, 20–31.
23. Lloyd Ogilvie, *Praying with Power* (Ventura, Calif.: Regal Books, 1983), 123.
24. Ogilvie suggests eight steps to effective prayer, but I have condensed this list to make it shorter.
25. Ibid., p. 26.
26. Psalm 118:1; 1 Thessalonians 5:18; Ephesians 5:20.
27. Psalm 49:3.
28. This is implied in the title of a book by Donald G. Bloesch, *The Struggle of Prayer* (New York: Harper & Row, 1980).
29. Nouwen, *Clowning in Rome,* 71–72.
30. Milton Rokeach, *The Open and Closed Mind* (New York: Basic Books, 1960).

Chapter 20

1. Helen Hooven Santmyer, . . . *And Ladies of the Club* (New York: Putnam's Sons, 1984).
2. ". . . in lowliness of mind let each esteem other better than themselves. . . . Let this mind be in you, which was also in Christ Jesus" (Philippians 2:3, 5, KJV).
3. Harry Blamires, *The Christian Mind* (Ann Arbor, Mich.: Servant Books, 1963). The book begins with the quoted sentence: "There is no longer a Christian mind."
4. Paul C. Vitz, *Psychology As Religion: The Cult of Self-Worship* (Grand Rapids: Wm. B. Eerdmans, 1977).
5. Francis A. Schaeffer, *The Great Evangelical Disaster* (Westchester, Ill.: Crossway Books, 1984).
6. Matthew 5:13–16.
7. Ibid., p. 83–4, emphasis added.
8. Romans 12:1, 2.
9. 1 Peter 1:13.
10. 1 Peter 4:7.
11. 2 Peter 3:1.
12. 1 Corinthians 2:16.
13. Philippians 3:3.
14. John 13:34–5.

15. Colossians 3:2.
16. Hebrews 10:5, 7.
17. Philippians 2:8.
18. Blamires, *The Christian Mind*, 132, 133.
19. These ideas are taken from Blamires' chapter on the acceptance of authority. See Blamires, ibid., 146, 132.
20. Gina Maranto, "The Mind Within the Brain," *Discover*, vol. 5, May 1984, 35–43.
21. Wilder Penfield, *The Mystery of the Mind* (Princeton, N.J.: Princeton University Press, 1975). See especially, the part of the book titled "Afterthoughts by the Author."
22. Karl R. Popper and John C. Eccles, *The Self and Its Brain* (Berlin: Springer International), 1977.
23. Quoted in Maranto, "The Mind Within the Brain."
24. Ronald K. Siegel, "Accounting for 'Afterlife' Experiences," *Psychology Today*, vol. 15, 64–75.
25. For a brief but recent report, see "The Near-Death Experience—How Thousands Describe It," *U.S. News & World Report*, 11 June 1984, 59–60.
26. Raymond A. Moody, *Life After Life* (New York: Bantam Books, 1975).
27. Adapted from Moody, ibid., 21–23.
28. Ronald K. Siegel, "The Psychology of Life After Death," *American Psychologist*, vol. 35, October 1980, 911–31.
29. A. Matson, *Afterlife: Reports from the Threshold of Death* (New York: Harper & Row, 1975). Matson titles one chapter, "The Thrill of Dying."
30. 1 John 1:5.
31. 2 Corinthians 11:14.
32. 1 Corinthians 15:26.
33. Hebrews 9:27.
34. Luke 16:19–31.
35. Quoted in Mark Albrecht, *Reincarnation: A Christian Appraisal* (Downers Grove, Ill.: InterVarsity Press, 1982).
36. Helen Wambach, *Reliving Past Lives: The Evidence Under Hypnosis* (New York: Harper & Row, 1978).
37. For evidence to support this conclusion, see Albrecht, *Reincarnation*, 53–56.
38. Stevenson's conclusions are presented in Ian Stevenson, *Twenty Cases Suggestive of Reincarnation* (Charlottesville, Va.: University Press of Virginia, 1966). Albrecht, *Reincarnation*, 56–60, gives a sympathetic, but evaluative review of Stevenson's work.
39. *San Francisco Examiner*, 17 March 1977, 24. Quoted in Albrecht, *Reincarnation*, 68.
40. Ibid.
41. 1 Samuel 28:7–19.
42. Leonard Zusne and Warren H. Jones, *Anomalistic Psychology: A Study of Extraordinary Phenomena of Behavior and Experience* (Hillsdale, N.J.: Lawrence Erlbaum, 1982), 280.
43. Leviticus 19:31; 20:6, 27.
44. Deuteronomy 18:10–12.
45. See Acts 8:9–23; 16:16–18; 19:18–19.
46. Acts 16:18.
47. 2 Corinthians 5:8.

48. John 5:28, 29; Acts 17:31; Romans 14:10; 2 Corinthians 5:10; Revelation 11:18; 20:11–15.
49. Matthew 25:41, 46; John 3:36; 5:29; Revelation 20:15.
50. 1 Corinthians 15:42–44.
51. See J. A. Schep, "Resurrection," in Merrill C. Tenney ed., *The Zondervan Pictoral Encyclopedia of the Bible*, vol. 5 (Grand Rapids: Zondervan, 1975), 70–75.
52. 2 Corinthians 5:9.

INDEX